Minority Politics
at the
Millennium

Contemporary Urban Affairs
volume 9
Garland Reference Library of Social Science
volume 1452

CONTEMPORARY URBAN AFFAIRS
RICHARD D. BINGHAM, *Series Editor*

MINORITY POLITICS AT THE MILLENNIUM

EDITED BY

RICHARD A. KEISER
KATHERINE UNDERWOOD

The Maxine
Goodman Levin
College of
Urban Affairs at
Cleveland State
University

GARLAND PUBLISHING, INC.
A MEMBER OF THE TAYLOR & FRANCIS GROUP
NEW YORK AND LONDON
2000

Published in 2000 by
Garland Publishing, Inc.
A member of the Taylor & Francis Group
19 Union Square West
New York, NY 10003

10 9 8 7 6 5 4 3 2 1

Library of Congress Cataloging-in-Publication Data

Minority politics at the millennium / edited by Katherine Underwood,
    Richard A. Kiser
        p.   cm.—(Garland reference library of social science ; v. 1452.
    Contemporary urban affairs ; v. 9
    Includes bibliographical references and index.
    ISBN 0-8153-3519-9 (alk. paper)
        1. Minorities—United States—Political activity.   2. Minorities—United
    States—Political activity—Forecasting.   3. Twenty-first century—Forecasts
    4. Urban policy—United States.   5. Municipal government—United States.
    6. United States—Ethnic relations.   7. United States—Race relations.
    8. United States—Politics and government—1989.   I. Underwood, Katherine.
    II. Keiser, Richard A.   III. Garland reference library of social science ;
    v. 1452.   IV. Garland reference library of social science. Contemporary
    urban affairs ; v. 9.

E184.A1 M5445 1999
324.7'2'08900973—dc21
                                                                        99-052031

Printed on acid-free, 250-year-life paper
Manufactured in the United States of America

Contents

List of Tables

Acknowledgments

This volume originated with a suggestion made by Susan Clarke, who encouraged us to pursue a volume devoted to minority incorporation. We are grateful to Sallie Marston and David Perry, who read the complete manuscript and offered us guidance in both the writing and publication phases of this project. Early versions of these chapters were presented during two panels of the 1997 American Political Science Association meeting in Washington D.C. We would like to thank John Mollenkopf and Adolph Reed, Jr., who served as discussants for these panels, for their helpful feedback. Many heartfelt thanks go to Vilas Genke (University of Wisconsin Oshkosh), who graciously provided expert technical assistance in the manuscript preparation phase. Finally, Rich would like to thank Carleton College for financial support of this project.

MINORITY POLITICS
AT THE
MILLENNIUM

CHAPTER 1

The Changing Structure of Minority Group Political Opportunities
Looking Ahead to the Twenty-First Century

RICHARD A. KEISER

The ambitious project of this book is to offer a scholarly perspective on the future of minority political incorporation in cities in the twenty-first century. We normatively endorse the struggle of subordinated groups such as communities of color and gays and lesbians for social and political equality. Tremendous strides have been made in three closely linked areas: the elimination of discriminatory electoral arrangements due largely to passage and enforcement of the Voting Rights Act (Parker, 1990; Davidson & Grofman, 1994); the formation of political coalitions that include rather than exclude these subordinated groups (Browning, Marshall & Tabb, 1984); and the attainment by representatives of these groups of mayoral and city council offices as well as administrative control over housing authorities, school systems, and police departments (Browning, Marshall & Tabb, 1990). Minority elected officials in cities have gone beyond representation and achieved political incorporation via membership in the dominant political coalitions. This has meant that minority officials have played a key role in making public policy that directly impacts constituents. Moreover, activist community organizations that purport to represent minority interests have been able to advise and influence the policymakers (Clavel & Wiewel, 1991). Political incorporation has yielded genuine benefits for members of subordinated groups in big and small ways. Income and employment opportunities have been improved through affirmative action and business set-aside policies; civil rights have been protected through numerous policies, including the creation of mechanisms for redress against policy brutality; and the distribution of the benefits from many of the housekeeping functions of city

1

government, such as the paving of streets, distribution of building permits, and placement of libraries, have been equalized (Keiser, 1997; Browning, Marshall & Tabb, 1997). These benefits represent major achievements and have had profoundly positive effects on the lives of minority citizens.

Yet much work remains to be done in the next millennium. In each minority community the proportion unaffected by the achievements of political incorporation rivals the proportion of beneficiaries. Communities of color remain overwhelmingly concentrated in central cities, have lower education and income levels, and are more likely to be the target of crime as well as police harassment than their suburban, Anglo counterparts (Massey & Denton, 1993; Orfield & Ashkinaze, 1991; Fainstein, 1995). Building metropolitan or statewide coalitions that seek to rectify these inequities is one challenge for the future agenda of political leaders seeking to advance minority incorporation, a topic discussed by Arnold Fleischmann (Chapter 5).

Improving the political participation rates of members of minority groups represents a second challenge for those who seek to advance the political power of minorities in the twenty-first century. The low socioeconomic status of large proportions of all minority communities, alluded to above, is correlated with depressed levels of political participation. While we acknowledge that democratic institutions imperfectly aggregate preferences, we contend that more participants in the political process is better than fewer. For Latinos and Asian Pacific Islanders, participation represents a special problem. Groups with lots of active voters tend to receive the most attention from elected officials and are more likely to see policies that reflect their interests. Louis DeSipio (Chapter 4) and James Lai (Chapter 9) both argue that the electoral clout of Latinos and Asian Pacific Islanders, respectively, is not proportionate to their population size. They explain that the low levels of electoral participation found in these groups are related to issues of youthful population profiles, low citizenship rates, and low rates of voter registration. Changing this dynamic will require the passage of time, the emergence of issues that increase the political attentiveness of these groups (e.g., anti-immigrant legislation), and the efforts of a coalition of leaders committed to empowering segments of the public that have not voted at high rates in the past.

Naturalization of immigrants and registration of voters once was a task performed capably by urban political parties. But as we approach the millennium there is little indication, even in the East and Midwest where they were strongest, that urban political parties are interested in mounting broad mobilization efforts and expanding their bases in new, inclusionary ways. Donald Rosenthal's discussion (Chapter 10) suggests this is equally true for New York state county party organizations and their relationship to gay and lesbian communities.

The weakness of urban parties creates an opportunity for community-based organizations (CBOs) to play a more consistent role in naturalizing new citizens, registering voters, and providing voter education and mobilization. The third challenge for those leaders who seek to advance minority political empowerment and social equality is to prod and work with CBOs in the creation of political coalitions dedicated to going beyond the status quo of minority power. In cities in which past political struggles have delivered minority empowerment gains, albeit unevenly, CBOs are too often and too easily satisfied with regime maintenance. In cities where conservative coalitions have sharply limited minority political empowerment, CBOs can provide the organizational guidance for a politics of protest and opposition.

To summarize, minority groups have been successful in altering the formal rules of the political game and in winning elected representation at the local level. Yet the chapters in this volume also indicate that substantive political equality remains a challenge to be conquered. Why is this so? What strategies exist for those who wish to rise to this challenge? Answering these twin questions is the goal of this volume.

This volume offers to students, scholars, and policymakers analyses of the struggles for political power in cities by African Americans, Latinos, Asian Americans, and gays that specifically discuss their relationships to mayors, city councils, urban bureaucrats, and private sector actors at the twentieth century's end. Although individual chapters certainly stand on their own and may obviously be read in any order, we have organized the contributions into two sections. The first section of this book focuses on external and contextual factors that shape political outcomes for minority groups, while the second section of the book focuses on the political struggles for equality of specific groups. In Chapter 2, Richard Engstrom discusses the impact that the U.S. Supreme Court's repudiation of the strategy of creating majority-minority districts has had on the playing field for minority political representation. Engstrom's analysis also offers minority community activists and policymakers a guide to alternative structural arrangements that they can utilize in the twenty-first century in light of the court's position. Amy Bridges and Katherine Underwood present both quantitative and qualitative data in

Chapter 3 from four large southwestern cities that have moved from at-large to district elections. Their analysis of city councils explains the effect that electoral arrangements can have not merely on representation but on politics and policy. Louis DeSipio provides an analysis of the dynamic impact that immigration and naturalization are having on the demographics and on the issue agendas of cities across the country in Chapter 4. DeSipio distills from his research on Latino immigrants three models for immigrant political incorporation that respectively emphasize the role of community-based organizing, the development of ethnic solidarity around immigrant issues, and the political opportunities for immigrant populations that become majority populations. The panacea of new structural arrangements, in this case metropolitan or regional arrangements that supersede cities, is the topic of Chapter 5 by Arnold Fleischmann. Fleischmann's chapter discusses the problems of coalition formation that minority and non-minority advocates of metropolitan arrangements will face in the twenty-first century and he offers a sober analysis of the impact that such arrangements may have on the struggle for political equality.

The five substantive chapters in the second section of this volume provide a look at specific minority groups with particular emphasis on the group's political resources, electoral strategies, issue agendas, influence over local government, and perhaps most importantly, the struggle to overcome divisions and produce group identity. Rufus Browning, Dale Rogers Marshall, and David Tabb, whose work has defined the dominant paradigm for urban scholars of minority power, review the achievements and limitations of minority empowerment in big cities in Chapter 6. They explain that the recent defeat of coalitions headed by African Americans is due to both the loss of coalitional cohesiveness caused by the decline of liberalism and the emergence of competing interest among old and new coalition members. Still, they counsel guarded optimism about the future based on their view that the institutionalized achievements won through a multi-decade struggle are unlikely to be erased. In Chapter 7, Richard Keiser offers a theoretical discussion that distinguishes between successful and failed efforts at regime change and provides a framework for analyzing the significance of the elections of white mayors in cities previously governed by blacks. He then provides an empirical analysis of mayoral and city council elections and policy outcomes that yields the conclusion that neither the election of Mayor Edward Rendell in Philadelphia nor the election of Rudolph Giuliani in New York represent regime changes or the rollback of black political power. Thomas Longoria, Jr., argues, in Chapter 8, that our understanding of Latino politics is too exclusively based on research in the Southwest. He argues that considerable historical and sociopolitical variation exists among Latinos across the country and that this variation will grow in the twenty-first century. In the Midwest, smaller and more dispersed Latino populations have produced a different construction of racial identity for Latinos and different patterns of intra- and interethnic coalitions than are evident in the Southwest. James Lai also analyzes identity politics in his discussion of Asian Pacific American political empowerment in Chapter 9. Through two detailed case studies of elections involving Asian Pacific candidates, Lai offers insights about why groups sometimes choose a pan-ethnic bridge building strategy and other times choose to go it alone and the consequences of these choices for mobilization, representation, and empowerment. In Chapter 10 Donald Rosenthal examines the efforts of gays and lesbians in four cities in New York to move from political subordination in the 1960s to varying degrees of empowerment by the 1990s. Rosenthal's analysis is very sensitive to the need to distinguish between symbolic and substantive gains, yet he sees success in the creation of a political and attitudinal environment that is not hostile to gays and lesbians. Although it may appear as if gays and lesbians have not achieved many concrete policy demands, Rosenthal cautions that the goal that engendered the most agreement was winning access and representation within the political system and that has been accomplished. When diversity transcends unity or identity of interest, perhaps the most that may be achieved is the capture of positions of electoral representation that will provide avenues for group influence when circumstances unify the group.

But, as the first half of this volume stresses, even when a group is unified, exogenous factors can have a huge impact on the ability of the group to redistribute political and economic power in its favor. One of the most important exogenous factors has been the role of the federal government. The federal government does not face the same constraints that states and particularly cities face, as Paul Peterson (1981) argued in *City Limits*. When the federal government has been committed to reducing the subordination of minorities, dramatic change has been achieved (Sundquist, 1968). The relationship in the twenty-first century between the federal government and the cities, where the vast majority of minorities continue to reside, is the topic of the remainder of this chapter. I will explain how demographic changes that favor suburbs over cities, structural changes that have devolved political power and accountability from the federal government to the states, and the ideological transformation of the Democratic party all will combine to create a twenty-first century environment that is hostile to the interests of politically and economically subordinated groups including minorities.

THE END OF REDISTRIBUTIVE POLITICS

The twentieth century was a period of massive growth in federal aid to cities. During the 1930s and 1940s New Deal politics and Keynesian economics sent streams of federal dollars to cities. The Great Society programs of the 1960s and 1970s turned these streams to rivers. These policies were the product of both progressive, compassionate policy toward those hardest hit by the exigencies of capitalism and pragmatic, calculated policies aimed at delivering benefits to the largest numbers of voters, urban residents. During the Reagan era, the Republican party sharply broke from the approach to federal spending on cities that was evident in the Eisenhower and Nixon administrations. At this point it appeared that the GOP would follow a policy of neglect toward cities (except where their policies of military Keynesianism benefited cities of the Southwest and West), while the Democrats would continue to use federal policy to redistribute benefits to the cities (Ginsberg & Shefter, 1990). Even though the Democrats remain reticent about budget cuts that negatively impact cities, I argue that in the twenty-first century cities will not enjoy a privileged position in the administrations of either party. This represents a dramatic difference with the Democratic party that played such a role in the empowerment of minorities analyzed by Browning, Marshall, and Tabb in *Protest Is Not Enough.*

In their study of ten California cities, Browning, Marshall, and Tabb (1984) considered the *ideological* shift in the country from the civil rights movement, the growth in *federal government* programs that targeted the cities, and the *population dynamics* that swelled the ranks of minorities among Democratic partisans to be three crucial variables that contributed to the replacement of conservative coalitions by liberal, biracial coalitions. Representatives of these liberal, biracial coalitions captured city council and mayoral offices and incrementally delivered policy benefits to communities of color; Browning, Marshall, and Tabb called this process "political incorporation." The remainder of this chapter will explore changes in these three factors and how they contribute to the political isolation that cities face as they enter the twenty-first century.

Population Dynamics

In 1949 Samuel Eldersveld persuasively argued that the largest cities in the nation were having a decisive and profound effect on presidential elections. Presidential election results in twelve of the nation's cities with populations over 500,000 were examined to determine the impact that their votes had on outcomes in their ten states.[1] His analysis of results in the ten states for the five presidential elections between 1932 and 1948 found that in thirty-five of the fifty elections Democratic pluralities in these big cities overcame Republican margins in the rest of the state and proved decisive. These victories had profound effects in the Electoral College, according to Eldersveld: "From 1932 to 1948, the Democrats secured in these ten states from 40 percent to 80 percent of the Electoral College vote needed by a political party (266) to win the presidential election. And this was because of the urban Democratic pluralities in these states" (Eldersveld, 1949, p. 1199). Without the pluralities accumulated in these 12 cities, the party would have lost the presidential elections of 1940, 1944, and 1948. Presidents and Congresses (as well as governors) were well advised to be responsive to these large and powerful electorates. The proverbial smoke-filled rooms of the Democratic party caucus were dominated by city leaders and both candidate selection and policymaking after elections were heavily influenced by urban representatives (Polsby, 1983). These urban representatives and their constituencies were much more representative of the minority populations of the era, in terms of ethnicity or race and interests, than were those of the suburbs.

Migration from cities to suburbs during the last thirty years has eroded the electoral power of cities at the same time that it has increased minority concentration in the cities. As Table 1.1 shows, all of the cities studied by Eldersveld have suffered absolute declines in population since 1950 (or 1960 for Milwaukee) except Los Angeles. Of course, other cities such as Houston, San Diego, Dallas, Phoenix, and San Antonio have, by 1990, joined the top ten in population.

Yet population has not merely moved from the Northeast and Midwest to the Southwest and West; it has moved from cities to suburbs. Table 1.2 suggests that the population losses of the cities have been accompanied by huge gains in their suburbs. Suburban growth is not, however, merely a byproduct of the decay of America's older cities. By 1970, suburban residents outnumbered residents of cities across the nation. By

Table 1.1. 1990 Population of the Twelve Largest Cities of 1950 as Percent of 1950 Population

City	1990 Population as Percent of 1950 Population
New York	92.7
Los Angeles	177.0
Chicago	76.9
Philadelphia	76.5
Detroit	55.6
Baltimore	77.5
San Francisco	93.4
Milwaukee	85.0
Boston	71.7
St. Louis	46.3
Pittsburgh	54.7

Source: C. Gibson. (1998). "Population of the 100 Largest Cities and Other Urban Places in the United States: 1790–1990." Population Division Working Paper No. 27. Washington, DC: U.S. Bureau of the Census, Table 23.

1990, 48 percent of the U.S. population lived in suburbs, with 29 percent living in cities and 23 percent in rural areas; the first census of the twenty-first century will no doubt show an absolute majority of Americans living in suburbs. Given the conventional wisdom about the relationship between electoral turnout and socioeconomic status, it is not surprising that suburban voters already constitute an absolute majority of the electorate. The declining urban share of the nation's population bodes ill for the cities, their residents, and their political agendas. The twenty-first century that we are about to embark on might appropriately be labeled "the Suburban Century." As Table 1.3 suggests, urban representation in Congress has declined dramatically in the last two decades and it will continue to decline as the urban share of the total population decreases. Most importantly, in nominations and elections for the presidency, the office that holds the greatest potential for redistributive agenda-setting and policymaking, the decline in the electoral power of the cities will have a negative effect on residents (Ripley & Franklin,

Table 1.2. 1990 Population of the Eleven Largest Cities of 1950 and Their Suburbs

City	Population (in thousands)	Suburban Population (in thousands)	Suburban Advantage
New York	7,323	8,721	16% larger
Los Angeles	3,485	7,918	56% larger
Chicago	2,784	4,008	31% larger
Philadelphia	1,586	2,636	40% larger
Detroit	1,028	2,670	61% larger
Baltimore	736	1,154	36% larger
San Francisco	724	2,906	75% larger
Milwaukee	628	598	5% smaller
Boston	574	2,201	74% larger
St. Louis	397	1,550	74% larger
Pittsburgh	370	1,309	72% larger

Source: C. Gibson. (1998). "Population of the 100 Largest Cities and Other Urban Places in the United States: 1790–1990." Population Division Working Paper No. 27. Washington, DC: U.S. Bureau of the Census. Data for Cleveland, the twelfth city studied by Eldersveld (1949), was unavailable.

1991). Minority residents who typically stand to gain the most from redistributive policy will suffer the most from the decline in federal interest in the cities.

Will the Democrats Restore the Federal Role?

William Schneider has argued that the electoral implications of these demographic changes favor the Republicans and negatively affect the Democratic party. Schneider's view is that the Democrats will continue to see themselves as the party of the cities and will fight a defensive, rearguard action to aid the cities financially. Schneider compares today's Democrats to the Democrats of the 1890s who backed William Jennings Bryan's defense of rural America as it was being eclipsed by the burgeoning cities financially. That political miscalculation left the Democrats

Table 1.3. Increase in Suburban Districts in the House of Representatives, 1973–1993

Year	Suburban districts[a]	Urban districts[b]	Rural Districts[c]	Mixed districts[d]
1973	88	78	92	177
1985	129	73	61	172
1993	160	67	57	151

Source: Cook (1997).

[a] A suburban district is defined as one in which at least 60 percent of the Metropolitan Statistical Area population lives within a defined metropolitan area but outside a central city.

[b] An urban district is defined as one in which at least 60 percent of the population of the Metropolitan Statistical Area lives inside a central city.

[c] A rural district is defined as one in which at least 60 percent of the Metropolitan Statistical Area population lives outside a metropolitan area (and outside towns of 25,000 or more).

[d] A mixed district is defined as one in which neither cities nor suburbs nor rural areas account for 60 percent of the population of the Metropolitan Statistical Area.

shut out of presidential politics for much of the next thirty-six years and Schneider suggests that the party is poised to travel a similar road by remaining loyal to urban residents and ceding suburbanites to the Republicans (Schneider, 1992).

Schneider's claim that this suburban century is "good news" for the GOP and that "the suburbs are that party's lock on the presidency" has not been borne out (Schneider, 1991, p. 2335). The results of suburban voting in the last two presidential elections suggest that the Republicans may be too closely identified with the South, religious fundamentalism, and antigovernment libertarianism (Dionne, 1996; Caldwell, 1997). In other words, the GOP is in danger of being defined as extremist and out of touch with mainstream, middle-class, suburban America. Dan Balz of the *Washington Post* has written about the Democrats' resurgence in suburbs that had been staunchly Republican. President Clinton won in Macomb County, Michigan, the suburban area that so many analysts have pointed to as the bellwether for Reagan Democrats (Edsall & Edsall, 1991). A Democratic presidential candidate had not won there since 1968. According to Balz (1996, 24),

> The same pattern held true throughout the states that in past elections were considered the prized battlegrounds of presidential elections. In New Jersey, Clinton carried Bergen and Monmouth counties, both of which Bush won in 1988 and in 1992. In Ohio, the president carried Lake County, east of Cleveland, which Bush won in both his campaigns. In Pennsylvania, Clinton expanded his victory margins of four years ago in three counties surrounding Philadelphia: Montgomery, Bucks and Delaware. Bush carried all three in 1988.

Balz also found numerous suburban counties in which Clinton lost, but by much narrower margins than did Dukakis in 1988. Such narrow defeats give the Democrats a very good shot at winning statewide if they merely maintain, rather than expand, their margins in the state's big cities.

The upshot for students of urban politics is that the Democrats are not being forced to take the position as diehard defenders of the cities. Nor are they trying to manufacture policies that will reach out to disaffected urban residents and increase low levels of registration and turnout. Instead the New Democrats (discussed later) are seeking to win suburban voters who were independents or Republican leaners. A credible argument can be made that this is a sound strategy for the Democrats, but that is not the question we address here. Rather, our concern is with the impact on cities and on minority residents of cities. To the extent that the Democrats choose to join the Republicans in formulating policies and programs to appeal to suburban constituencies, the cities and their residents will suffer. For example, although the second Clinton administration has not deepened the cuts in funding for urban programs of the first administration or the Reagan-Bush years (Eisinger, 1998), the administration also has not advanced an agenda that acknowledges a federal responsibility to cities and to the least fortunate citizens who live there.[2]

The Democrats' attention to suburban voters may have some benefits for minority populations who live in the suburbs. In electorally competitive suburban districts, Hispanic and African American voters may be wooed because their votes can play a decisive role in presidential and congressional elections. Such was the case in the 1996 presidential election in Florida for Hispanics and in Georgia for African Americans (Brownstein, 1996; Alexander & Soto, 1996). Even in noncompetitive areas the upsurge in Democratic voting by suburban Latinos in Arizona (which went to the Democrats for the first time since 1948), California (where Hispanic turnout increased by 40 percent over 1992), and Texas (where Hispanic turnout increased by 60 percent over 1992) cut deeply enough into GOP margins that Democrats were able to win based on the larger margins they built in urban areas. Continued growth in Hispanic turnout will depend on many of the factors analyzed by DeSipio in Chapter 4. Whether Latinos divide their votes or give the majority of their support to the Democrats may depend on whether the GOP remains the party of anti-immigrant policies such as Proposition 187.

But the issue agendas of African Americans and Hispanics who have migrated from the city to the suburbs to continue their trek up the employment ladder is not the same as that of inner-city minority populations who are underskilled, hold jobs that do not pay a living wage, and recognize that their children are going to schools that are not readying them for the twenty-first century. There is no available evidence that suggests that minorities in the suburbs do not share the suburban agenda of demanding that government be more fiscally efficient (in contradistinction to the GOP position of ending most government intervention), that budgets be balanced, and at the same time that political leaders protect universal programs that benefit the middle class. Concomitantly, among suburban voters there is little support for narrowly targeted, redistributive programs that aid lower income residents of cities. The New Democrat platform of protecting Medicare, Social Security, and student loans and offering tax cuts for college tuition all exemplify the party's desire to use universal policies to appeal to middle-class suburbanites.

The Democratic party's willingness to abandon the federal government's role in a welfare system for the poor shows its desire to redefine itself in a way that excludes redistributive liberalism. Finally, the party's desire to woo suburban voters and to avoid redistributive policies has very negative implications for metropolitanization policies, discussed by Fleischmann in Chapter 5, because such efforts typically involve use of suburban taxes to aid ailing cities.

Ideological Shift within the Democratic Party

President Clinton's decision to engage in electoral battle with the Republicans in the suburbs and the decisions his administration has made about its programmatic priorities in an era of budget cutting by a Republican Congress are part of a coherent ideological vision. This vision owes more to the Democratic Leadership Council (DLC) than any other source and goes beyond both Bill Clinton and Al Gore, both of whom are proponents of the DLC philosophy. The DLC began as a faction within the Democratic party that was intent on remaking the image and agenda of the party in a more centrist manner. The DLC has argued that the party has become captive to special interests, particularly white liberals and minorities, who promulgate tax and spend policies that have alienated the pocketbook-conscious middle class. In 1989–1991, while Bill Clinton was governor of Arkansas, he served as chairman of the DLC and orchestrated the DLC's effort to move from a Beltway organization to a grass roots organization with more than twenty state chapters. By the 1990s, the DLC had become a widely respected voice within the party and had succeeded in creating the image that the agenda it advocated represented an innovative path that differed from modern liberalism (Rae, 1994). It also succeeded in its goal of nominating a moderate Southerner, Bill Clinton, as the Democratic candidate for president in 1992.

Al From, one of the founders of the DLC, endorsed Schneider's comparison of the contemporary Democratic party to the party of William Jennings Bryan. Writing prior to the 1992 presidential election in *The New Democrat,* the house organ of the DLC, he warned that, "if the Democrats cast their lot with the cities—and against the suburbs— they sharply diminish their chances of winning the White House" (From, 1992, p. 32). From's suggestions for policies that will enable the party to "make inroads into the suburban vote without turning their back on the cities" include the creation of empowerment zones where federal tax abatements would serve as an incentive for business location (all too often relocation from an area that can ill afford to lose employers), the formation of community credit financial institutions, and the strengthening of the Community Reinvestment Act (aimed at reducing redlining-type restrictions that inhibit bank loans to minority entrepreneurs and would-be homeowners). These are market mechanisms that cost few bucks and will deliver few bangs. The DLC is as critical of the "Nanny State" as the nonlibertarian factions of the GOP and their philosophy, if not all of their policy recommendations, gibes with the tough-love "Daddy State" ethos (Starobin, 1998).

Most analyses of the DLC conclude that New Democrats do not advocate many policies that differentiate them from the liberals that they criticize (Faux, 1993; Rae, 1994; Hale, 1995; Dionne, 1996; Judis, 1996). The few salient differences in policy agendas are in the DLC's rejection of policies that offer redistributive benefits without demanding personal responsibility (e.g., they oppose welfare and subsidies for public housing but favor workfare and tenant ownership of public housing) and in trade, where the DLC promotes free trade and the liberal wing of the party seeks to protect unionized workers and others threatened by job loss. Yet, the DLC has created an identity and persona that sharply distinguishes it from the party's liberal wing whom DLCers deride as "liberal fundamentalists." Although elections remain candidate-centered, the candidates compete on shifting ideological terrain. As Hale (1995, p. 224) explains, the DLC has redefined what constitutes legitimate rhetoric among Democratic candidates:

> In the end, the New Democrats' message is one thing, its agenda another. In attacking the liberal fundamentalists, the DLC is signaling to swing voters in the white middle class [i.e., suburbia] that Democrats are not exclusively black, feminist, gay and liberal. While this message is offensive to the groups just mentioned, it holds the potential to wedge the Democrats' foot in the door of voters who make the difference in presidential elections and many subpresidential elections. In its policy positions, the DLC has fleshed out a liberal-leaning platform couched in soothing centrist rhetoric for a party that has been unable to do so and one that has considerable potential appeal to much of the party's liberal base. On the other hand, the DLC program seems vulnerable to an attack from the right claiming that it is just a cleverly concealed version of liberalism.

The verbal attack on minorities has not been accompanied by a policy attack on minorities. Neither the DLC nor the Clinton administration have joined conservative Republicans in attacks on gay rights, affirmative action, or the rights of women to control their reproductive decisions, just to name a few issues of salience for so-called liberal fundamentalists. But the DLC rhetoric has been an important piece of symbolic politics because it has provided a stalking horse for the New Democrats to differentiate themselves from the party's previous direction which had been discredited among middle class, suburban voters. Unions have become a second stalking horse for the DLC, as is discussed later. The popularity of unions has declined dramatically over the last three decades as any politician who pays attention to the polls knows. Moreover, unions represent a powerful opposition constituency in the fight over free trade, the North American Free Trade Agreement (NAFTA), and fast-track trade legislation. The rise of the DLC as the party's most prominent faction, then, and the ideological shift away from redistributive policies that disproportionately benefit urban minorities, represents a dramatic and negative change in the environment of minority groups seeking political incorporation.

This new Democratic party ethos is relevant for minority politics at the millennium in a second way. The new breed of mayors who have generated so much recent media hype pine away for money to be thrown at them. They know that if the federal government does not repeal the aspects of welfare reform that end the eligibility of legal immigrants for AFDC, food stamps, and SSI, the cities where immigrants are concentrated will have to bear a heavy burden. But they also know that federal help is not on the way. The lecture circuit speech of Philadelphia's Mayor Ed Rendell often contains the following plea:

> If we are going to cut people off welfare, it's going to increase Philadelphia's costs for providing services to the homeless. If 30 percent of the people who would be cut off AFDC go into our shelter system, we estimate that our shelter costs will rise from $24 million to $93 million.
>
> The states can have a choice. Either they make up the difference, often causing them to raise taxes—or they can look at the city and county governments and say, "Aha, we don't have to raise taxes, we can just drop this problem down to them."
>
> We've just eliminated a billion-dollar-plus deficit. We produced the first cut in our wage tax in fifty years. But this one thing—the additional shelter-care costs that will come from cuts in AFDC—could eradicate our tax cut, and maybe force us to raise taxes. If we raise taxes, all we do is drive people out in the long run, and worsen the city's problems. (O'Neill & Sheehan, 1995)

Rendell's statement points out that, in the absence of federal redistributive policy, mayors now must turn to governors and state legislators for help. It is imperative that city officials win the confidence and support of largely suburban constituencies increasingly governed by Republican legislators and governors. To pull off this difficult feat, the mayors are adapting on the fly. One tactic that is evident is the willingness of these mayors to develop cozy relations with any sympathetic governor, even if this means crossing party lines. Republican Rudolph Giuliani endorsed Democratic Governor Mario Cuomo in 1994; both Mike White of Cleveland and Tom Murphy of Pittsburgh have developed close relations with the Republican governors of their states and seem unlikely to give more than nominal support to Democratic gubernatorial candidates (O'Toole, 1998). A second tactic of these mayors in their bid to appeal to suburbanites and their elected representatives is the adoption of DLC rhetoric about privatization and the inefficiency of unionized urban bureaucracies. Mayors Rendell, White, Richard Daley, Kurt Schmoke, and John Norquist have varied connections to the DLC and Republicans Giuliani and Richard Riordan are often described as advocates of DLC philosophy (Siegel, 1994; Hale, 1995). All preach a desire to improve the fiscal health of their cities and make government more responsive and less bureaucratic through privatization and assaults on the wage and benefit packages of unionized municipal employees. Given that urban bureaucracies have been more hospitable to minority employment than the private sector, and that minorities have finally penetrated beyond the lowest bureaucratic ranks in many cities, any attacks on the city workforce will have a disproportionately negative effect on minorities (Browning, Marshall & Tabb, 1990).

The likelihood that cities can expect little support from the federal government and, therefore, that those who seek to advance the struggle for minority equality have lost an important source of support and resources makes the other structural and political factors that influence minority politics even more salient. It is with this sense of urgency that the contributors to this volume have authored their chapters.

NOTES

[1]Fourteen cities had populations over 500,000; Buffalo and Washington, DC were omitted from the study. The twelve cities are in ten states because both Philadelphia and Pittsburgh are in Pennsylvania and San Francisco and Los Angeles are in California.

[2]The Clinton administration is responsible for cuts in public housing rent subsidies and the elimination of funding for the construction of new public housing. The consequence of these decisions will be that public housing authorities will have to look for new sources of funding to maintain service levels. This will likely prompt a redefinition of their mission from a last resort provider of housing to the poor to catering to tenants who can afford market rates. See Fulton (1997).

REFERENCES

Alexander, K., & Soto, L. (1996, December 15). Georgia's evolving politics. *Atlanta Journal and Constitution,* p. 6G.

Balz, D. (1996, November 10). Clinton broke Republican grip on some suburban county strongholds. *Washington Post,* p. 24.

Browning, R.P., Marshall, D.R., & Tabb, D. (1984). *Protest is not enough: The struggle of Blacks and Hispanics for equality in urban politics.* Berkeley: University of California Press.

Browning, R.P., Marshall, D.R., & Tabb, D. (eds.) (1990). *Racial politics in American cities.* New York: Longman.

Browning, R.P., Marshall, D.R., & Tabb, D. (eds.) (1997). *Racial politics in American cities* (2nd ed.). New York: Longman.

Brownstein, R. (1996, November 4). Florida battle mirrors wider conflict. *Los Angeles Times,* p. 1.

Caldwell, C. (1997). The southern captivity of the GOP. *Atlantic Magazine,* 281, 55–72.

Clavel, P., & Wiewel, W. (eds.) (1991). *Harold Washington and the neighborhoods: Progressive city government in Chicago, 1983–1987.* New Brunswick, NJ: Rutgers University Press.

Cook, R. (1997, May 24). Suburbia: Land of varied faces and a growing political force. *Congressional Quarterly Weekly Report,* 55, 1209–1217.

Davidson, C., & Grofman, B. (eds.) (1994). *Quiet revolution in the South.* Princeton, NJ: Princeton University Press.

Dionne, Jr., E.J. (1996). *They only look dead: Why progressives will dominate the next political era.* New York: Simon and Schuster.

Edsall, T., & Edsall, M. (1991). *Chain reaction: The impact of race, rights, and taxes on American politics.* New York: W. W. Norton.

Eisinger, P. (1998, January). City politics in an era of federal devolution. *Urban Affairs Review,* 33, 308–325.

Eldersveld, S.J. (1949). The influence of metropolitan party pluralities in presidential elections since 1920: A study of twelve key cities. *American Political Science Review,* 43, 1189–1206.

Fainstein, N. (1995). Black ghettoization and social mobility. In M. P. Smith & J. R. Feagin, *The bubbling cauldron: Race, ethnicity, and the urban crisis* (pp. 123–141). Minneapolis: University of Minnesota Press.

Faux, J. (1993, Fall). The myth of the New Democrat. *The American Prospect,* 15, 20–29.

From, Al. (1992, July). The surburban factor. *The New Democrat,* 32.

Fulton, W. (1997, December). Do housing authorities have a future? *Governing,* 11, 40–43.

Hale, J.F. (1995, Summer). The making of the New Democrats. *Political Science Quarterly,* 110, 207–232.

Judis, J.B. (1996, September 16, 23). Beyond the Clinton presidency. *The New Republic,* 215, 24–26.

Keiser, R.A. (1997). *Subordination or empowerment? African American leadership and the struggle for urban political power.* New York: Oxford University Press.

Massey, D.S., & Denton, N.A. (1993). *American apartheid: Segregation and the making of the underclass.* Cambridge, MA: Harvard University Press.

O'Neill, H., & Sheehan, M. (1995). The impact of new federal budget priorities on America's cities. Taub Urban Research Center, New York University.

Orfield, G., & Ashkinaze, C. (1991). *The closing door.* Chicago: University of Chicago Press.

O'Toole, J. (1998, July 29). Murphy taps Ridge over Itkin for office. *Pittsburgh Post-Gazette,* p. 8B.

Parker, F. (1990). *Black votes count.* Chapel Hill: University of North Carolina Press.

Peterson, P.E. (1981). *City limits.* Chicago: University of Chicago Press.

Polsby, N. (1983). *Consequences of party reform.* New York: Oxford University Press.

Rae, N. (1994). *Southern Democrats.* New York: Oxford University Press.

Ripley, R., & Franklin, G. (1991). *Congress, the bureaucracy, and public policy.* Pacific Grove, CA: Brooks/Cole.

Schneider, W. (1991, September 28). Rule suburbia. *National Journal, 39,* 2335.

———. (1992, July). The suburban century begins. *Atlantic, 270,* 33–44.

Siegel, F. (1994, April–May). Rudy in disguise: Giuliani talks like a New Democrat, can he walk like one? *New Democrat, 6,* 9–14.

Starobin, P. (1998, March 28). The daddy state. *National Journal,13,* 678–683.

Sundquist, J.L. (1968). *Politics and policy: The Eisenhower, Kennedy, and Johnson years.* Washington, DC: The Brookings Institution.

CHAPTER 2

Electoral Arrangements and Minority Political Incorporation

RICHARD L. ENGSTROM

The theory of minority political incorporation has focused on the empowerment of minorities through coalitions with white liberals. The concept of incorporation, therefore, involves more than what Browning, Marshall, and Tabb refer to as "simple representation," or the "mere presence" of minorities on decision-making bodies (1984, p. 141). But the concept does begin with precisely that, the presence of minorities in elected office (1984, pp. 168, 241). White liberals, in their theory, are coalition partners with, not the primary representatives of, minority group members. This important distinction is based on the belief that "minority interests are most likely to be effectively represented by minority persons" (1984, p. 274). The absence of minority elected officials within a political jurisdiction, therefore, results in the lowest possible score, 0, on their quantitative measure of incorporation, regardless of the types of whites that constitute the governing coalition within a city (1984, pp. 272–273; 1997, p. 9).

The election of minority group members, the first step toward incorporation, has usually been heavily dependent on minority group voters. The ability of minority voters to translate their votes into the election of minority representatives, however, has often been dependent in turn on the type of election system employed. At the time Browning, Marshall, and Tabb wrote *Protest Is Not Enough* (1984), the election system widely viewed as the most minority-friendly was the single-member district. Indeed, the basic election system issue at that time, when it came to minority representation in local government, was whether governing bodies should be elected at-large, through single-member districts (in some of which minority group members were expected to constitute a majority of the voters), or through a combination of the two (1984, pp. 68, 202–203). At-large elections were widely viewed as dilutive of minority voting strength, and demands to switch to single-member districts (SMDs) in order to enhance minority electoral opportunities were common (see Helig and Mundt, 1984, pp. 10–12).

Recently, however, the utility of the SMD format as a medium for minority electoral opportunities has come under question. The U.S. Supreme Court has placed new constraints on the creation of majority-minority districts, constraints that will no doubt reduce, in many settings, the number of opportunities that minority voters will have to elect candidates of their choice within that format. The Court has also made it more difficult for minorities to force local governments, through litigation, to change from at-large to SMD arrangements. These changes in the law, not surprisingly, have stimulated interest in alternative ways to structure electoral competition, particularly within the at-large context.

At-large elections can be cleansed of their dilutive tendencies if the voting rules employed within that format are changed. In the typical multiseat at-large election in this country, every voter is allocated as many votes as there are seats to be filled, but then restricted to casting only one vote for any particular candidate. But other voting rules, equally if not more democratic than these, can also be applied to this format. Alternative voting rules can be employed that will provide minority voters with opportunities to elect the candidates they prefer, even when their preferences are not shared by other voters. The alternative systems receiving the most attention, in this respect, are limited, cumulative, and preference voting arrangements. Rather than serving as impediments to minority electoral opportunities, in some settings at-large elections may actually enhance those opportunities, provided limited, cumulative, or preference voting rules are attached to them.

The revisions in the law that threaten to reduce the utility of SMDs as a medium for minority electoral opportunities, and that now stimulate interest in alternative at-large arrangements, will be reviewed below. Modifications in at-large systems based on limited, cumulative, and preference voting will be identified, and their utility as media for enhancing minority electoral opportunities evaluated, both theoretically and empirically. The later will rely on the recent experience with such systems in local elections in several states.

AT-LARGE ELECTIONS AND MINORITY ELECTORAL OPPORTUNITIES

At-large elections under the traditional voting rules were part of a larger package of structural revisions advocated for local governments around the turn of the twentieth century (see, e.g., Bridges, 1992). The first Model City Charter, for example, which was issued by the National Municipal League in 1899, recommended that the at-large format be used in place of the districted arrangements common at the time. At-large elections were widely adopted on the premise that they would result in the election of better qualified council members and that those council members, accountable to a citywide electorate, would base decisions on what was good for the entire city. The combination of superior personnel and a citywide decisional referent was expected to improve dramatically the quality of municipal governance (Engstrom & McDonald, 1986, pp. 203–204).

It is usually very difficult to demonstrate what, if any, impact a particular structural feature has on municipal governance. This has certainly been the case with at-large elections. There is little if any evidence, however, that the at-large format has fulfilled the predictions of its advocates. Welch and Bledsoe have provided the most extensive examination of the nonracial consequences associated with the use of at-large elections and concluded that "whether a person was elected by district or at-large, played a modest role in determining who was elected to office and how that person behaved in office" (1988, p. 104).

The racial consequence of the choice of at-large or district elections has been far from modest, however. When candidate preferences are racially divided, the submergence of the minority's vote within that of the majority in the traditional at-large arrangement makes the election of minority candidates difficult. Given the residential segregation in this country, single-member districting schemes, in contrast, have often resulted in majority-minority districts in which minority candidates have reasonable, if not excellent, chances of being elected. It was well documented at the time that Browning, Marshall, and Tabb wrote that African Americans were more likely to be elected in cities with districted rather than at-large arrangements (see the literature review in Engstrom & McDonald, 1986). In three of the cities they studied, a change from at-large to district elections resulted in an immediate increase in African American representation (1984, pp. 202–203). Changes to district elections have had the same effect in numerous other jurisdictions as well (see, e.g., Grofman and Davidson, 1994). Latinos have also benefited from districts, although not to the same extent as African Americans. The residential segregation of Latinos has been less intense than that of African Americans, and consequently districting tends to be less advantageous for them (see McDonald & Engstrom, 1992; Welch, 1990).

The change from at-large to district elections has often been the result of lawsuits, or the threat of lawsuits, invoking provisions of the Voting Rights Act (VRA) (79 Stat. 667). While initially adopted to eliminate discriminatory voter registration practices, the Act has also provided important protections against the subsequent problem of minority vote dilution. A nationwide protection against election systems that result in the dilution of minority voting strength, as well as a special constraint on changes in election arrangements in areas with a history of discriminatory electoral practices (both discussed below), have been important stimuli to the adoption of majority-minority districts. The growth in the number of minority elected officials has been directly related to the adoption of such districts (see Engstrom, 1994; Grofman & Davidson, 1994; Handley & Grofman, 1994; Arden, Grofman, & Handley, 1997; and Lublin, 1997).

As noted above, the utility of SMDs as a medium for minority electoral opportunities may not be as great in the future as it has been in the past. The Supreme Court has placed new constraints on the creation of majority-minority districts, and also made it more difficult for minorities to force local governments to change from at-large to SMD arrangements. We now turn to these changes in the law and their impact on minority electoral opportunities.

RACE AND THE DISTRICT FORMAT

New constraints on the creation of majority-minority districts have been adopted by the Supreme Court in *Shaw v. Reno* (1993) and its progeny.[1] These constraints are the Court's response to complaints about the manipulation of the district format that followed the census of 1990. In an effort to comply with the requirements of the VRA, majority-minority districts were deliberately included in the post-1990 districting plans adopted by many state and local governments.

Given the absence of any federal constitutional constraints on the design of specific districts, other than that they satisfy the basic "one person, one vote" requirement,[2] some state and local governments employed a search and include approach to the creation of minority districts. Districting cartographers, with the aid of computers, searched for potential minority voters and combined them into a district or districts in which they would have a realistic opportunity to elect a representative of their choice. This motivation, as well as simultaneous partisan, incumbent protection, and various other political considerations, sometimes resulted in districts that were severely contorted in shape. These affirmative efforts to provide minorities with electoral opportunities provoked a hostile response among many whites, who despite continuing to control a greater than proportional number of districts within most of these plans, challenged the constitutionality of this approach to districting.

The Court's response to these complaints has been to elevate the importance of "race-neutral" criteria in the design of districts. In *Shaw,* a case involving North Carolina congressional districts, the Court held that race-based districting must satisfy the "strict scrutiny" test for compliance with the Fourteenth Amendment's equal protection clause even though there is no allegation that the voting strength of any racial group has been adversely affected by the districts. A challenge can be based, instead, on an allegation that "traditional districting principles" have been disregarded in the design of majority-minority districts. In *Shaw* the Court identified "compactness, contiguity, and respect for political subdivisions" as such principles (at 647). In *Miller v. Johnson* (1995), a case concerning congressional districts in Georgia, the Court added respect for "communities defined by actual shared interests" to this list, and held that strict scrutiny was required whenever these criteria (and perhaps others) were "subordinated" to racial considerations in the construction of the districts (at 916). (This limitation, it must be noted, applies only to racial considerations. None of these districting criteria is constitutionally required, and therefore each may be subordinated to nonracial considerations.)

There is great ambiguity concerning exactly what triggers strict scrutiny under the *Shaw/Miller* standard. The absence of clear definitions for some of these criteria, and clear standards for identifying departures from them, have resulted in districting becoming a conceptual as well as a political thicket. Lower court applications of these precedents have employed capricious definitions and conflicting measurements. Contiguity has been confused with compactness, for example, and compactness with communities of interest (see Engstrom, 1995). It is also unclear, in determining whether these principles have been "subordinated," if departures from them are to be compared to absolute standards or to the actual traditions revealed by past districting practices. Justice Sandra Day O'Connor, widely viewed as the swing justice on these matters, suggests it is the latter. She has written, in a brief concurrence in *Miller,* that "certainly the standard does not treat efforts to create majority-minority districts *less* favorably than similar efforts on behalf of other groups" (at 928, emphasis in original). No other justice in the five-person majority in *Miller,* however, joined her in this concurrence.[3]

If these districting criteria are found to have been subordinated to racial considerations, the district or districts at issue must satisfy the strict scrutiny standard. In order to survive such scrutiny, a district must be "narrowly tailored" to achieve a "compelling governmental interest" (*Shaw,* 1993, at 642, 644, 657–658). This standard is very demanding. Indeed, the popular description of strict scrutiny is that it is "strict in theory but fatal in fact." The Supreme Court's application of this test to majority-minority districts subsequent to *Shaw* has been fatal in all cases.[4] While these cases have concerned congressional districts, they serve as precedents directly applicable to majority-minority districts at the local level as well. The need to deviate from these "traditional principles" to create minority councilmanic districts will not be as great in many urban areas as it is in statewide congressional plans, but the elevation of these criteria will no doubt reduce the number of such councilmanic districts created following the census of 2000, especially the number that is majority-Latino.[5]

WEAKENING VOTING RIGHTS PROTECTIONS

Compliance with the Voting Rights Act was a major stimulus to the adoption of majority-minority districts following the 1990 census, especially those with bizarre appearances. Section 2 of that Act, as amended in 1982, contains a "results" test that prohibits districting plans that dilute a protected minority's voting strength (see *Thornburg v. Gingles,* 1986).[6] The provision prohibits electoral arrangements in which minority voters have "less opportunity than other members of the electorate to participate in the political process and to elect representatives of their choice." In addition, one of the special provisions of the Act, section 5, imposes a "preclearance" requirement on some governmental jurisdictions that precludes them from adopting districting plans that have a discriminatory purpose or effect.[7] Preclearance may be granted by either the Attorney General or the federal district court for the District of Columbia. The burden of proof in these determinations rests with the government adopting the plan. Recent decisions by the Supreme Court, however, in addition to *Shaw* and its progeny, raise serious questions about the future impact of these provisions.

Section 2 has been the focus of legal challenges to at-large election systems, and also to multimember districts that have a similar tendency to submerge the electoral strength of minorities. The "results" test of section 2 was adopted in 1982 in response to the Supreme Court's determination, in *City of Mobile v. Bolden* (1980), that dilutive election arrangements do not violate the Fourteenth Amendment unless they had been adopted, or continued to be used, for racially discriminatory reasons. Section 2 was revised to eliminate the necessity of proving intent in order to win a dilution lawsuit. Three reasons were given in the legislative history for this modification. Proof of intent was found to present plaintiffs with an "inordinately difficult" burden, while the inquiry itself is "unnecessarily divisive." But "the main reason" identified for rejecting a need to prove intent was that it "asks the wrong question." The appropriate inquiry is *whether* the voting strength of a minority group is being diluted by the system, not *why* the dilution is tolerated (S. Rep. No. 97-417, at 36).[8] Section 2, therefore, was amended to provide that a demonstration of a system's discriminatory effects would be a separate basis, in addition to discriminatory intent, for invalidating a dilutive arrangement.

The determination of whether a system has a dilutive effect is to be based, according to the statute, on "the totality of circumstances" in the governmental jurisdiction at issue. Several things were identified in the legislative history of the amendment as "typical factors" that judges might examine in assessing the circumstances, such as the extent to which minority group members have been elected, whether voting has been racially polarized, whether candidate slating processes have been open to minorities, and whether racial appeals have been made in campaigns. But judges were not limited to examining only those identified, nor was there any requirement that a specified number of factors be found to be present in order to reach a conclusion about a system's effects (S. Rep. No. 97–417, at 19–20). This is an extremely flexible decisional standard. Justice Clarence Thomas has described it, correctly, as:

> ... a list of possible considerations that might be consulted by a court attempting to develop a *gestalt* view of the political and racial climate in a jurisdiction, but a list that cannot provide a rule for deciding a vote dilution claim (*Holder v. Hall,* 1994, at 938).[9]

The totality of circumstances standard places, in short, "breathtaking discretion" in the hands of federal judges, promising "wide variation in outcome based on a judge's subjective beliefs" (Mulroy, 1997, pp. 59, 60). It is fair to say that in the first wave of dilution cases under

this standard, which party won often depended less on the evidence mar-
shalled than, as with the intent test, on "the luck of the judicial draw"
(Kousser, 1984, p. 37; see also Engstrom, 1985).

One approach employed in defending at-large systems was to reinsert an intent requirement through the evidentiary issue of racially polarized voting, which is "ordinarily the keystone of a dilution case" (*United
States v. Marengo County Commission*, 1984, at 1566). Not surprisingly,
clear and consistent racial divisions in the candidate preferences of voters were documented in numerous settings faced with dilution allegations. Defendant jurisdictions attempted to dismiss these divisions by
arguing that additional evidence demonstrating that the voters' choices
were racially *motivated* was required of plaintiffs. This was done through
two basic approaches. One was to argue that voting was not racially polarized, regardless of how acute the racial divisions were, unless evidence of other racially motivated behavior was available, such as special
efforts to mobilize white voters when minority candidates were on the
ballot. An adverse "racial climate," it was maintained, was a necessary
condition for dilution to occur. The second approach was to assert that a
multivariate analysis of voting behavior was required. The argument was
that variables other than race, such as the income level of voters, or their
assessments of the relative merits of the candidates, or their issue preferences, were the *causes* of the divisions in candidate preferences. If plaintiffs had not demonstrated that these other factors, which, of course, were
themselves related to race, had not been the "cause" of the divisions, it
was argued that voting was not racially polarized.

Reinserting an intent requirement into the dilution determination,
through the polarized voting issue, proved to be a successful strategy in
some courtrooms. These efforts to "cleanse" racial divisions in voting of
any racial content were seized upon by some federal judges as reasons to
conclude that plaintiffs had failed on this critical evidentiary matter. Vote
dilution, they therefore concluded, had not occurred, despite the fact that
minority candidates favored by minority voters were being consistently
defeated (see Engstrom, 1985).

The Supreme Court placed significant constraints on the discretion
that lower court judges had under the totality of circumstances test in
1986 in *Thornburg v Gingles*. The case concerned the dilution of the minority vote by submergence in multimember state legislative districts,
but provides a direct precedent for allegations of submergence through
at-large elections as well. Focusing on evidentiary considerations that related directly to the problem of dilution, the Court in *Gingles* stated that

two of the factors explicitly identified in the legislative history of section 2 were "the most important" ones for judges to consider in a submergence case—the extent to which members of the minority group at issue had been elected, and the extent to which voting had been racially polarized. The other factors, if present, were said to be "supportive of, but *not essential to,* a minority voter's claim" (at 48–49, n.15). The Court then proceeded to identify three "necessary preconditions" for a dilution by submergence claim to succeed. These are (1) a demonstration that a possible remedy for any dilution is available, in the form of a majority-minority SMD, (2) evidence that the minority at issue is "politically cohesive," and (3) evidence that the majority of voters is able, usually, to defeat the candidates preferred by the minority (at 50–51).

The second and third preconditions were essentially a restatement of the polarized voting issue. Justice William Brennan, in a portion of the *Gingles* opinion joined by three other justices, explicitly rejected both approaches to reinserting an intent requirement through the polarized voting inquiry (at 63–74). Brennan stated that "the reasons black and white voters vote differently have no relevance to the central inquiry of section 2" (at 63), and that requiring proof of "*racial hostility* toward black candidates" was inconsistent with the congressional intent to free plaintiffs of the need to prove intent (at 71). The four concurring justices also agree with this position, although they would consider evidence of nonracial causes for voting divisions to be relevant to "the overall vote dilution inquiry" (O'Connor, J., concurring, at 100).

Gingles provided a much needed focus to the vote dilution inquiry, one that did provide a basic rule for adjudicating dilution by submergence claims. The vastly more ambiguous totality of circumstances standard of course still had to be satisfied, but it was now much less likely that judges, after finding that the three preconditions of *Gingles* were present, would find a system somehow free of dilution. Justice Thomas has noted that, following *Gingles,* the totality of circumstances inquiry became an "empty ritual." The other factors identified in the legislative history had become "essentially superfluous" to the dilution determination (*Holder v. Hall,* Thomas, J., dissenting, at 939). After *Gingles* it was, without question, easier for minority plaintiffs to prevail in challenges to at-large systems, and thereby force jurisdictions to adopt SMD arrangements containing majority-minority districts.

The preconditions identified in *Gingles* have also been applied to dilution allegations involving SMDs (*Growe v. Emison,* 1993, and *Voinovich v. Quilter,* 1993). Recognizing that a districting arrangement may well contain a number of majority-minority districts yet still dilute the voting strength of a minority, the Court, in *Johnson v. DeGrandy* (1994), modified the first precondition to require, in this context, that plaintiffs demonstrate that additional "reasonably compact" majority-minority districts could have been adopted by the jurisdiction (at 1008).

In *DeGrandy,* however, the Court relied on the totality of circumstances standard to reverse a lower court finding that a state legislative districting plan was dilutive. Justice David Souter, writing for a seven-member majority, noted that the presence of the *Gingles* preconditions is not, by itself, a sufficient basis for finding a section 2 violation. Judges, he stated, must also examine "other evidence in the totality of circumstances, including the extent of the opportunities minority voters enjoy to participate in the political processes" (at 1011–1012). The plan at issue provided the minority group with a "roughly proportional" number of minority districts, a feature of the plan that Souter found to be a "relevant fact in the totality of circumstances" (at 1000). While proportionality, Souter stated, is not always dispositive of the dilution inquiry, in this particular situation it was found to be.

The *DeGrandy* decision has had the effect of removing much of the constraint on judicial discretion that *Gingles* had imposed. While the focus in *DeGrandy* was on the proportionality feature of the plan, lower courts have accepted the invitation to look far beyond the *Gingles* preconditions to conclude that, despite their presence, and despite the absence of a proportional number of opportunities for minorities to elect the candidates of their choice, no violation of section 2 has occurred. Indeed, some judges have treated *DeGrandy* as an invitation to, once again, reinsert an intent requirement into the dilution inquiry, this time through the totality of circumstances conclusion.

This is the approach taken, for example, in *Uno v. City of Holyoke* (1995), a challenge by Latinos to the at-large portion of a municipal election system. A three-judge panel of the First Circuit Court of Appeals, in vacating a district court decision in favor of the plaintiffs, held that, after *DeGrandy,* if a court finds that white or Anglo voters veto the candidates preferred by minority voters (the third prong of *Gingles*), the court may still, as part of its totality of circumstances determination, "mull other factors, apart from racial bias, that may have caused the white bloc voting" (at 980). Indeed, a lack of "racial animus," the *Holyoke* panel held, is in effect a "safe harbor" for defendants. As expressed by the panel:

> We believe it follows that after *DeGrandy,* plaintiffs *cannot prevail* on
> a VRA section 2 claim if there is significantly probative evidence that

whites voted as a bloc for reasons wholly unrelated to racial animus. (at 981, emphasis added)

If there is an absence of "racial antagonism" behind the white veto, the panel maintained, then the defeat of the minority's preferred candidate "does not prove the lack of electoral opportunity but a lack of whatever it takes to be successful in politics" (at 981). The court provided examples of these other explanations, which were, with parenthetical material added, "failure to support popular [among Anglos] programmatic initiatives, or failure to reflect the [Anglo] majority's ideological viewpoints, or failure to appreciate the popularity [among Anglos] of an incumbent" (at 981).

Holyoke is, needless to say, a rerun of the pre-*Gingles* effort to reinsert an intent standard into the dilution inquiry. Only the medium for doing so, not the method, has changed. The method is simply to reference more proximate, yet themselves racially related, "causes" for voting behavior. Racial divisions in candidate preferences are, it is argued, somehow cleansed of racial context by this exercise. The medium through which this intent requirement is inserted into the dilution determination is no longer the racially polarized voting inquiry, but rather the more ambiguous totality of circumstances determination.

The *Holyoke* panel's approach seriously erodes the ability of minority plaintiffs to force, through section 2 litigation, a jurisdiction to switch from an at-large to a districted arrangement.[10] It similarly affects a minority's ability to challenge districting plans on vote dilution grounds, as well as its ability, and that of a state or local government, to defend majority-minority districts that have been challenged under *Shaw* as necessary to avoid a violation of the VRA.[11]

RETREAT ON PRECLEARANCE

A major impediment to the adoption of dilutive districting arrangements has been the preclearance provision of section 5 of the VRA. Since the adoption of the VRA, the Department of Justice has denied preclearance to over 7,000 districting plans under this provision for being discriminatory either in purpose or effect. In the post-1990 round of redistricting, the department has been accused by many of requiring jurisdictions covered by section 5 to maximize the number of majority-minority districts in their new plans as a condition for preclearance. While maximization has not been the policy of the department (see Dunne, 1993, p. 1128), it has been the result, in some contexts, of the department's policy of denying preclearance to plans that constitute a "clear violation" of the results test of section 2 (28 CFR sec. 51.55(b)(2) (1996). Many of the contorted majority-minority districts adopted after the 1990 census were adopted in response to, or in anticipation of, the Justice Department rejecting plans that would, in its view, violate section 2. This interpretation of its authority under section 5, however, has recently been rejected by the Supreme Court in *Reno v. Bossier Parish School Board* (1997).

The "effects" portion of section 5 had been interpreted by the Supreme Court, in 1976, as prohibiting only those new districting plans that had a *retrogressive* impact on minority voters (i.e., were worse for the minority than the plan they replaced) (*Beer v. United States*). Following the addition of the results test to section 2 in 1982, the Justice Department added the section 2 consideration to its preclearance calculus. In *Shaw*-based challenges to contorted districts, the Court in 1995 and 1996 had registered disagreement with the department's interpretation of what section 2 required of districting plans (*Miller v. Johnson*, 1995, at 920–927, and *Shaw v. Hunt*, 1996, at 911, 915–918; see also *Abrams v. Johnson*, 1997, at 90–95), but it had not stated that section 2, properly interpreted, could not provide the basis for a section 5 objection. In *Reno v. Bossier Parish School Board*, however, the Court did just that, holding that a perceived violation of section 2's results test cannot serve, by itself, as the basis for an objection. Section 5's protection against discriminatory effects was again limited to those that are retrogressive. [The Court left for another day the question of whether the section's protection against purposeful discrimination extends beyond retrogression (at 486).]

The Supreme Court has placed new constraints on the use of race as a referent in districting decisions, emphasized the totality of circumstances as the decision rule in section 2 challenges to election systems, and rejected the Department of Justice's policy of denying preclearance under section 5 to plans viewed as violating section 2. The traditional medium for minority electoral opportunities, the majority-minority district, will no doubt be harder to implement under these conditions. Fewer local governments can be expected to shift from at-large to districted election systems in the future, and fewer majority-minority districts can be expected within the districting schemes adopted by jurisdictions employing that format. It is not surprising, therefore, that among those concerned with minority electoral opportunities, interest has increased in alternative ways to structure electoral competition. This interest has focused on systems that retain the at-large feature but contain significant changes in the voting rules employed. The alternative arrangements that have received the most attention have been limited, cumulative, and preference voting systems.

ALTERNATIVE ELECTION SYSTEMS

Interest in providing minority voters with electoral opportunities through alternative election systems predates the Supreme Court's recent restrictions on SMDs (see, e.g., Zimmerman, 1978; Note, 1981, 1982; and Still, 1984). Limited, cumulative, and preference voting in particular have long been recognized as systems in which politically cohesive but residentially dispersed minority groups can compete effectively. When these systems are employed, electoral units do not need to be majority-minority in order to provide minority groups with realistic opportunities to elect candidates favored by them. Prior to the 1990 census, cumulative and limited voting had even been adopted as remedies for dilutive electoral arrangements in a number of municipalities, counties, and school districts (see Engstrom, 1992; Engstrom, Kirksey & Still, 1997b; and Arrington & Ingalls, 1998).

Limited, cumulative, and preference voting systems have been called modified multiseat election systems.[12] They can be used in any multiseat election context, whether "at-large" across an entire political jurisdiction or within a multimember geographical district. They vary from the typical multiseat elections in this country, however, in that the rules concerning how votes may be cast are different. As noted above, the voting rules traditionally employed in multiseat elections in this country are (1) every voter is allowed to cast as many votes as there are seats to be filled, but (2) only one of those votes may be cast for any particular candidate. The winners of the seats are then determined by a plurality vote rule; the N candidates receiving the most votes win the N available seats. It is these voting rules employed with the multiseat format, not the format itself, that is responsible for the dilutive results of multiseat elections. If other voting rules are employed, minority voters can have a realistic opportunity to elect candidates of their choice within that format. Limited, cumulative, and preference voting are three systems through which such opportunities can be provided.

Limited Voting

Limited voting makes the simplest change in the voting rules. In this system each voter in a multiseat election is provided with a number of votes that is less than the number of seats to be filled. For example, if five people are to be elected at-large, each voter in that electoral unit may be limited to casting only a single vote. The limitation could also be set at two, or three, or even four. The defining characteristic of limited voting is simply that the number of votes be fewer than the number of seats. Voters are still restricted to casting only one vote for any particular candidate, and winning candidates continue to be determined by a simple plurality rule; the top N vote recipients are elected to the N seats at issue.

Limited voting can provide minority voters with an opportunity to elect candidates of their choice by reducing the plurality's ability to win every seat. The restriction on the number of votes reduces the larger group's ability to submerge the votes of a minority. The smaller the number of votes allocated to each voter, the fewer votes that group has to distribute across the candidates of its choice, and the less dominant it is likely to be. The more limited the vote compared to the number of seats, therefore, the greater the opportunity minority voters will have to place a candidate or candidates of their choice among the winners.

Cumulative Voting

Under cumulative voting rules, each voter may continue to be provided with as many votes as there are seats to be filled, but the restriction that only a single vote may be cast for any particular candidate is removed. Voters may still vote in the more traditional fashion, providing several candidates with one vote apiece. But if they wish, they may cumulate their votes behind fewer candidates than there are seats being filled. Generally, the only restriction in distributing votes among the candidates is that the votes be cast in whole units. In a five-seat, five-vote election, for example, voters retain the option of voting for five different candidates, giving each of them a single vote. But if a voter prefers some candidates more intensely than the other candidates, he or she may cast the five votes for fewer than five candidates. A voter with a strong preference for two particular candidates, for instance, could cast two votes for each of them and another vote for a third candidate. If a voter strongly preferred the election of one particular candidate over all of the others, that voter could cast all five of his or her votes for that candidate (a practice known as "plumping").[13] As with limited voting, winning candidates are determined by a simple plurality rule.

Despite the absence of any limitation on the overall voting strength of the plurality, minority voters can have opportunities to elect candidates of their choice when cumulative voting rules are employed. The removal of the one vote for any particular candidate limitation permits minority voters to cast, in effect, a more efficacious type of "single-shot" vote than they can in other multiseat elections. The single-shot voting strategy entails group members voting for only one particular candidate (or perhaps a few, depending on the relative size of the group). Under the more traditional voting rules, when a group employs the single-shot strategy it does not fully exercise its franchise. The group's voters cast a vote for the candidate that they want elected, and simply withhold the rest of their votes from all of the other candidates so as not to add to the vote totals of those other candidates. The idea behind single-shot voting is that by voting for one particular candidate and not contributing votes to the others, the candidate preferred by the group might finish among the top N vote recipients and win one of the seats.[14] With cumulative voting, a group will not need to withhold its remaining votes, but can cast those votes as well for the candidate of it choice. Cumulative voting allows minority voters to concentrate their votes much more powerfully, and thereby increases their opportunity to elect a candidate or candidates preferred by them.

Preference Voting

Preference voting, also known as the single transferable vote, is like a one vote limited system in that every voter is allocated a single vote. Under this system, however, voters are allowed to indicate more than simply which candidate they most prefer. They may also, if they wish, rank order candidates to reflect their relative preferences among them. A voter may rank his or her first choice as "1," second choice as "2," third choice as "3," and so forth, until they no longer care to distinguish among the remaining candidates.

Voters are allowed to rank order candidates because in this system votes that would be "wasted" on one candidate can be transferred to another candidate. A vote can be wasted in either of two ways. It could be cast in support of a losing candidate, or it could be a "surplus" vote cast in support of a candidate who would win without it. Rather than waste a vote in such situations, preference voting allows a vote to transfer to the next choice of the voter. This transfer feature is designed to increase the number of voters in an election whose vote will ultimately contribute to the election of a candidate.

The winning candidates in a preference voting election are those whose votes equal or exceed a specified number. This number is usually based on the *Droop quota,* which is the lowest number of votes that can be required for election and yet limit the number of individuals elected to the number of seats to be filled. This quota is 1 more than the quotient obtained when the total number of votes cast in an election is divided by 1 plus the number of seats to be filled. If three seats are to be filled and 1,000 votes are cast, for example, the quota will be 251, the value that results from dividing 1,000 by (3+1), and then adding 1.

The first step in counting the votes in a preference voting election is to allocate to each candidate the ballots on which he or she is listed as the first preference. If none of the candidates has a number of first preferences equal to or exceeding the quota, then the candidate with the fewest first preference votes is considered defeated and the votes received by that candidate transferred to the candidates listed as the second preferences on those ballots. Each candidate's votes are then recounted. If a candidate exceeds the quota, however, then that candidate is declared elected and any surplus votes (above the quota) received by the candidate are redistributed to the candidates listed as the next preference. Whereas transferring the votes of defeated candidates is straightforward (all of that candidate's votes are transferred to the next most preferred candidates among the remaining candidates), transferring surplus votes is more complicated. Several methods are available for transferring surplus votes. The simplest is to declare a candidate elected once his or her vote matches the quota and then transfer all of the subsequent ballots that go to that candidate. Another method, used in Ireland where preference voting is employed to elect the Dail, the lower (and most significant) house of parliament, is to select randomly a number of ballots equal to a candidate's surplus and transfer those ballots to the next available preference. A third method, probably the most preferable now that computers can be used to count votes, is to redistribute the surplus in a proportional manner. Each remaining candidate (not already elected or eliminated) would be given a share of the surplus votes equal to the proportion of the ballots on which he or she was the next choice of the voters.[15]

A count of the ballots in a hypothetical preference voting election involving five candidates competing for three seats is contained in Table 2.1. It assumes that 2,000 votes are cast, so the Droop quota is 501. The first preferences of the voters are distributed as reflected in the column labeled First Count. Candidate C1 receives 480 first preference votes, candidate C2 receives 470, C3 450, C4 350, and C5 250. Given that none of the candidates has met the quota, the lowest vote recipient, C5, is eliminated and his votes redistributed. Most of C5's voters, 200, identified C4 as their second preference, and therefore C4 receives 200 votes

Table 2.1. Hypothetical Single Transferable Vote (STV) Election for Three Seats

Candidate	First Count	Transfer	Second Count	Transfer	Third Count
C1	480	+15	495	+25	520 elected
C2	470	+25	495	+20	515 elected
C3	450	+10	460	+4	464
C4	350	+200	550 elected		
C5	250 eliminated				

via transfer from C5. The other candidates receive only a few of C5's votes, 15, 25, and 10, respectively, for C1, C2, and C3. When the second preferences are added to the first preferences, reflected in the column labeled Second Count, C4's new vote total is 550, which exceeds the quota. C4 is therefore declared elected and his 49 surplus votes redistributed. If these surplus votes are transferred proportionally, and C1 is the next preference among the remaining candidates on 281 of C4's ballots, C2 the next preference on 224 of them, and C3 the next preference on 45, then the C1 would receive 25 of the surplus votes, C2 20, and C3 only four. When these votes are added to the candidates' totals, the results, reported in the column labeled Third Count, put C1 and C2 over the quota. C1 and C2 are, therefore, declared elected to the two remaining seats and the counting of the votes concluded.

Preference voting, as noted above, is like limited voting when the number of votes is limited to one. It also reduces the ability of a cohesive plurality to win all of the seats by limiting each voter to one vote. The transfer feature allows a minority group to transfer wasted ballots among candidates preferred by the group, a feature that makes intragroup competition less likely to cause the defeat of candidates the group prefers.

ELECTORAL OPPORTUNITIES UNDER
ALTERNATIVE SYSTEMS

All three of these modified multiseat systems, which satisfy the basic "one person, one vote" rule because every voter has the same number of votes and the same options with which to cast them,[16] can cleanse the at-large format of its tendency to dilute the vote of a minority group. These alterations in the voting rules counter the submergence effect that so often accompanies the traditional rules, and thereby can provide minority voters with opportunities to elect candidates of their choice, even when voting occurs along group lines.

The opportunities to elect candidates that these systems provide minority voters can be demonstrated theoretically through a coefficient known as the *threshold of exclusion* (see Rae, Hanby & Loosemore, 1971). This coefficient identifies the percentage or proportion of the electorate that a group must exceed in order to elect a candidate of its choice *regardless of how the rest of the voters vote*. This coefficient is based on a set of worst case assumptions, from the minority group's perspective, about the behavior of the other voters. These assumptions are:

1. the other voters cast all of the votes available to them, but
2. none of their votes are cast for the candidate preferred by the minority voters, but rather are
3. concentrated entirely on a number of other candidates equal to the number of seats to be filled, and are
4. divided evenly among those other candidates.

The other voters, in short, are assumed to cast their votes as efficiently as possible in a multiseat election.

The value of the threshold of exclusion for limited voting systems depends on both the number of seats to be filled and on how limited the vote is. The formula for calculating this threshold for limited voting, expressed as a percentage, is:

$$\frac{(\text{Number of Votes})}{(\text{Number of Votes}) + (\text{Number of Seats})} \times 100$$

If the vote is limited to one, for example, the threshold value for a three-seat election is $[1/(1+3)]*100$, or 25.0 percent. In other words, if 251 voters out of 1,000 (25%+1) all voted for candidate A, then candidate A must be elected to one of the three seats. Even if the other 749 voted according to the worst case assumptions, casting all of their votes for only three candidates, B, C, and D, with B receiving 250, C also receiving 250, and D 249, candidate A would be the highest vote recipient and therefore win a seat. If the other voters did not vote according to the worst case assumptions, but instead cast their votes unevenly so that B received 260 and C 255, for example, then the most D can receive is 234

Table 2.2. Threshold of Exclusion Values

Number of Seats	Cumulative Voting	Limited Voting		
		1 Vote	2 Votes	3 Votes
2	33.3	33.3	—	—
3	25.0	25.0	40.0	—
4	20.0	20.0	33.3	42.9
5	16.7	16.7	28.6	37.5
6	14.3	14.3	25.0	33.3
7	12.5	12.5	22.2	30.0
8	11.1	11.1	20.0	27.3
9	10.0	10.0	18.2	25.0

and the minority preferred candidate, A, still wins one of the three seats. Illustrative values of the threshold for limited voting, for various seat and vote combinations, are reported in Table 2.2. For any number of seats, the more limited the vote is, the lower will be the value of the threshold. Likewise, for any number of votes, the larger the number of seats, the lower the threshold value. The threshold for a two-vote, three-seat election, for example, is 40.0 percent, while that for a one-vote, five-seat election is 16.7 percent.

The formula for calculating the threshold of exclusions values for cumulative voting systems, expressed as a percentage, is:

$$\frac{1}{1 + (\text{Number of Seats})} \times 100$$

This is the same as that for limited voting when the number of votes is one. In the three-seat cumulative context, for example, the value of the formula is again 25.0 percent. In other words, if those 251 voters out of 1,000 (25 percent + 1) each "plumped" all three of their votes for candidate A, giving him 753 votes, then A again must win one of the seats. The other 749 voters could distribute their 2,247 votes evenly across only three candidates, so that B, C, and D each receive 749, and A would still be a winner. Again, if the other voters deviated from the worst case assumptions, giving more votes to two of their choices, their third choice would have even fewer votes and A would still win a seat. As with the one-vote limited context, the more seats at issue the lower will be the value of the threshold for cumulative voting. Illustrative values of the threshold for the cumulative context, for different numbers of seats, are also reported in Table 2.2.

If the Droop quota used in preference voting systems, which identifies the number of votes a candidate must receive in order to be elected, is expressed as a percentage, it is also the same as the threshold of exclusion (plus 1 vote) for a one vote limited system or a cumulative system. As noted above, the Droop quota for a three-seat election with 1,000 voters is 251. This is the result of dividing 1,000 by (3+1), and adding 1. Any group, in short, that can provide a candidate with at least 25 percent plus one of the votes is elected to one of the three seats in a preference voting election, just as in a one vote limited or cumulative voting election. The threshold values for preference voting, therefore, also vary inversely with the number of seats, just as in the other systems.

The threshold of exclusion, it must be remembered, identifies the percentage of the voters in a particular election that a group sharing the same candidate preference must exceed in order to elect that candidate with no assistance whatsoever from the other voters. If the behavior of other voters deviates in any way from the worst case assumptions, then a minority group may be smaller and/or less cohesive in its preferences and still have a realistic opportunity to elect a candidate or candidates of its choice through one of these voting systems.

Deviations from perfect cohesion among minority voters can, of course, negate their opportunity to elect a candidate, even when their presence in the electorate exceeds the threshold. In the previous illustration involving a three-seat, one vote election, for example, if just 10 percent of the minority voters (25 of the 251) had as their first preference another candidate, say E rather than A, then A would have received only 226 votes and failed to have won a seat. In the three-vote cumulative election, if a second candidate, E, received just 10 percent of the votes cast by minority voters (75 votes), candidate A would be left with 678 and again fail to win a seat. Electoral opportunities provided by limited and cumulative voting can be negated, in short, by intragroup competition.

Preference voting is more conducive to intragroup competition than either limited or cumulative voting. As long as minority voters share a preference for a set of candidates, there can be competition among those candidates for minority voter support without that competition precluding the election of one or more of them because votes can transfer among them. Preference voting in effect offers minority voters, as well as other voters, the equivalent of a primary election (or a series of primary elections) and a general election through a single ballot on the same day. In the previous illustration, for example, if those voting for candidate E preferred A to all of the other candidates, then in a preference voting election A would have been elected when E's votes transferred to him following E's elimination for being the last place candidate. Likewise, in the illustrative preference voting election in Table 2.1, if C4 and C5 were candidates whose 600 votes came from minority voters, the fact that minority voters had initially divided their votes between them would not have precluded either from being elected. Rather, the minority voter cohesion, reflected by most of C5's voters listing C4 as their second preference, would allow C4 to win one of the seats. This feature of preference voting is particularly advantageous when the minority might have enough electoral strength to elect more than one candidate in a multiseat election. An uneven distribution of support across candidates is much less problematic, given the transfer feature, in a preference voting election than a limited or cumulative voting contest.

ELECTORAL EXPERIENCE WITH ALTERNATIVE SYSTEMS

Electoral systems are alleged to have numerous consequences, some of which are good, some of which are bad, and some of which commentators disagree about the value. As was the case with the more traditional at-large election, many of these claims concerning limited, cumulative, and preference voting are exaggerated (see Engstrom, 1998). Most either have not been, or cannot yet be, documented. One claim about which there cannot be serious disagreement, however, is that these modified multiseat election systems do provide minority voters with opportunities to elect candidates of their choice.[17]

Minority electoral opportunities within these systems are not just theoretical (see, e.g., Gerber, et al., 1998). Both cumulative voting and limited voting systems have been adopted in response to lawsuits, or the threat of lawsuits, alleging minority vote dilution. Courts have approved the adoption of these systems when they provided the basis for the settlement of such suits, and the Department of Justice has almost invariably granted preclearance to them (see Mulroy, 1995). Cumulative voting has been adopted by almost sixty counties, municipalities, and school boards in five states, while limited voting has been adopted by almost forty such units, also in five states.[18] Elections have now been held under these voting rules in almost all of these settings. These elections have demonstrated that when the minority's percentage of the electorate exceeds, or even approaches, the threshold of exclusion value in one of these systems, minority candidates have almost always been elected (see, e.g., Engstrom, 1992; Engstrom, Kirksey & Still, 1997a; Brischetto & Engstrom, 1997; Arrington & Ingalls, 1998). Exit polls conducted at a number of these elections have further confirmed that these minority candidates, often the first minority ever elected to the particular governing body, have been the choices of minority voters. These results have been found regardless of whether the relevant minority has been African Americans (Engstrom, Kirksey & Still, 1997b), Latinos (Engstrom, Taebel & Cole, 1989; Cole, Engstrom & Taebel, 1990; Cole & Taebel, 1992; and Brischetto & Engstrom, 1997), or Native Americans (Engstrom & Barrilleaux, 1991).[19]

The critical factor in providing minority voters with electoral opportunities through these arrangements has been how close the minority presence in the electorate matches the threshold of exclusion for a particular system. Brischetto and Engstrom, for example, conducted exit polls at fifteen cumulative voting elections in Texas in 1995 in which at least one Latino was a candidate. These elections were for either a municipal council or a local school board. In all seven of the elections in which the ratio between the percentage of those signing in to vote that was Latino and the threshold of exclusion value exceeded .9, Latino candidates favored by Latino voters were elected. In the one setting where the percentage of Latino voters was almost twice the threshold of exclusion (1.93), two Latino candidates favored by Latino voters were elected. A Latino candidate favored by Latino voters was also elected in a setting where the Latino percentage of those signing in constituted almost two-thirds (.66) of the threshold (Brischetto & Engstrom, 1997).[20]

In the other seven settings no Latino was elected, despite Latino candidates being the choice of Latino voters in all but one of them. One might speculate that because of its complexity the cumulative system will be difficult for voters to comprehend, particularly minority voters because they tend to be less educated than other voters. The Texas exit polls, however, like those in other settings, provide no evidence that minority voters, or other voters, have particular difficulty understanding or using cumulative options (Engstrom & Brischetto, 1998; see also Cole, Engstrom & Taebel, 1990; Engstrom & Barrilleaux, 1991; Cole & Taebel, 1992; and Engstrom, Kirksey & Still, 1997b).

Intragroup competition, as noted above, can negate the electoral opportunities provided minority groups through cumulative voting (see Engstrom, 1993; Aspin & Hall, 1996). Yet, in only one of these settings was there more than a single candidate. If all of the votes cast for the last place Latino candidate in that election had been cast for the other Latino candidate, the other would still have failed to win a seat (Brischetto & Engstrom, 1997, p. 984).

The primary reason the Latino candidates lost in the other Texas settings was an insufficient mobilization of the Latino electorate. The ratio of the percentage of those signing in to vote that was Latino and the value of the threshold of exclusion for the cumulative system in these settings ranged from .64 to .06. In some of these settings too few seats were being contested to give Latino voters a realistic chance of electing Latino candidates, given the percentage of registered voters that was Latino. In all of these settings Latino turnout was much lower than that of the other voters (Brischetto & Engstrom, 1997). Alternative election systems have been criticized as systems that guarantee proportional representation. The Texas results clearly demonstrate that while these systems can be structured to provide minority voters with opportunities to elect candidates of their choice, they guarantee no particular election outcomes. They provide electoral opportunities, and nothing more.

Recent experience with preference voting in the United States has been much more limited. Only New York City and Cambridge, Massachusetts, currently employ the system. While twenty-two cities have used preference voting for councilmanic elections at some time during the 1900s, Cambridge is the only city continuing to use the arrangement (Weaver, 1986). In many of the cities that used preference voting in the past, African Americans were elected for the first time, and continued to be elected, under that arrangement (see Barber, 1995: *passim*). The success of minority candidates has been cited as a major reason for the abandonment of these systems at the time, as opponents of the system often used the "race card" in their campaigns for repeal (Amy, 1997, p. 18; see also Barber, *passim;* and Burnham, 1997). Cambridge continues to use the preference system to elect both its city council and school committee, bodies on which African Americans have been consistently represented (Amy, 1993, p. 166). In New York the system has been used since 1970 to elect thirty-two community school boards, on which African Americans and Latinos have generally won a close to proportional number of seats over the years (Amy, 1993, p. 138).

Unlike limited and cumulative voting, preference voting has not been adopted in response to vote dilution allegations. Minority group leaders have been instrumental in getting it placed on the ballot for voter consideration in Cincinnati in 1988 and 1991 and in San Francisco in

1996, however, and touted the electoral opportunities it provides minority voters (see Engstrom, 1990, 1993, pp. 800–804; DeLeon, Blash & Hill, 1997). The system was rejected in both cities as the result of racially divided votes in which African Americans were supportive of the system but whites were not (Engstrom, 1993, pp. 801, 804; DeLeon, Blash & Hill, pp. 21–26, 48–55). In all three instances preference voting received around 45 percent of the total vote, an encouraging response to many of its supporters (see, e.g., Electoral Reform Society, 1996).

CONCLUSION

The political incorporation of minorities begins, according to Browning, Marshall, and Tabb, with the election of minority group members (1984, pp. 168, 214; 1997, p. 9). This first step toward incorporation has usually been dependent on the presence of not only a sufficient number of minority voters, but also on the use of electoral systems that do not systematically dilute the minority's voting strength. The major election system issue concerning minority electoral opportunities in local politics has been, for many years, the choice between the traditional at-large system or SMDs. This has been an unnecessarily truncated choice, however, as many other electoral systems, equally if not more democratic than these, can provide minorities with reasonable electoral opportunities. Limited, cumulative, and preference voting are three such systems.

These three alternative systems began to receive considerable attention in the late 1980s. Limited and cumulative voting rules were even adopted, in response to vote dilution complaints, by a number of local governments at that time. Interest in these systems has intensified, however, in the 1990s, as Supreme Court decisions have created questions about the number of minority electoral opportunities that SMDs will provide in the future. New constraints on the creation of majority-minority districts, plus recent decisions concerning the anti-dilution protections contained in sections 2 and 5 of the VRA, have created conditions that could result in that medium providing fewer minority electoral opportunities than it has in the past.

Limited, cumulative, and preference voting are receiving increased attention as alternative arrangements through which minorities, without the need for geographical districts, can gain such opportunities. Experience with these voting rules has confirmed their utility. As long as the threshold of exclusion associated with the specific applications of these systems is not set too high relative to the minority's voting strength, these systems can provide opportunities at least comparable to, and sometimes exceeding, those provided through SMD arrangements. The at-large election format, in short, need not be dilutive, even in the face of racially polarized candidate preferences, if these voting rules are employed with that format.

NOTES

[1]See *Miller v. Johnson* (1995), *Bush v. Vera* (1996), *Shaw v. Hunt* (1996), *Abrams v. Johnson* (1997), and *Lawyer v. Department of Justice* (1997).

[2]See *Wesberry v. Sanders* (1964), *Reynolds v. Sims* (1964), *Avery v. Midland County* (1968), and *Hadley v. Junior College District of Metropolitan Kansas City* (1970).

[3]The *Shaw/Miller* standard has been imposed by a five-person majority on the Court consisting of Chief Justice William H. Rehnquist and Justices Anthony Kennedy, Antonin Scalia, and Clarence Thomas, as well as Justice O'Connor. The other four justices, John Paul Stephens, David H. Souter, Ruth Bader Ginsburg, and Stephen Breyer, have opposed the adoption of this standard.

[4]*Miller v. Johnson* (1995), *Bush v. Vera* (1996), *Shaw v. Hunt* (1996), and *Abrams v. Johnson* (1997). The Court has affirmed, however, without full review, a lower court decision concluding that a majority-Latino congressional district in Chicago satisfied the strict scrutiny standard. *King v. State Board of Elections* (1998).

[5]For lower court invalidations of other majority-minority congressional and state legislative districts, see *Hays v. State of Louisiana* (1996), *Johnson v. Mortham* (1996), *Moon v. Meadows,* (1997), *Diaz v. Silver* (1997), and *Able v. Wilkens* (1996). A majority African American councilmanic district in Jefferson Parish, Louisiana, survived a *Shaw*-based challenge when a federal district court found its bizarre shape to be the result of political rather than racial considerations. *Theriot v. Parish* of Jefferson (1997). For more extensive commentary on the *Shaw* line of cases and their implications, see Peacock (1997).

[6]Protected minorities include African Americans, Latinos, Native Americans, Native Alaskans, and Asian Americans.

[7]Jurisdictions covered by section 5 are determined by formulae contained in section 4 of the Act. These jurisdictions include state and local governments that are located primarily, but not exclusively, in the South.

[8]The Senate Judiciary Committee's Report on the Voting Rights Act Extension has been the most widely referenced source for the legislative intentions behind the revisions in the Act. See, for example *Thornburg v. Gingles* (1986, at 43 n.7).

[9]See also *Barnett v. City of Chicago* (1998), in which an appellate court panel observes, "The statute tells the courts to consider 'the totality of circumstances,' and that has turned out to be, if anything, worse than useless advice, as it has discouraged the Supreme Court from trying to particularize the standard" (at 702).

[10]Another threat to the continued viability of section 2 as a medium for invalidating dilutive at-large election systems is the recent acceptance, by the majority of a Fourth Circuit panel, of the argument that the inability of a minority group to elect the candidates of its choice, when those candidates are themselves minority group members, may be of no probative importance if minority voters have the ability to get on the winning side of elections in which members of their group are not candidates. The opportunity to elect, in short, can be limited by the race of the candidate for one group but not the other yet still be considered equal (*Lewis v. Alamance County,* 1996). This is an old argument that has been repeatedly rebuffed in the past (see, e.g., *East Jefferson Coalition v. Jefferson Parish,* 1988, at 1001, 1004, and *Smith v. Clinton,* 1988, at 1316–1318), but the ability to be on the winning side in white-on-white contests appears to be gaining acceptance as another factor to be considered in the totality of circumstances inquiry (see *Jenkins v. Manning,* 1997, at 695–696, and *Uno v. City of Holyoke,* 1995, at 988 n.8).

[11]A majority of the Supreme Court has indicated that complying with section 2 of the VRA qualifies as a "compelling interest" under the strict scrutiny standard (see *Bush v. Vera,* 1996, O'Connor, J., concurring, at 990–992; Stevens, J., dissenting, at 1004, 1013, 1033–1034; and Souter, J., dissenting, at 1046, 1065).

[12]This and the following section rely heavily on Engstrom (1993).

[13]It is not necessary that voters cast votes in whole units, however. In Peoria, Illinois, for example, a five-vote cumulative system has been adopted whereby voters simply identify up to five candidates for whom they wish to vote, and then their five votes are allocated evenly among those candidates. If a voter votes for only one candidate, five votes are allocated to that candidate. If a voter votes for two candidates, then two and one-half votes are allocated to each. If a voter votes for three, four, or five candidates, then one and two-thirds votes, one and one-fourth votes, or one vote, respectively, are allocated to each of the chosen candidates.

[14]The successful application of the single-shot strategy depends not only on a group's voters complying with it, but also on the other voters dispersing their votes across more candidates than there are seats to be filled. Single-shot voting can occur only in multiseat elections in which the seats are not divided into separate places or posts for election purposes and in which voters are not required by "full-slate" provisions to cast as many votes as there are positions to be filled. On

the incidence and impact of these anti-single shot features, see Engstrom and McDonald (1987 and 1993).

[15]Voters are not necessarily required to rank all of the candidates on a preference voting ballot. When this is the case, some ballots may become nontransferable, resulting in the quota not being obtained by the required number of candidates. When this happens, the remaining seat(s) may be filled by applying a simple plurality rule after the final set of transfers.

[16]See *Kaelin v. Warden* (1971); *LoFrisco v. Schaffer* (1972); and *Orloski v. Davis* (1983).

[17]For a review of the evidence concerning some of the other alleged implications of the use of these systems, see Engstrom (1998).

[18]Cumulative voting has been adopted by local governments in Texas, Alabama, New Mexico, South Dakota, and Illinois. Limited voting has been adopted by local jurisdictions in Alabama, North Carolina, Texas, Georgia, and Arizona.

[19]A study that matched the actual ballots cast in the 1991 cumulative voting election for the city council in Peoria, Illinois, with the racial composition of the city's precincts, however, found that while an African American was elected, he was not the preferred candidate of African American voters. The African American voters divided most of their votes among three other African American candidates, resulting in none of the three being elected (Aspin & Hall, 1996).

[20]Only two of the nine Latino candidates that were elected were also among the candidates preferred by the Anglo voters. One was an incumbent who three years earlier, in the city's first cumulative voting election, had become the first Latino ever to be elected to the city council. He was the Anglo voters' second choice among three candidates (one a write-in candidate) in a two-seat election. The other was elected in a three-seat election in which only two Anglos and one other Latino were candidates.

REFERENCES

Amy, D.J. (1993). *Real choices/new voices: The case for proportional representation elections in the United States.* New York: Columbia University Press.

Amy, D.J. (1996–1997). The forgotten history of the single-transferable vote in the United States. *Representation,* 34, 13–20.

Arden, W., Grofman, B., & Handley, L. (1997). The impact of redistricting on African American representation in the U.S. Congress and state legislatures in the 1990s. *National Political Science Review,* 6, 35–43.

Arrington, T.S., & Ingalls, G.L. (1998). The limited vote alternative to affirmative districting. *Political Geography,* 17, 701–728.

Aspin, L.T., & Hall, W.K. (1996). Cumulative voting and minority candidates: An analysis of the 1991 Peoria city council elections. *American Review of Politics,* 17, 225–244.

Barber, K.L. (1995). *Proportional representation and electoral reform in Ohio.* Columbus, OH: Ohio State University Press.

Bridges, A. (1992). Winning the West to municipal reform. *Urban Affairs Quarterly,* 27, 494–518.

Brischetto, R.R., & Engstrom, R.L. (1997). Cumulative voting and Latino representation: Exit surveys in 15 Texas communities. *Social Science Quarterly,* 78, 973–991.

Browning, R.P., Marshall, D.R., & Tabb, D.H. (1984). *Protest is not enough: The struggle of Blacks and Hispanics for equality in urban politics.* Berkeley, CA: University of California Press.

Browning, R.P., Marshall, D.R., & Tabb, D.H. (1997). Can people of color achieve power in city government? The setting and the issues. In R.P. Browning, D.R. Marshall, & D.H. Tabb, (eds.) *Racial politics in American cities,* (pp. 3–14). 2d ed; New York: Longman.

Burnham, R.A. (1997). Reform, politics, and race in Cincinnati: Proportional representation and the City Charter Committee, 1924–1959. *Journal of Urban History,* 23, 131–163.

Cole, R.L., & Taebel, D.A. (1992). Cumulative voting in local elections: Lessons from the Alamogordo experience. *Social Science Quarterly,* 73, 194–201.

Cole, R.L., Engstrom, R.L., & Taebel, D.A. (1990). Cumulative voting in a municipal election: A note on voter reactions and electoral consequences. *Western Political Quarterly,* 43, 191–199.

DeLeon, R.E., Blash, L., & Hill, S. (1997). The politics of electoral reform in San Francisco: Preference voting versus districts versus plurality at-large. Paper presented at the 1997 Annual Meeting of the Western Political Science Association, March 13–15, Tucson, AZ.

Dunne, J.R. (1993). Remarks of John R. Dunne. *Cardozo Law Review,* 14, 1127–1133.

Electoral Reform Society. (1996). *Report on the San Francisco voting reform referendum 96.* London: Electoral Reform Society.

Engstrom, R.L. (1985). The reincarnation of the intent standard: Federal judges and at-large election cases. *Howard Law Journal,* 28, 495–513.

Engstrom, R.L. (1990). Cincinnati's proportional representation initiative. *Electoral Studies,* 9, 217–225.

Engstrom, R.L. (1992). Modified multi-seat election systems as remedies for minority vote dilution. *Stetson Law Review,* 21, 743–770.

Engstrom, R.L. (1993). The single transferable vote: An alternative remedy for minority vote dilution. *University of San Francisco Law Review, 27,* 781–813.

Engstrom, R.L. (1994). The Voting Rights Act: Disfranchisement, dilution, and alternative election systems. *PS: Political Science and Politics, 27,* 685–688.

Engstrom, R.L. (1995). *Shaw, Miller* and the districting thicket. *National Civic Review, 84,* 323–336.

Engstrom, R.L. (1998). Minority electoral opportunities and alternative election systems in the United States. In M. Rush (ed.). *Voting rights and redistricting in the United States* (pp. 227–243). New York: Greenwood Publishing.

Engstrom, R.L., & Barrilleaux, C.J. (1991). Native Americans and cumulative voting: The Sisseton Wahpeton Sioux. *Social Science Quarterly, 72,* 388–393.

Engstrom, R.L., & Brischetto, R.R. (1998). Is cumulative voting too complex? Evidence from exit polls. *Stetson Law Review, 27,* 813–834.

Engstrom, R.L., & McDonald, M.D. (1986). The effect of at-large versus district elections on racial representation in U.S. municipalities. In B. Grofman & A. Lijphart (eds.). *Election laws and their political consequences* (pp. 203–225). New York: Agathon Press.

Engstrom, R.L., & McDonald, M.D. (1987). The election of Blacks to southern city councils: The dominant impact of election arrangements. In R.P. Steed, L.W. Moreland, & T.A. Baker (eds.). *Blacks in Southern Politics* (pp. 245–258). New York: Praeger Publishers.

Engstrom, R.L., & McDonald, M.D. (1993). "Enhancing" factors in at-large plurality and majority systems: A reconsideration. *Electoral Studies, 12,* 385–401.

Engstrom, R.L., Kirksey, J.F., & Still, E. (1997a). Limited and cumulative voting in Alabama: An assessment after two rounds of elections. *National Political Science Review, 6,* 180–191.

Engstrom, R.L., Kirksey, J.F., & Still, E. (1997b). One person, seven votes: The cumulative voting experience in Chilton County, Alabama. In A. Peacock (ed.). *Affirmative action and representation: Shaw v. Reno and the future of voting rights* (pp. 285–313). Durham: Carolina Academic Press.

Engstrom, R.L., Taebel, D.A., & Cole, R.L. (1989). Cumulative voting as a remedy for minority vote dilution: The case of Alamogordo, New Mexico. *Journal of Law and Politics, 5,* 469–497.

Gerber, E.R., Morton, R.B., & Rietz, T.A. (1998). Minority representation in multimember districts. *American Political Science Review, 92,* 127–144.

Grofman, B., & Davidson, C. (1994). The effect of municipal election structure on Black representation in eight southern states. In C. Davidson & B. Grofman (eds.) *Quiet revolution in the South: The impact of the Voting Rights Act, 1965–1990* (pp. 301–334). Princeton, NJ: Princeton University Press.

Grofman, B., & Handley, L. (1992). Preconditions for Black and Hispanic congressional success. In W. Rule & J. Zimmerman (eds.). *United States electoral systems: Their impact on women and minorities* (pp. 31–39). New York: Greenwood Press.

Handley, L., & Grofman, B. (1994). The impact of the Voting Rights Act on minority representation: Black officeholding in southern state legislatures and congressional delegations. In C. Davidson & B. Grofman (eds.), *Quiet revolution in the South: The impact of the Voting Rights Act, 1965–1990* (pp. 335–350). Princeton, NJ: Princeton University Press.

Helig, P., & Mundt, R. (1984). *Your voice at city hall: The politics, procedures and policies of district representation.* Albany: State University of New York Press.

Kousser, J.M. (1984). The undermining of the First Reconstruction. In C. Davidson (ed.). *Minority vote dilution* (pp. 27–46). Washington, DC: Howard University Press.

Lublin, D. (1997). The election of African Americans and Latinos to the U.S. House of Representatives, 1972–1994. *American Politics Quarterly,* 25, 269–286.

McDonald, M.D., & Engstrom, R.L. (1992). Minority representation and city council electoral systems: A Black and Hispanic comparison. In A. Messina, L.R. Fraga, L.A. Rhodebeck, & F.D. Wright (eds.), *Ethnic and racial minorities in advanced industrial democracies* (pp. 127–142). New York: Greenwood Press.

Mulroy, S.J. (1995). Limited, cumulative evidence: Divining Justice Department positions on alternative electoral systems. *National Civic Review,* 84, 66–71.

Mulroy, S.J. (1997). The way out: Toward a legal standard for imposing alternative electoral systems as voting rights remedies. Manuscript dated June 29, 1997.

Note. (1981). Affirmative action and electoral reform. *Yale Law Journal,* 90, 1811–1832.

Note. (1982). Alternative voting systems as remedies for unlawful at-large systems. *Yale Law Journal,* 92, 144–160.

Peacock, A. (ed.). (1997). *Affirmative action and representation: Shaw v. Reno and the future of voting rights.* Durham, NC: Carolina Academic Press.

Rae, D., Hanby, V., & Loosemore, J. (1971). Thresholds of representation and thresholds of exclusion: An analytic note on electoral systems. *Comparative Political Studies,* 3, 479–488.

Still, E. (1984). Alternatives to single-member districts. In C. Davidson (ed.). *Minority vote dilution* (pp. 249–267). Washington, DC: Howard University Press.

Weaver, L. (1984). Semi-proportional and proportional representation systems in the United States. In A. Lijphart & B. Grofman (eds.). *Choosing an electoral system: Issues and alternatives* (pp. 191–206). New York: Praeger Publishers.

Weaver, L. (1986). The rise, decline, and resurrection of proportional representation in local governments in the United States. In B. Grofman & A. Lijphart (eds.). *Electoral laws and their political consequences* (pp. 139–153). New York: Agathon Press.

Welch, S. (1990). The impact of at-large elections on the representation of Blacks and Hispanics. *Journal of Politics,* 52, 1050–1076.

Welch, S., & Bledsoe, T. (1988). *Urban reform and its consequences: A study in representation.* Chicago: University of Chicago Press.

Zimmerman, J.F. (1978). The Federal Voting Rights Act and alternative election systems. *William and Mary Law Review,* 19, 621–660.

COURT CASES

Able v. Wilkins. 1996. 946 F.Supp. 1174 (D. S.C.).

Abrams v. Johnson. 1997. 521 U.S. 74.

Avery v. Midland County. 1968. 390 U.S. 474.

Barnett v. City of Chicago. 1998. 141 F. 3d. 699 (7th Cir.).

Beer v. United States. 1976. 425 U.S. 130.

Bush v. Vera. 1996. 517 U.S. 952.

City of Mobile v. Bolden. 1980. 446 U.S. 55.

Diaz v. Silver. 1997. 978 F. Supp. 96 (E.D. N.Y).

East Jefferson Coalition v. Jefferson Parish. 1988. 691 F.Supp. 991 (E.D. La).

Gomillion v. Lightfoot. 1960. 364 U.S. 339.

Growe v. Emison. 1993. 507 U.S. 25.

Hadley v. Junior College District of Metropolitan Kansas City. 1970. 397 U.S. 50.

Hays v. State of Louisiana. 1996. 936 F.Supp. 360 (W.D. La.).

Holder v. Hall. 1994. 512 U.S. 874.

Jenkins v. Manning. 1997. 116 F. 3d 685 (3d Cir.).

Johnson v. DeGrandy. 1994. 512 U.S. 997.

Johnson v. Miller. 1994. 864 F.Supp. 1354 (S.D. Ga.)

Johnson v. Mortham. 1996. 926 F. Supp. 1460 (N.D. Flda.).

Kaelin v. Warden. 1971. 334 F.Supp. 602 (E.D. Pa).

King v. Illinois Board of Elections. 1998. 522 U.S. 1087.

Lawyer v. Department of Justice. 1997. 521 U.S. 567.

Lewis v. Alamance County. 1996. 99 F. 3d 600 (4th. Cir).

LoFrisco v. Schaffer. 1972. 341 F. Supp. 743 (D. Conn.).

Miller v. Johnson. 1995. 515 U.S. 900.

Moon v. Meadows. 1997. 952 F.Supp. 1141 (E.D. Va.).

Orloski v. Davis. 1983. 564 F. Supp. 526 (M.D. Pa.).

Reno v. Bossier Parish School Board. 1997. 520 U.S. 471.

Reynolds v. Sims. 1964. 377 U.S. 533.

Shaw v. Hunt. 1996. 517 U.S. 899.

Shaw v. Reno. 1993. 509 U.S. 630.

Smith v. Clinton. 1988. 687 F.Supp. 1310 (E.D. Ark.).

Theriot v. Parish of Jefferson. 1997. 966 F. Supp. 1435 (E.D. La.).

Thornburg v. Gingles. 1986. 478 U.S. 30.

Wesberry v. Sanders. 1964. 376 U.S. 1.

Voinovich v. Quilter. 1993. 507 U.S. 146.

United States v. Marengo County Commission. 1984. 731 F. 2d 1546.

Uno v. City of Holyoke. 1995. 72 F. 3d 973 (1st. Cir).

CHAPTER 3

Life after Districts

AMY BRIDGES AND KATHERINE UNDERWOOD

For nearly all of this century the cities and towns of the South and West have been governed by institutions designed by municipal reformers. A key feature of that design was citywide election to the city council. In the 1960s and 1970s citywide elections came under attack by proponents of civil rights, neighborhood advocates, and antigrowth activists. By the early 1990s, these coalitions had won their fight for district elections in many southwestern cities. Change was not confined to the Southwest: although half of all big cities (more than 250,000) in the United States elected their councils in citywide elections in 1970, only about a quarter did so in 1991 (see Table 3.1). As citywide elections have become rare, cities have adopted district elections and mixed systems (systems with some council members elected from districts, and some citywide). By 1991, 71 percent of cities elected councils by district or mixed system.

African Americans and Latinos were central players in the coalitions that fought the sometimes protracted legal and electoral battles for district elections. The shift away from at-large councils began in the mid-1970s as a result of their lawsuits challenging at-large elections for diluting the votes of minority residents (see Engstrom in this volume; Davidson, 1992; Cotrell & Stevens, 1978). Their hope was that district elections would provide increased representation for minorities, facilitate their inclusion into urban governing coalitions, and lead to policy equity for underserved areas of the city (Bridges, 1997; Heilig & Mundt, 1984; Polinard, Wrinkle, Longoria & Binder 1994; Welch & Bledsoe, 1988; Christensen & Gerston, 1984).

**Table 3.1. Selected Institutional/Electoral Characteristics
for Large Cities*: 1971, 1977, 1986, 1991**

	1971	1977	1986	1991
At-large	49%	46%**	28%	28%
District	29.3%	54%**	19%	10%
Mixed	17%	—	53%	61%
Nonpartisan	—	66%	75%	81%
Council–manager	—	34%	—	48%

*Population 100,000+ for 1971, all other years population 250,000+; **includes mixed at-large/district election systems.
Sources: Klevit, 1972, p. 24; Sanders, 1979, pp. 98–99; Renner, 1988, pp. 14, 17; Renner & DeSantis, 1993, pp. 59, 67–68.

This chapter is a preliminary, qualitative exploration of whether these expectations have been borne out in four large southwestern cities that have switched from at-large to district elections within the past three decades: Albuquerque (1974), Phoenix (1982), San Jose (1978), and San Diego (1988).[1] Each city had a clear majority of Anglo residents in 1990 and currently has two minority-majority districts (see Table 3.2). Our investigation is inspired by prior research on the impact of changing from citywide to district elections, most notably that by Heilig and Mundt (1984), Welch and Bledsoe (1988), and Polinard et al. (1994), and by Browning, Marshall, and Tabb's (1984) work on political incorporation. The questions we seek to answer are: What new norms have emerged from districted representation? To what extent have district elections benefited minority groups? What do council–manager relationships look like, and how might these relationships affect low-income, heavily minority districts? What are the prospects for minority inclusion in stable, governing coalitions in districted systems?

We report three sets of findings. First, we found that subsequent to the adoption of district elections, individual council members in our four cities possess significantly increased responsibility and discretion. Certain types of decisions, most notably minor economic development and federal Community Development Block Grant (CDBG) spending, have been decentralized to the district level. With slight exaggeration one might say that city council members have become district executives. Like Polinard et al. (1994), we observe that the dominant norm on these

Table 3.2. Population by Race and Ethnicity, 1990*

	Total Population	White	Black	Latino	Asian Pacific Islander**	Native American
Albuquerque	384,736	58%	3%	35%	2%	3%
Phoenix	983,403	72%	5%	20%	2%	2%
San Diego	1,110,549	59%	9%	20%	11%	1%
San Jose	782,225	50%	5%	26%	19%	1%

*Totals may not equal 100 percent due to rounding.
**Less than .5 percent.
Source: 1990 U.S. Census of Population and Housing, Table 3.

councils is deference to the wishes of council members on issues that concern their own districts. This decentralized pattern appears to maximize council members' ability to deliver to their constituents, and certainly maximizes their ability to take credit for what is delivered.

Second, like other authors, we found council coalitions to be uncertain and fleeting (Polinard et al., 1994; Welch & Bledsoe, 1988). In our four cities council coalitions tend to be fluid, sometimes crossing racial, geographic, and ideological lines. The fluidity of alliances places a premium on the ability of individual council members to build amicable relationships with their colleagues. In addition, although municipal elections in all of these cities are nonpartisan, party identification is a good predictor of like-mindedness among council members.

Third, we observe the creation of districts has affected the roles of city manager and public bureaucracies in complex ways. Council members elected by district seek and receive more information from managers and agencies; they also expect the manager to be responsive to direction from elected officials. Yet a district focus on the part of representatives (especially, we think, combined with term limits in San Jose and San Diego), may mean that the responsibility for long-term and strategic planning has been delegated to bureaucrats, or abandoned altogether. The short term and partial perspectives of elected officials mean city staff (from the city manager on down) feel they must "educate" council members about policy goals.

District representation occupies the underexamined middle ground on a continuum of political inclusion from exclusion to incorporation (Browning et al., 1984, p. 47). District representation is a clear improvement in the political position of communities of color. District representation provides not only a voice at city hall, but also tangible *collective* benefits to communities of color (not just favors to individuals). On the other hand, district elections do not provide incentives for council office-seekers to create electoral coalitions, and there are reasons to doubt the prospects for their inclusion in stable governing coalitions.

We view this essay as the first step of a larger research endeavor that will address the same questions, but using more cities and a combination of research techniques. The methodology used here is explicitly qualitative. Our findings are drawn from semistructured interviews with sixteen individuals (former and current elected officials, high-ranking bureaucrats, and staff) in our four cities, as well as newspaper coverage of local politics. Unlike other authors, we have not yet explored council appointments of minorities to boards and commissions or the share of municipal employment held by minority groups as measures of progress. These are useful and rigorous indicators of change and will be included in our next iteration.

We begin our discussion with a review of the current academic wisdom on the consequences of change from citywide to district selection of city councils. The second section presents our findings about changes in local politics after the adoption of districts and their impact on communities of color. The concluding section considers how we might evaluate the nature of such change: Is there progress towards more equitable municipal politics? What are the prospects for the future?

THEIR VOICES AT CITY HALL

Our brief account of major works that explore the relationship between electoral rules and political outcomes begins with the conceptual framework articulated by Browning et al. in *Protest Is Not Enough*. They investigated minority group mobilization in ten northern California cities and found that the most successful degree of political inclusion occurred where African Americans were included in a liberal electoral coalition that replaced a conservative city council majority. Subsequently the victorious biracial, liberal alliance become the dominant or governing coalition that was responsive to minority group policy demands (1984, p. 241). For most of Browning et al.'s study (1960–1980), the ten cities held at-large elections for their city council, and thus progressive, change-oriented candidates had a significant incentive to form coalitions with sympathetic allies; pooling resources and running coordinated campaigns increased the chances of a collective (and thus meaningful) victory. However, by 1980, and in a move that mirrored changes taking place across the nation, five of their cities adopted district elections (pp. 201–203). Unanticipated by Browning et al. was that these new, districted systems would discourage candidates from pursuing collective electoral strategies and coalition building with the potential for governing payoffs.

The impact of changing from citywide to district elections for city council has been the subject of two studies; a third searched for differences between council members elected at large and those elected from districts. Like Browning et al., these researchers are also concerned with the link between representation and policy equity. Peggy Heilig and Robert J. Mundt, in *Your Voice at City Hall* (1984), explored the consequences of change in eleven cities across the United States. J.L. Polinard et al., *Electoral Structure and Urban Policy* (1994) searched for the effects of increased Mexican American representation in Texas cities. Susan Welch and Timothy Bledsoe, *Urban Reform and Its Consequences* (1988), surveyed elected officials in 218 cities to compare council members elected from districts with those elected citywide. Below we outline their findings about districted systems as the conceptual framework for our project, and do so by concentrating on three areas: the representational focus of members; council dynamics; and council–bureaucratic relationships.

There is consensus that district elections produce council members with district focus and priorities, although not to the complete exclusion of citywide issues. Welch and Bledsoe found that "Those elected by district are more likely to feel that they represent neighborhoods than do those elected at large, and those elected at large are more likely to see themselves as representing the city as a whole" (1988, p. 67).[2] Polinard et al. report data from Texas that shows district elections facilitated the election of both more Mexican Americans and "council members with a decidedly neighborhood orientation" (1994, p. 92). In a similar vein, Heilig and Mundt discovered that "district representation has provided residents of the poorer areas of all our cities with council members eager to help with individual, immediate problems that involve city services or facilities" (1984, p. 96). This form of representation, according to Heilig and Mundt, has "improved local government by giving their part of the city a 'voice at city hall'," with the result that local governments were more popular with minority communities (p. 96). The ten city managers interviewed by Polinard et al. corroborated this view: they "were in almost total agreement that the change to districts had enhanced minority representation" (1994, p. 88). Thus a change to districts, in the city managers' view, tied together the Mexican American community and the city council (p. 89).

Whether district elections increased the level of conflict and factionalism on city councils generated more divergent findings. Heilig and Mundt reported that district elections did not result in more conflict on the city council (1984, p. 113). They also found that "districts have had some effect on the formation of voting blocs on our councils" but cautioned that "it is difficult to predict what kind of impact districts will have on coalition voting in general and in the long run" (pp. 128–129). Council turnover certainly affected coalition maintenance.

Welch and Bledsoe found that conflict exists on all types of councils, but that "It is more apparent . . . in district than at large councils" (1988, p. 97). Self-reported data from their study indicated "members elected by district are more likely to acknowledge the presence of sharp factionalism on the council (49 percent compared to 40 percent) . . . " (p. 97). Welch and Bledsoe's bivariate and multivariate analysis indicates that "the impact of district elections on council factionalism remained significant . . . election by district does slightly predispose a council to break into factions, independent of the size of the group" (p. 99). The substance of these conflicts was most often whether growth should be managed, and second in frequency, conflict between business and neighborhood interests (pp. 100, 101).

Texas data collected by Polinard et al. essentially support Welch and Bledsoe. While over two-thirds of Polinard et al.'s respondents (from at-large, district, and mixed systems) indicated that "75 percent or more" of city council decisions are unanimous; 26 percent also indicated "the presence of voting blocs on the council" (1994, p. 86). Council representatives elected by district, however, "were more likely to indicate a low percentage of decisions as unanimous . . . to report an increase in council conflict . . . and to report that an increase in conflict had occurred since the change to a district form of elections . . . " (p. 86). Yet city managers interviewed by Polinard et al. observed that "after an initial period of conflict between ethnic council members and nonethnics, most council members began to work together" (p. 89). These councils developed norms of deference on issues affecting each member's district, thus allowing each representative to "act as 'lead' for the council on that particular issue" (p. 89).

Changes in electoral rules have altered council–administrative relationships. Welch and Bledsoe did not explore this relationship. Heilig and Mundt hypothesized that "at-large representatives will approve of a strong leadership role for the manager, while district members will prefer a technician who will follow their orders" (1984, p. 95). Their data showed that district representatives are less likely to perceive a city manager as being too weak (not sufficiently assertive) than those elected at-large (p. 95). In addition, Heilig and Mundt found that city managers they interviewed reported "some differences in the demands of at-large and district representatives . . . our data support the hypothesis that administrators will see district council members as more likely to interfere in administration" (p. 94). Similarly, city managers in Polinard et al.'s Texas study said that district representatives asked for more information from their offices (p. 89).

To summarize, considerable research by Heilig and Mundt (1984), Welch and Bledsoe (1988), and Polinard et al. (1994) suggest basic agreement that districted systems produce representatives with a more distinct neighborhood focus; increase council conflict; and alter council–manager relationships. District representatives tend to pay more attention to their neighborhood constituency and this has benefited minority groups who previously lacked voice and government access. Districted councils, with the exception of those in Heilig and Mundt's study, appear to experience more conflict and factionalism. Yet Heilig and Mundt argue that who is elected may affect the nature of council coalitions. Intra-council relationships, at least in Texas, are shaped by norms of mutual deference. Finally, district representatives use their city managers as sources of information (and as problem solvers), and perceive the appropriate role of the manager as one subordinate to council direction.

Heilig and Mundt found little progress towards equity. New facilities were more equitably distributed than in the past, as were routine services, but beyond these changes they saw little policy change as a result of district elections. Although some minority residents might receive "personalized attention," Heilig and Mundt saw little suggesting that changing city councils affected the "daily lives" of minority communities (pp. 150–154). Polinard and his colleagues saw greater changes as a result of increased Mexican American presence on city councils: more Mexican Americans on city commissions, great representation in middle range, professional, and senior positions in municipal bureaucracies, and better compensation for these employees all followed from greater numbers on the city council (pp. 127, 132).

LIFE AFTER DISTRICTS

To place life after districts in perspective, we need to revisit briefly political life in these cities when there were citywide elections. All of our cities were governed by big city reform regimes. Not only did they have citywide elections, city managers, nonpartisanship, and very low voter turnout, but they also were governed by strong pro-growth coalitions. The dominant rhetoric insisted on pursuit of the "good of the whole" (Bridges, 1997a, 1997b). In Phoenix and Albuquerque their governing coalitions were organized by nonpartisan slating groups. In the political life of these cities, poor people and people of color were nearly invisible. Phoenix, Albuquerque, and San Diego did not participate in federally assisted low-income housing programs; Albuquerque provided no public parks in its lower income neighborhoods, and the same neighborhoods lacked drainage systems and paving. Descriptive representation was slight; geographic representation nonexistent. In these and other big reform cities, rewriting the rules to elect city council members from districts was part of a broader shake-up in politics as usual, the fallout of which has not been systematically appraised.

Nationwide, a key result of the change to election by districts has been an increase in descriptive representation. Because African American communities are more segregated than Latino communities, there have been greater gains for African Americans. In our four cities, two have followed this pattern and two have not. In San Diego and Phoenix, which each have one district created for Latinos and one district created for African Americans, city councils typically had two representatives of color before the change to districts. Phoenix has had one African American on the council since the mid-1960s; in San Diego there has been an African American since 1969, and a Latino since 1975. Typically, these representatives were appointed in mid-term, and then elected, or (in Phoenix) were part of the slate nominated by the dominant nonpartisan slating group.[3]

In Albuquerque and San Jose the councils have experienced more change. Albuquerque usually had one Mexican American on the council before the change to districts; today's nine member council has three Latinos. San Jose's first representative of color was Norman Mineta, a Japanese American, appointed to a vacant seat in 1967 and then elected to the seat in 1969. Two years later Mineta was elected mayor and a Mexican American, Al Garza, appointed to a vacant council seat. Today San Jose's ten member council includes one African American, two Mexican Americans, and one Japanese Mexican American.

Citywide elections structured both political campaigns and public policy in big reform cities, including our four cases. Our San Diego and San Jose interviewees explained that when their council was at-large, members had the political "space" to ignore issues salient to minority neighborhoods because they won elections by campaigning only in more affluent, vote rich areas of the city. The adoption of districts significantly alters both electoral incentives and behavior on the council for members. To win election and re-election in a districted system, individuals must at least appear to care for their neighborhood communities. Not only individual council members, but city government as a whole, is responsive to the presence of new rules and new voices. In Phoenix, for example, the mayor delivers not only a "state of the city" address, but also an annual "state of the neighborhoods" report.

We see our research as a preliminary follow-up to the earlier studies reviewed here, and the beginning of an effort to appraise more systematically the dynamics of political life after districts. We use a qualitative methodology to test questions similar to those posed by others. We are especially interested in how evolving council norms and political–bureaucratic relationships might affect what minority communities receive from local government. Our interviews and newspaper research in Albuquerque, Phoenix, San Diego, and San Jose suggest that council members in these cities hold more power through decentralization of decision making and norms of mutual deference; that council coalitions are fluid rather than stable; and that managers still exert considerable authority over long-range, strategic issues.

The Executive Representative

Our first observation about politics after districts is that the role of individual council members has been considerably enhanced. Like Polinard et al. we find that the dominant ethos is mutual deference among individual council members on matters concerning their own districts. More, we observe that councils award resources to members to distribute as they see fit. The result is that council members have become "district executives," making decisions about policy priorities for their own constituents.

Minority council members in our four cities have used this executive power to provide collective benefits for their constituents. Other authors (Welch & Bledsoe, 1988; Heilig & Mundt, 1984) have focused on whether the ombudsman aspect of representation is significantly increased under districted systems.[4] Minority constituents do call their district representatives (more than under the at-large system) and sometimes, as was the case in San Jose, requests for assistance come from fellow ethnics outside the district. Yet we emphasize these calls are about problems that confront *many* constituents, such as gang activity, police brutality, and street flooding due to lack of curbs and adequate drainage, rather than fixing parking tickets or requests for tree trimming. We found that the top priority for minority representatives was substantive improvement in their constituents' quality of life. Their wish lists have included greater employment and retail opportunities, modernized infrastructure, improved public safety, and an end to police brutality.

Council members now have the authority to take the lead in managing land use issues (both new property development and redevelopment), and in negotiating small-scale economic development. One city manager reported that:

> the rest of the council, so long as whatever is being done is in compliance with our overall general plan, will show deference to that council member . . . The full council will expect that council member to resolve that issue and that issue cannot come to the council until they've got the community on board . . . that is what they are supposed to do.

Albuquerque requires developers to consult with neighborhood groups. Although the Council is the court of last resort for developer–neighborhood disputes, the district representative is in practice the arbiter of these disagreements. In a typical instance, the developer wanted a large scale project in a largely Latino, median- to low-income neighborhood. Current residents argued for a smaller project on the grounds that the proposal was out of scale with the neighborhood as a whole, and that the impact on traffic and parking would be unacceptably high. "Here we have the developer who wants everything," Albuquerque council representative Vincent Griego explained, and "I have to tell them you can't have everything . . . you have to put something that's compatible with the people there." This suggests district council representatives have the ability to protect their constituents from further deterioration in the quality of their life, which is especially important to minority groups previously left out of local political equations.

Minority council members have also played critical roles in redirecting public money towards the construction of new, low-income housing. San Jose's first Latina council member co-authored an ordinance, over the strong objections of the mayor, that created a new housing department to oversee the development and construction of affordable housing all over the city; previously housing funds were managed by the city's redevelopment agency with the effect that projects were concentrated in the downtown area. In the opinion of this member, a "shining example" of the housing department's accolade winning work is "Pocoway," a redevelopment project [in her district] that transformed a "drug-ridden, high crime" area with "deplorable" housing into a "phenomenal" development, complete with a new park. In San Diego, African American council member George Stevens is a member of the city's Housing Commission. In this capacity he has identified properties suitable for the construction of affordable housing units in his district, and then successfully lobbied for their purchase. He has also worked with the Southeastern Economic Development Corporation to encourage private developers to build in his district (Fried, 1995; Weisberg, 1994).

The pursuit of economic development by council members may also be proactive. Certainly those who represent low-income districts have a strong incentive to do so. In Albuquerque, Griego and council colleague Steve Gallegos worked together to recruit Hyatt Hotels to the city, and to insist Hyatt hire minorities and residents of particular neighborhoods. In San Diego, both George Stevens and Juan Vargas have worked to bring retail services back to their constituents: Stevens successfully waged a years-long battle to get a major grocery store in his district. Stevens also vehemently and vocally opposed the closure of a major savings and loan's branches in his district, calling its actions "irresponsible." Several months later the company announced it would promote a home loan program targeted to Stevens' district (and two other low-income, minority areas) (*San Diego Union-Tribune,* 1994a; Bunch, 1994; Handley, 1994; Riggs, 1994). Stevens' council colleague, Juan Vargas, has advocated a growth strategy for the city (emphasizing trade with Mexico) that would have direct fallout for his district.

Certain types of spending decisions have also been decentralized (although specifics vary from city to city), which also contributes to the executive role of district representatives. Money in hand, council members make decisions about policy priorities. In San Diego the Council voted in 1994 to dedicate 40 percent of its $16.3 million federal CDBG funds to citywide programs that served the poor, while the remaining 60 percent of the CDBG money was given to Council members (Davison, 1997, p. 5). Each member's prerogative is to select from among competing CDBG applications submitted by various organizations and programs. How Vargas and Stevens used their power of discretion to distribute CDBG money reveals some of their priorities. Vargas supported applications from the San Diego Business Incubator, the Logan Heights

Family Health Center, the San Ysidro Health Center, and Neighbors United. He turned down requests for funding from two St. Vincent de Paul programs that serve the homeless (Powell, 1994a, 1994b). For his part, Stevens "continued a pattern of largely supporting youth-oriented programs": money went toward the construction of the Malcom X Library, Jackie Robinson YMCA, the Elementary Institute of Science, and the Sunshine Little League (Powell, 1994a, 1994b).

Similarly, in San Jose, Park and Recreation money is allocated on the basis of the dollar value of new development. According to a former council member, district representatives have "a major influence on where the dollars that were available for parks and recreation would go within the district." At least one council member collaborated with his colleagues to develop a large, region-serving park, allowing "my district funds to go into" the Almaden Lake Park. Also in San Jose each council member currently has $100,000 to spend on homework centers, which may provide after school care, recreation, or tutorial assistance to students.

Decentralization and mutual deference give minority council members some leverage in the quests to bring their infrastructure, services, and amenities to parity with other areas. The minority district representatives in our four cities can boast of a long list of concrete improvements delivered to their district (as could their counterparts in Houston, Dallas, and other cities that have recently adopted districts). In Albuquerque, Vincent Griego and Steve Gallegos point to new or renovated libraries in the Valley, and a new $1.8 million cultural center in the South Valley, a $6 million family and community center in the North Valley, three or four smaller centers scattered through the Valley, a new public park to adjoin a public school, a new theater and dance hall (this from a bond issue that received support citywide), a nationally recognized program to assist single mothers, $2 million annually for paving and street maintenance, another $2 million annually for improving drainage, raises for firefighters, and fifty additional police officers. In San Diego, Vargas has secured a new police station for the Otay Mesa area, two new fire stations (the only new fire stations in the whole city), a new neighborhood services center, and a southern division police satellite station office. Moreover, Vargas secured $9 million to widen, repair, and improve a five-mile stretch of San Ysidro Boulevard northward from the border (*San Diego Union-Tribune*, 1994b; *San Diego Union-Tribune*, 1995). Stevens, too, has delivered. The summer of 1995 saw the opening of the Malcom X Library and Performing Arts Center—a 28,000 square foot, $7 million library and 300-seat theater. A cultural center will be placed across the street, in a 7,000 square foot building purchased by the city for around $300,000 (Turegano, 1995). In Phoenix, Calvin Goode presided at the opening of a historical museum and cultural center for African Americans.

It is significant, we think, that district representatives, most especially those with disadvantaged constituencies, boast of the *collective benefits* they provide. Albuquerque's Griego described himself as "an advocate in terms of people in the neighborhoods. I feel that as the city councilman I'm there to help them. . . . ." When Griego talked about phone calls from constituents, these were about problems that required *collective* solutions (of which the most pressing was street drainage), not individual assistance. Blanca Alvarado, the first Latina elected to the San Jose City Council, received numerous calls from her constituents (as well as Latinos from outside her district) about San Jose Police Department harassment. While police brutality occurs incident by incident, the problem is a collective and persistent one for communities of color. Our findings here stand in contrast to Heilig and Mundt's finding about the importance of district representative assistance to individuals. Indeed, in our four cities, the single report we had of demands for individual assistance was from affluent Anglo residents who asked council members to approve their requests for zoning changes and variances so they could improve or expand their residential properties.

Friends and Allies

Despite the decentralization of many decisions to district representatives, decisions remain which require finding political allies. Like the politicians surveyed by other political scientists, those we studied saw few reliable allies or stable voting patterns in their councils. All council members we interviewed (current and former) indicated that coalitions were fluid, crossing racial, geographic, and ideological lines. However, we perceive several sources of coalitional glue: partisanship, geographical proximity, positions on development, personality, and interpersonal skills.

Party is a recurring axis of division or bond for councilmanic solidarity. Although district representatives were quick to remind us they are elected in nonpartisan systems, their stories reveal that partisanship remains a convenient shorthand for real policy differences within the council. Remembering the San Jose City Council in the early and mid-1980s, a former member said, "We were pretty much all liberal Democrats. It was a great time for us." In another city, one Democrat reported bitterly, the Republicans "never talk to us." In a third city, one representative hoped to position himself as a swing voter between partisan camps.

Although party affiliation is a good predictor of like-mindedness and facilitates collaborative relationships, partisanship does not determine the shape of council decisions. Specific issues often prompt council members to reach across ideological divides to solve common problems. Representatives talked about working with colleagues from neighboring districts on development issues, especially those with interjurisdictional impacts. The strong working relationship of Gallegos and Griego in Albuquerque is a case in point. For two years (1989–1991), San Diego's council saw a coalition of five members (the "Gang of Five") unified by their support for limited growth initiatives and a redistricting map that protected incumbents. This coalition did not advance a coherent policy agenda, and individual members downplayed the group's cohesion (Schloyer, 1993). A former San Jose city council member recalls that there was general agreement on the importance of downtown redevelopment.

Often we heard about the importance of developing strong personal relationships with colleagues, confirming Heilig and Mundt's argument that who is elected has an impact on coalition formation (1984, p. 129). One San Diego respondent observed that in districted systems, close working relationships are needed for votes. A former San Jose council member, a self-identified conservative Republican, claimed that "personal relationships were the real key rather than issues," and gave as evidence a diverse working group that joined a "Mexican American," an African American, "and two Republicans." San Diego's Stevens and Vargas represent the two ends of the personality–coalition-building spectrum. Stevens' relationships with his council colleagues are markedly cool, largely as a result of combative, undiplomatic remarks made in Council chambers. Stevens refuses to alter his methods of interaction, saying, "I'm not going to change it, because it is one that is emotional, and it is necessary to use that style to impress upon someone else the needs of my district" (La Velle, 1994a; Dolbee, 1994). A political outsider on the council, Stevens is nevertheless very popular with his constituents. Vargas, on the other hand, uses light quips and humor to make points, is comfortable with a range of personalities, and enjoys a strong working relationship with Mayor Susan Golding, and clearly has greater political ambitions (Young, 1995; La Velle, 1994b; Huard, 1995).

Finally, able mayors, like San Jose's Tom McEnery, were able to count on a plurality of council votes for their initiatives. We do not yet know how these pluralities were created, what combination of reward, shared principle, common goals, political threat, and personal skill brought them into being. Our interviews point in the direction of mayoral committee appointments and control over budgets as potentially important resources for influencing council member behavior on key votes. Yet in these weak mayor systems resources are few. Our interviewees attested to mayors' very limited resources and their inability to organize a reliable majority of votes. Future research should explore the executive's power and limitations in shaping coalitions.

Relations with Bureaucracy

City managers are key players in public policy in our cities. Their assistance in the transition from citywide to district elections has been central to council members' satisfaction with the change. Where, as in Phoenix, managers worked to facilitate the new system, they were roundly applauded and strong positive relations with the council developed. Where they were resistant, as in Dallas, ill will and resentment still characterize council–bureaucracy relations. At the same time, the role of managers and the public bureaucracies they supervise has changed.

In the era before districts, managers were more prominent in some cities than others, but everywhere the office carried important prerogatives. Borrowing from social choice theory, we can say that significant authority was delegated to city managers in big reformed cities because there was a strong and clear consensus on policy and priorities on the part of elected officials and their supporters in the growth machine. Thus, even in cities where managers were very prominent, nowhere did public bureaucracies gain the status of "islands of functional power" they had in northeastern cities (Lowi, 1967).[5] If bureaucracies and the manager were powerful it was, as Weber explained, because of their efficiency, discretion, and reliability in executing public policy. The influence of managers and bureaucrats could be particularly enhanced where councils were part time, as in San Jose. When asked if the San Jose planning department had more power twenty years ago, the current director responded by saying, "Let's say we had a lot more unfettered discretion. And now the council knows everything because they want to."

In politics after districts the authority of the manager's office (drawing on other resources Weber explained) rests more squarely on monopoly of information and expertise. To help solve problems and make policy, district representatives and their staff regularly request information and assistance from city managers and agencies. And, not surprisingly, they want information on bureaucratic routines and outcomes by district. Our interviews indicate that district representatives interact frequently with the bureaucracy, and they also hold the expectation that the city manager should respond to policy directions set by the mayor and the council.

In San Jose, the bureaucracy has proactively responded to changes in political context. There, the city manager holds two meetings a month with each council member (in addition to attending council committee sessions and the weekly full council meeting). She has a standard format that includes district issues, citywide issues, and a follow-up section for issues raised in the past. Infrastructure service and repairs are performed on a regular schedule, and records are computerized so that the manager and agency directors can respond to inquiries and complaints made by council members. The city's director of planning and the director of economic development hold monthly briefing sessions with each council member and their top staff assistant. Council members thus learn about pending development projects and projects which are in the discussion or "pre-application phase." As the planning director explained, council members "want to know in advance what projects are coming down the road." The result of such meetings, in his view, is that "council members are much more aware and naturally they get much more involved in the decisions. Prior to that we never talked to the council members until there was an application on file, and it was part of the public record."

District perspectives combined with term limits reinforce bureaucratic impulses; managers and bureaucrats educate and remind council members of long-term, citywide, and professional perspectives. While the progressive ideal of a city manager was that of a neutral expert, our research suggests that the professional values held by bureaucrats do shape allocative/distributive issues in ways that are beneficial (or not) to low-income, minority communities. In San Jose, for example, a proposal for equal budgets for street paving drew support from council members, but the city manager successfully argued that this idea was so wholly irrational that the proposal was abandoned. Also in San Jose the planning department has begun an initiative to organize and involve low-income communities in neighborhood revitalization efforts; a program that holds the promise of increasing the influence of minorities who have been excluded from planning decisions.

Even where managers and bureaucrats are strongly committed to sharing information with council members, it may be difficult to arrange for each side. Even where councils are full time, for example, members might not have sufficient or expert enough staff to research or write legislation on complicated policy matters. San Diego's city council, for example, sends its legislative proposals to the city manager's staff to be drafted as ordinances. Thus the level and type of information provided by city managers and bureaucrats to council members, and the extent to which it advances minority policy agendas, depends on a combination of values, routines, and resources.

DISCUSSION: SO WHAT?

There was general agreement among our respondents that district elections have benefited communities of color. Districts have created a more open, accessible, and democratic local politics, with a more equitable distribution of public goods.[6] On the other hand, in every city the disadvantaged remain disadvantaged, and nowhere have the enormous political advantages of the growth machine been laid to rest. In this section we offer some reflections on these tensions.

The good news first. In assessing the progress that has been made, we recall Charles Hamilton's argument that while in the 1940s and 1950s policy-makers were indifferent (at best) to the consequences of their actions for people of color, in the wake of the civil rights movement, political life took on a "new normalcy" in which the concerns of people of color were routinely considered. In our cities the new normalcy awaited district elections. District elections have not created minority empowerment, or even the "contested liberalism" of cities in other regions, but they have created a contested conservatism. Although the number of minority representatives elected to the city council in each of our cities is modest (one in Phoenix, two in San Diego, three in Albuquerque, and four in San Jose), the truly new and critical development is that long neglected, heavily minority, low-income neighborhoods now have a seat at the table.

Second, council members who represent majority-minority districts have helped to produce a more equitable decision making environment and have won important collective benefits for their constituents. We do not minimize the collective benefits council members have secured for their constituents, and we insist on the collective quality of these benefits. Even those council members who see themselves as community and neighborhood advocates speak not of assistance to individuals or families, but of solutions to common problems, for example, flooding, and public goods contributing to the quality of daily life (youth centers, low-income housing, public libraries). At the same time, their presence provides a louder public voice for these communities, an opportunity to "go public," validating the issues raised by neighborhoods previously excluded from consideration on the council or in the news media.

Third, we also see reasons to be optimistic that these accomplishments will be augmented. In California, the hostility of Governor Wilson to immigrants and Spanish-speakers (and nationwide, Congressional hostility to immigrants) has provoked a dramatic increase both in immigrant applications for citizenship, and in the proportion of Mexican Americans registering and voting. Citizenship applications have risen significantly, from 1.3 million in 1996 to 1.5 million in 1997, and are projected at two million for 1998 (Ojito, 1998). In California, the rise in naturalizations has been followed by a dramatic increase in the proportions of Mexican Americans going to the polls (Rohrlich, 1997). Latinos cast 12 percent of the votes in the June 1998 primary in California, double the number who voted in the 1994 primary (Del Olmo, 1998).

As a dispersed minority, Mexican Americans should benefit from this increased political activity by becoming an important constituency in many districts, not just the districts heretofore created for them (see Table 3.3). In San Diego, for example, in addition to District 8 (where the population is 61.5 percent Latino), there are two districts where one in four residents is Latino. In San Jose, in addition to the two districts (3, 5) with majority Latino residents, there are four districts (2, 6, 7, 8) where

Table 3.3. 1990 Latino Population by City Council District: San Diego and San Jose

Council District	San Diego	San Jose
1	7.5%	10.4%
2	12.4%	18.3%
3	23.0%	55.0%
4	27.5%	16.5%
5	8.7%	55.5%*
6	11.6%	20.5%
7	11.1%	42.3%
8	61.5%*	25.6%
9		11.1%
10		10.6%

*Districts represented by a Latino council member.
Source: San Diego Association of Governments, 1992; City of San Jose, 1992.

increased participation in elections should increase the political visibility and leverage of Latinos.

And fourth, at the same time that minority majority districts remain distinct, we see common issues between their residents and residents of other neighborhoods. More important, so do city council members. For example, in our four cities we see a rethinking of city government's relation to the school system, a consequence of the recognition of a critical issue common to communities of color and Anglo working people. For decades there has been a wall of separation between school administration and city government. Yet subsequent to the creation of districts, the city council in each of our cities has become interested in problems of schooling, and in particular, attentive to the need for before- and after-school care for the children of working parents.

Assessing the prospects for minority inclusion in stable governing coalitions is more sobering. District elections have not altered the dominant political ethos of these cities, which remains largely conservative and resistant to major changes in the status quo. From the instances of alliance described to us, representatives of communities of color, and their reliable friends, amount to fewer than half of the council members in each of our cities, and surely not a dominant majority in any of them. Many other supporters of district elections (antigrowth advocates, for example) shared little sentiment with minorities other than the desire for districts. Although the general political environment is more favorably inclined towards the communities once wholly ignored by city government, no one could claim that their priorities dominate city politics today. Thus beyond those amenities and improvements that follow from a district "share," a great deal depends on the ability of district representatives to bargain, negotiate, and persuade their colleagues. Moreover, while citywide elections encouraged the organization of citywide slates of candidates for office, district elections encourage candidates to campaign alone, without organizing coalitions or common platforms.

Where might minority citizens seek political allies? Browning, Marshall, and Tabb argued that the key to minority incorporation was the existence of liberal allies in the Anglo community. This formulation is somewhat less comfortable in 1998, when "liberal" solutions have fallen into disrepute, and conservatives are prominent in minority communities. Nevertheless, we thought it still sensible to count registered Democrats as a potential source of allies, and are modestly encouraged by the substantial Democratic registration in each of our cities (see Table 3.4). Democrats outnumber Republicans in San Diego, San Jose,

Table 3.4. Party Affiliation of Registered Voters (1998):
Albuquerque, Phoenix, San Diego, San Jose

	Democratic	Republican	Other*	Total
Albuquerque	47%	38%	15%	233,798
Phoenix**	40%	44%	16%	544,372
San Diego	41%	37%	23%	572,773
San Jose	49%	31%	20%	335,407

*Includes decline-to-state and minor parties registrants; **as of September 1997.
Source: Bernalillo County Clerk, Elections Division; Maricopa County Clerk
Elections Department; San Diego County Clerk, Elections Division; Santa Clara
County Clerk, Elections Division.

and Albuquerque. Yet Table 3.4 also shows that there are many citizens in
third parties, or unaffiliated, making Democrats, if a plurality, well short
of a majority. And if we look at party registration by districts, only San
Jose has more Democratic districts than Republican districts.

Minority representatives seeking council allies face considerable
obstacles. First, although we see common ground between communities
of color and others in the city, minority representatives suffer from the
difficulty that low-income and minority populations remain small, isolated, and distinctive enough that common issues for coalition building
with other constituencies are not obvious (see Table 3.5). In San Diego,
for example, the median income of Council District 8, which is more
than 60 percent Latino, is $23,780, well below the median income of the
city as a whole. Both that district and Council District 4 (which sent an
African American to the city council) have considerably more poverty
(26.3 percent and 15.6 percent) than the city as a whole (9.7 percent).
And residents in those districts also have less education, with 71 percent
of the residents in Council District 4 and 56.3% of the residents in Council District 8 having completed high school (compared to 82.3% of the
residents of the city as a whole). For these residents, good public policy
may well be very different than whatever the residents of more affluent
districts desire. And good times for the city as a whole may not be very
good times for the residents of Districts 4 and 8. For example, thriving
San Diego is incubating a major housing crisis for low-income residents.

When they seek to serve their constituents, representatives of poor
communities inevitably raise redistributive issues to which middle class

**Table 3.5. San Diego City Council Districts: Selected
Characteristics**

Council District	Poverty	Median Income	High School Graduate & Greater	Owner-Occupied Unit	Percentage Anglo Population
1	7.1%	$50,547	94.4%	60.2%	78.4%
2	11.1%	$30,854	87.5%	35.3%	79.1%
3	19.3%	$23,893	78.4%	26.2%	56.5%
4*	15.6%	$31,189	71.0%	60.3%	20.6%
5	6.1%	$45,550	90.0%	62.9%	69.8%
6	8.1%	$37,132	87.7%	53.2%	76.9%
7	13.3%	$35,445	86.2%	54.8%	72.6%
8**	26.3%	$23,780	56.3%	39.7%	19.3%
City-wide	9.7%	$33,686	82.3%	48.3%	58.7%

*CD 4 represented by an African American.
**CD 8 represented by a Latino.

voters and their representatives remain resistant. Even getting to equity in the provision of services that in other districts have been routine may be a very expensive matter. The provision of sewers to prevent neighborhood flooding is a case in point. On this and many other issues, Griego explains, "we had to fight for everything we got." When municipal budgets become tight, as during recessions, the fights can become particularly intense, or underserved areas might get half a loaf. This was the case in San Diego, where the city built a new fire station in Juan Vargas's district, but did not have money to hire additional firefighters to staff the facility. Also in San Diego, where CDBG monies are in part divided among districts, debts from past capital improvements must be retired from current allocations by district, giving our district executives fewer resources than at first appear to be theirs to spend.

We think that there can be no question that political life after districts is more democratic and more equitable than the politics of big city reform. Neighborhood concerns are accepted as legitimate subjects of public debate, municipal bureaucracies have become attentive to equity among districts, minorities have places at the city council table, and their representatives are able to deliver significant collective goods to their

districts. Our findings provide further evidence that institutional arrangements have an impact on politics and policy, although they are not a
panacea for the ills of our cities, or even for the disadvantages of the
poorer communities within them. Nevertheless, district elections have
expanded the range of those who have participated in politics and decisions, and we find this cause for optimism.

REFERENCES

Bernalillo Country Clerk. (1998). Elections Division.

Bridges, A. (1997a). *Morning glories: Municipal reform in the Southwest.*
Princeton, NJ: Princeton University Press.

———. (1997b). Textbook municipal reform. *Urban Affairs Review, 33* (1),
97–119.

Browning, R.P., Marshall, D.R., & Tabb, D.H. (1984). *Protest is not enough: The
struggle of Blacks and Hispanics for equality in urban politics.* Berkeley:
University of California Press.

Bunch, M. (1994, July 7). Grocery chain starts building in the inner city. *San
Diego Union-Tribune,* p. B-1.

Christensen, T., & Gerston, L.N. (1984). *The local connection: Grassroots challenges to elite control of city government.* Boston: Little, Brown.

City of San Jose. (1992). *Department of Planning and Building: San Jose population, race and sex by 1992, City Council Districts.*

Cotrell, C.L., & Stevens, R.M. (1978). The 1975 Voting Rights Act and San Antonio, Texas: Toward a federal guarantee of a republican form of local government. *Publius, 8*(1), 79–89.

Davidson, C. (1992). The voting rights act: A brief history. In B. Grofman &
C. Davidson (eds.), *Controversies in minority voting: The voting rights act
in perspective* (pp. 7–51). Washington, DC: Brookings Institution.

Davison, S. (1997). *Case study of community development block grant spending
in the city of San Diego: FY 1991 and 1995.* Senior thesis (Urban Studies
and Planning), University of California, San Diego.

Del Olmo, F. (1998, June 7). "Giant" is awake and is a force. *Los Angeles Times,*
p. M-5.

Dolbee, S. (1994, November 13). Councilman straddles line between church and
state. *San Diego Union-Tribune,* p. D-1.

Fried, D.L. (1995, April 8). Eyesore is demolished amid cheers in skyline. *San
Diego Union-Tribune,* p. B-3.

Handley, R. (1994, January 7). Thrift's plan to close sites is attacked. *San Diego
Union-Tribune,* p. C-1.

Heilig, P., & Mundt, R.J. (1984). *Your voice at city hall: The politics, procedures and policies of district representation.* Albany: State University of New York Press.

Huard, R. (1995, October 5). Vargas to enter race for Congress: Councilman seeks Filner's position. *San Diego Union-Tribune,* p. B-1.

LaVelle, P.J. (1994a, October 24). Recent city council battles leave colleagues cool towards Stevens. *San Diego Union-Tribune,* p. B-2.

———. (1994b, November 27). 'Tis now the Golding season for giving—and not giving. *San Diego-Union Tribune,* p. B-2.

Lowi, T. (1967). Machine politics, old and new. *The Public Interest, 9,* 83–92.

Klevit, A. (1972). City councils and their functions in local government. In International City Management Association, *The municipal year book* (pp. 15–28). Washington, DC: International City Management Association.

Maricopa County Clerk. (1997, September). Elections Department.

McClain, P.D., & Stewart, J., Jr. (1995). *"Can we all get along?": Racial and ethnic minorities in American politics.* Boulder, CO: Westview Press.

Ojito, M. (1998, April 20). A record backlog to get citizenship stymies 2 million. *New York Times,* p. A-1.

Polinard, J.L., Wrinkle, R.D., Longoria, T., & Binder, N.E. (1994). *Electoral structure and urban policy: The impact on mexican american communities.* Armonk, NY: M.E. Sharpe.

Powell, R. (1994a, May 29). Red tape is untangled from funding requests. *San Diego Union-Tribune,* p. B-3.

———. (1994b, May 29). Scramble for federal block grant funding is heated. *San Diego Union-Tribune,* p. B-1.

Renner, T. (1988). Municipal election processes: The impact on minority representation. In International City Management Association, *The municipal year book* (pp. 13–21).

——— and De Santis, V. (1993). Contemporary patterns and trends in municipal government structures. In International City Managers Association, *The municipal year book* (pp. 57–69).

Riggs, R. (1994, September 1). Lending plan set for low-incomes. *San Diego Union-Tribune,* p. C-1.

Rohrlich, T. (1997, December 31). Politics: Rise in naturalizations partly fueled turnout, data show. *Los Angeles Times,* p. A-1.

San Diego Associate of Governments. (1992). *1990 census population and housing profile: City of San Diego council districts 1–8.* San Diego: SANDAG/Source Point Regional Census Data Center.

San Diego Country Clerk. (1998). Elections Division.

San Diego Union-Tribune. (1994a, May 26), p. C-1.

San Diego Union-Tribune. (1994b, November 22), p. B-2.

San Diego Union-Tribune. (1995, January 22), p. G-2.

Sanders, H. (1979). Governmental structure in American cities. In International City Management Association, *The municipal year book* (pp. 97–109).

Santa Clara County Clerk. (1998). Elections Division.

Schloyer, D. (1993). *Ethnic politics in a sunbelt city: The case of San Diego.* M.A. thesis, University of California, San Diego.

Turegano, P. (1995, January 29). Center stage: African Americans draw on experiences to give roles life. *San Diego Union-Tribune,* p. G-2.

U.S. Bureau of the Census. (1991). *1990 Census of Population and Housing. Summary Population and Housing Characteristics: Arizona,* Table 3. Washington, DC: U.S. Government Printing Office.

———. (1991). *1990 Census of Population and Housing. Summary Population and Housing Characteristics: California,* Table 3. Washington, DC: U.S. Government Printing Office.

———. (1991). *1990 Census of Population and Housing. Summary Population and Housing Characteristics: New Mexico,* Table 3. Washington, DC: U.S. Government Printing Office.

Weisberg, L. (1994, April 24). Building boom in the southwest. *San Diego Union-Tribune,* p. H-1.

Welch, S., & Bledsoe, T. (1988). *Urban reform and its consequences: A study in representation.* Chicago: The University of Chicago Press.

Young, E. (1995, September 18). It's ticket time again if your car blocks sidewalk. *San Diego Union-Tribune,* p. B-2.

NOTES

[1]San Jose, San Diego, Albuquerque, and Phoenix were chosen because they are the largest cities in their states to follow this trajectory. In addition to districted city councils, all hold nonpartisan elections and have independently elected mayors that vote with the council.

[2]At the same time Welch and Bledsoe found that "Over 70 percent of the members elected from districts also view" concern for the entire city as a critical aspect of representation (1988, p. 68).

[3]In San Diego the creation of a district created for Mexican American representation resulted, in the first post-district campaign, in the election of an Anglo.

[4]Heilig and Mundt found that the poorest districts received the "most personalized and constant kind of attention" (1984, p. 89). This is because low-income constituents have "the most errands to be run: They depend more than

other citizens upon government not only for amenities but for many of the necessities of urban life" (p. 89).

[5]The exceptions are those income-generating authorities that are largely free of city government supervision, such as San Diego's Port Authority.

[6]While all of our respondents argue that districts have provided their constituents with advantages that were nonexistent when their councils were elected at-large, some did voice concerns about what they perceive to be negative impacts of decentralized decision making. In their view, the major consequence is that members tend to think of their district first, with the result that issues have been "midgetized." Secondly, term limits (in San Jose and San Diego) have created short time frames for representatives; their focus is the immediate and concrete rather than the long term and abstract. Some say this increases the need for strong leadership from the mayor's office; others point to increased burdens on municipal bureaucracies. Finally, one respondent believed that district elections eliminate voters' ability to replace an unsatisfactory council majority; that voters now only have the power to replace one member reduces their political control. It should be noted that politicians who also served in periods of citywide elections were especially uncomfortable with both the district-centered agendas of council members and with the bargaining and negotiating among council members to achieve district objectives. Here one politician's laudable trustworthiness, collegiality, and interpersonal skills are another's regrettable vote-trading, politicking, and logrolling.

CHAPTER 4

The Dynamo of Urban Growth
Immigration, Naturalization, and the Restructuring of Urban Politics[1]

LOUIS DeSIPIO

With the change in U.S. immigration law in 1965, large-scale immigration again became a regular part of American life. In the years since 1965, more than twenty million people have immigrated to permanent residence and an uncountable number of others have migrated without permanent status, including five million undocumented immigrants who resided in the United States in 1996 (U.S. Immigration and Naturalization Service, 1997b, pp. 25, 198). Overwhelmingly these immigrants have migrated to metropolitan areas, and within the metropolitan areas, the majority of immigrants have settled, at least initially, in the center cities.

These new populations present a challenge for the cities, a challenge that cities had not experienced in the period of low migration from the 1920s to the 1960s, but also a challenge to the study of urban politics. In this article, I examine the potential impact of these new immigrants on cities and on the questions that political scientists should be asking about urban politics. As will soon become evident, I raise questions here that cannot be answered with what we know today about immigrants and their political environments. Equally importantly, these questions cannot be answered because this migration is ongoing and questions of settlement that are yet to be confronted will shape the political interests and political opportunities of the new immigrants (DeSipio & de la Garza, 1998).

My focus is twofold. First, I examine the potential impact that comes simply from numbers of immigrants, whether naturalized or not. By this, I mean both demography—changed composition of major cities receiving immigrants—and the new issues around which immigrants will organize. Second, I look at the likelihood that urban immigrant populations will develop the ability to participate fully in urban politics through naturalization and political socialization. I suggest that to the extent that previous patterns of naturalization and naturalized citizen electoral participation continue, naturalized immigrant populations will always be represented at levels less than parity with their share of the population. As a result, political demand making will focus on means other than the ballot box. As will soon become evident, my primary focus in the final section of the article is urban Latino[2] immigrant populations. While this focus on Latinos reflects both my own research interests and the availability of survey data from which to identify patterns of immigrant-native urban relations, Latinos also merit study because of their numbers and their relative successes in organizing to make political demands. Latinos are the largest of the recent immigrant populations. Equally important, Latinos have been most successful among contemporary immigrant populations in influencing local and national politics. Thus, while Asians and immigrants from other parts of the world will undoubtedly develop their own strategies to influence politics, they will also learn from the experience of Latinos.

In sum, I develop a profile of the demographic foundations of urban relations over the next decade or two that accounts for new immigrants (including those already here and those likely to migrate in the coming years), both in terms of their indirect influence on ethnic group-majority relations and their more direct influence, once naturalized, as voters.

IMMIGRANTS AND AMERICAN CITIES

The history of U.S. immigration has long been a primarily urban phenomenon. While many immigrants before the Revolution did settle outside of cities, immigrants since have clustered in them (Muller, 1993). By the late nineteenth century, there were few exceptions to this pattern— Scandinavians in the nineteenth century, Mexicans in the late nineteenth and early twentieth centuries, and some Germans in the late nineteenth century. The urban immigrants joined with native-born Americans born in rural areas to build the great cities of the nineteenth century. The approximately twenty-six million people who immigrated to the United States between 1865 and 1920 exceeded the 1850 national population.

Immigration fueled tremendous increases in urban population and, simultaneously, these new immigrants played a critical role in the development of the nation's industrial economy. This labor, often unskilled in the nineteenth and early twentieth centuries, was the engine of U.S. economic growth in this era, particularly in manufacturing. It was the urban centers, initially of the East Coast cities, but over time in the Midwest and West that led this manufacturing boom. Estimates suggest that as late as the 1920s, immigrant workers comprised more than half of the labor force of New York and Chicago (Muller, 1993, p. 7).

The final contribution of these nineteenth and early twentieth century immigrants is often overlooked. By their presence, they challenged the political leaders of these cities and then of nation as a whole to live up to the nation's democratic ideals. Over time, they and their descendants participated in electoral politics. Initially, many immigrants faced a denial of voting rights, and those that could participate did not do so freely. Instead, their votes were controlled by the urban political machines. The machines eased the transition for some—particularly co-nationals and co-ethnics of the machines' leaders—and hindered it for others—later arriving ethnic groups in the cities and national-origin groups whose voting rights were challenged from the time of their arrival such as Asian and Mexican immigrants (Erie, 1988; Gómez-Quiñones, 1994). In cases where the machines facilitated political participation, they not only provided get-out-the-vote resources and some selective incentives to participate, but also two resources that are in short supply in today's immigrant communities—information about how to vote and assistance with naturalization and, after requirements were imposed, voter registration.

Over time, however, these earlier immigrants and their children participated in large numbers and were a key building block of the New Deal Coalition (Allswang, 1971; Cohen, 1990; DeSipio, 1996a; Gamm, 1986). Equally important for the purposes of this study, immigrants and their children became sufficiently empowered that they could routinely contest and often win political races against opponents who traced their ancestry to earlier periods of immigration. This point of ethnic political efficacy occurred at different times in different cities, but again offers a pattern against which later immigrants can be judged.

Turn-of-the-century immigrants did, occasionally, shape political outcomes, but focusing simply on that dimension of their experience misses a larger point. By the time of the New Deal, most European immigrants (and their American born children and grandchildren) participated in politics or did not participate because of the demographic factors and structural barriers that predicted participation among all Americans. Ethnicity—at least among European ethnics—played an increasingly diminished role in predicting political activity.

Contemporary Immigration and the Cities

Post-1965 immigrants have also migrated in large numbers to cities. Table 4.1 reports on immigrants to permanent residence in 1996. Of these immigrants, 93.6 percent reported that they would live, at least initially, in a metropolitan statistical area. Among the native population, just 79.4 percent resided in metropolitan areas. This concentration in urban areas is not simply a function of *new* immigrants. Among the foreign born counted in the 1990 census, more than 90 percent resided in urban areas.

Table 4.1. Intended Residential Metropolitan Statistical Area, FY 1996 Immigrants Admitted to Permanent Residence, Metropolitan Statistical Areas Receiving 1 Percent or More of Immigrants

	FY 1996 immigrants	
City	Number	% of total
1. New York, NY	133,168	14.5
2. Los Angeles–Long Beach, CA	64,285	7.0
3. Miami, FL	41,527	4.5
4. Chicago, IL	39,989	4.4
5. Washington, DC	34,327	3.7
6. Houston, TX	21,387	2.3
7. Boston, MA	18,726	2.0
8. San Diego, CA	18,226	2.0
9. San Francisco, CA	18,171	2.0
10. Newark, NJ	17,939	2.0
11. Orange County, CA	17,580	1.9
12. Dallas, TX	15,915	1.7
13. Oakland, CA	15,759	1.7
14. Bergen-Passaic, NJ	15,682	1.7
15. San Jose, CA	13,854	1.5
16. Philadelphia, PA	13,034	1.4
17. Detroit, MI	11,929	1.3
18. Jersey City, NJ	11,399	1.2
19. Nassau-Suffolk, NJ	10,594	1.2

Table 4.1. *continued*

City	FY 1996 immigrants	
	Number	**% of total**
20. Seattle, WA	10,429	1.1
21. Riverside–San Bernardino, CA	10,314	1.1
22. Ft. Lauderdale, FL	10,290	1.1
23. Atlanta, GA	9,870	1.1
24. Middlesex-Somerset-Hunterdon, NJ	9,286	1.0
Other Metropolitan Statistical Areas	273,254	29.8
Non-Metropolitan Statistical Areas	58,966	6.4
Total	915,900	

Source: U.S. Immigration and Naturalization Service, 1997b, pp. 66–68.

As with the turn of the century migration, the movement of immigrants into cities disproportionately favors a few of the larger cities. Again looking at the 1996 immigrants, New York alone received 14.5 percent of immigrants (see Table 4.1). Los Angeles received another 7.0 percent of immigrants. The top ten urban destinations were the intended residences of more than 44 percent of immigrants. This concentration is even clearer on examination of the states of intended residence. The top four states—California, New York, Florida, and Texas—received more than 56 percent of 1996 immigrants, remembering that approximately 94 percent of these immigrants are destined for urban areas (see Table 4.2). Thirty-five states, on the other hand, each received less than 1 percent of the 1995 immigrant flow. Combined these 35 states received just 15.3 percent of 1996 immigrants, slightly less than did New York.

Table 4.2. State of Intended Residence, FY 1996
Immigrants Admitted to Permanent Residence,
States Receiving 1 Percent or More of Immigrants

State	FY 1996 immigrants	
	Number	**% of total**
1. California	201,529	22.0
2. New York	154,095	16.8
3. Texas	83,385	9.1

Table 4.2. *continued*

| | FY 1996 immigrants | |
State	Number	% of total
4. Florida	79,461	8.7
5. New Jersey	63,303	6.9
6. Illinois	42,517	4.6
7. Massachusetts	23,085	2.5
8. Virginia	21,375	2.3
9. Maryland	20,732	2.3
10. Washington	18,833	2.1
11. Michigan	17,253	1.9
12. Pennsylvania	16,938	1.8
13. Georgia	12,608	1.4
14. Connecticut	10,874	1.2
15. Ohio	10,237	1.1
Other states	139,675	15.3
Total	915,900	

Source: U.S. Immigration and Naturalization Service, 1997b, pp. 62–64.

The destinations of undocumented immigrants are necessarily less clear. Traditionally, undocumented immigrants have migrated to rural areas to work in agriculture. Over the past thirty years, however, undocumented immigrants—particularly undocumented immigrants who remain in the United States for lengthy periods and are captured in the population estimate presented below—have increasingly come to live in cities (Heer, 1990). An Immigration and Naturalization Service (INS) estimate of undocumented immigrants resident in the United States in 1996 matches the state-level concentrations found in data for immigrants to permanent residence. Of the five million undocumented immigrants estimated to reside in the United States, more than 71 percent lived in the same four states that received the highest number of legal immigrants (see Table 4.3). Fully 40 percent of these resided in California. Again, a large number of states are home to few of these immigrants. Thirty-one states are home to 330,000 undocumented immigrants, a number smaller than the undocumented population of the any of the four largest states.

Table 4.3. Undocumented Immigrant Population by State, October 1996

State	Population	State	Population
1. California	2,000,000	12. Maryland	44,000
2. Texas	700,000	13. Michigan	37,000
3. New York	540,000	14. Pennsylvania	37,000
4. Florida	350,000	15. New Mexico	37,000
5. Illinois	290,000	16. Oregon	33,000
6. New Jersey	135,000	17. Georgia	32,000
7. Arizona	115,000	18. District of Columbia	30,000
8. Massachusetts	85,000	19. Connecticut	29,000
9. Virginia	55,000	20. Nevada	24,000
10. Washington	52,000	Other states	330,000
11. Colorado	45,000	Total	5,000,000

Source: U.S. Immigration and Naturalization Service, 1997a, p. 183.

There are no reliable national city-level estimates of undocumented immigrant residence patterns.

The contemporary immigrant flow is quite heterogeneous, both in terms of country of origin and region. This heterogeneity can again be seen by examining 1996 immigrants and their intended cities of residence. Table 4.4 reports on the top ten cities for intended residence and the four largest national-origin populations intending to reside in these cities. The table highlights how diverse the flow of immigrants is to these cities. In none of the ten cities do immigrants from any one country make up half of the total immigrants destined for that city. Miami sees the greatest concentration, with Cubans making up approximately 48 percent of the city's new immigrants. Another notable characteristic is that the top nationalities going to these cities, for the most part, come from different parts of the world. So, the immigrant population in these cities is not only not dominated by a single nation, there is also little regional unity within them. The possible exception to this pattern is Miami, where all of the large immigrant populations are from the Americas. Because Miami's large immigrant populations are from the English-, French-, and Spanish-speaking countries in the Americas, however, there is, again, little likelihood of "regional" unity among the city's immigrants.

Table 4.4. Top Four National-Origin Groups Intending to Reside in Top Ten Cities of Intended Migration, FY 1996

New York, NY (133,168)

1. Dominican Republic (19,665)
2. People's Republic of China (10,376)
3. Ukraine (8,460)
4. Jamaica (7,010)

Los Angeles–Long Beach, CA (64,285)

1. Mexico (17,035)
2. Philippines (6,733)
3. El Salvador (4,434)
4. Soviet Union (3,248)

Miami, FL (41,527)

1. Cuba (20,061)
2. Haiti (3,139)
3. Colombia (2,054)
4. Jamaica (1,540)

Chicago, IL (39,989)

1. Mexico (11,138)
2. Poland (5,474)
3. India (3,596)
4. Philippines (2,379)

Washington, DC-MD-VA (34,327)

1. El Salvador (3,282)
2. Vietnam (1,918)
3. India (1,861)
4. Philippines (1,407)

Houston, TX (21,387)

1. Mexico (6,697)
2. Vietnam (3,151)
3. El Salvador (1,605)
4. India (1,374)

Boston-Lawrence-Lowell-Brockton, MA (18,726)

1. Dominican Republic (1,928)
2. People's Republic of China (1,426)
3. Haiti (1,332)
4. Vietnam (1,085)

San Diego, CA (18,226)

1. Mexico (7,791)
2. Philippines (3,342)
3. Vietnam (1,165)
4. People's Republic of China (456)

San Francisco, CA (18,171)

1. People's Republic of China (3,095)
2. Philippines (2,956)
3. Mexico (1,549)
4. Hong Kong (990)

Newark, NJ (17,936)

1. Haiti (1,352)
2. India (1,259)
3. Colombia (1,103)
4. Peru (876)

Source: U.S. Immigration and Naturalization Service, 1997b, pp. 66–68.

With this heterogeneity in mind, it is important to see that immigrants as a group are crucial to the growth (or to the slowed decline) of the larger U.S. cities. Although these are undoubtedly slight overestimates[3], approximately 3.2 million immigrants migrated, at least initially, to the ten largest cities in the 1980s (see Table 4.5). In the seven cities that experienced population growth in the decade, immigration exceeded the number of new residents in three of the cities. The most dramatic impact was in the two largest cities—New York and Los Angeles—where immigration exceeded growth by a factor of 4 and nearly 2.5, respectively. Without new immigration New York's population would have declined by more than 10 percent and Los

Table 4.5. Change in Population in the Ten Largest Cities, 1980–1990, and Immigrant Share of the Change

City	1980 Population	1990 Population	Change	Estimated Immigration 1981–1990[a b]
New York	7,071,631	7,322,564	+250,933	1,043,392
Los Angeles	2,966,850	3,485,557	+518,707	1,248,234
Chicago	3,005,072	2,783,726	–221,346	299,363
Houston	1,595,138	1,629,902	+34,764	153,010
Philadelphia	1,688,210	1,585,577	–102,633	89,615
San Diego	875,538	1,110,623	+235,085	164,669
Detroit	1,203,368	1,027,974	–175,394	60,390
Dallas	904,078	1,007,618	+103,540	102,494
Phoenix	789,704	983,403	+193,699	37,920
San Antonio	785,880	935,393	+149,513	40,866

Notes: [a]Estimated immigration 1981–1990 includes recipients of legalization under the Immigration Reform and Control Act of 1986 who had already been resident in the United States.
[b]Reports on intended residence of immigrants to permanent residence. The INS does not verify that immigrants move to these areas. Subsequently, they may move. Finally, these data report intention to move to the metropolitan statistical area named which includes suburban areas. So, this estimate overestimates the number of immigrants who moved to these cities in the 1980s.
Sources: U.S. Immigration and Naturalization Service, *Statistical Yearbook of the Immigration and Naturalization Service,* various years.

Angeles' by 20 percent. The impact of immigrants' numbers is also felt in smaller cities, particularly in the West, Northeast, in Florida, and in Texas.

These immigrants create immediate costs as well as benefits for these cities. While they tap overextended municipal social services, particularly public education, they create a benefit for these cities in every program that allocates benefits based on population figures. New York, for example, would have lost an additional member of Congress (holding other migration patterns constant) had it not been for immigration in the 1980s. Los Angeles owes at least one and part of a second of its new members of Congress in 1992 to 1980s immigration. Block grants also grew in each of these cities based on the numbers of immigrants.

Clearly, this is a very rough calculus. In the short term, the costs of providing services to these new residents exceeds the intangible benefits of added congressional representation and increased federal funding. The most intangible impact of immigrants on these cities is the availability of their labor. While it fuels the service sector in the large immigrant receiving cities, the availability of low-skill, low-wage immigrant labor may slow the transition to more technologically intensive production in some of these cities. But many immigrants also bring entrepreneurial skills to these cities and foment the creation of small business. Some also create economic ties to their home countries, expanding trade. In the case of Miami, these entrepreneurial skills and international focus (as well as high levels of human capital and aid from the U.S. government) combined to make Miami the banking center for Latin America and the center of regional trade networks. While the economic impact of immigration can be studied for each of the major immigrant receiving cities, it is important to recognize that the long-term economic contribution of the current wave of immigration is an open question the answer to which is dependent on the process of settlement for the immigrants and, particularly, their children. If the work ethic and drive that is evident in many of today's immigrants cannot be maintained in their children or the economy falters and cannot absorb the labor of these immigrants and their children, the long-term costs of this period of immigration will be high, not just to these cities where they reside, but also to the society as a whole.

Immigration at these levels also speeds the process of ethnic diversification in American cities by facilitating the movement of native-born whites and African Americans out of the cities. This, of course, is not new to this era of American immigration history. In the modern era, however, there is a very specific cost. The people that move are generally higher income wage earners who take with them taxes needed by the cities. The impact varies based on the city and its relationship with neighboring areas, but generally weakens the ability of the cities to provide the services that immigrants need to adapt to American life. Thus, while immigration laws are determined by the national government, the specific demographic impact occurs in highly localized contexts and the day-to-day costs of incorporating immigrants are financed by local governments. The success or failure of immigrant settlement will, in the long run, be borne by the society as a whole. In the short run, however, cities are asked to pay the first installment.

These new residents cannot, initially, use the ballot box to make demands on city services. Immigrants to permanent residence attain eligibility for citizenship after five years of residence, and the undocumented never attain this eligibility. Even after eligibility for naturalization, many immigrants remain denizens for many years. The reasons for this are numerous and can not be examined here (DeSipio, 1996a). What is important to note is that immigrants from different parts of the world and different countries have vastly different naturalization rates (see Table 4.6). Those nationalities that have been in the country longer generally have a greater likelihood of having naturalized. Also, Asian immigrants, controlling for year of entry, are generally quicker than immigrants from other parts of the world to naturalize. Thus, the rate of non-naturalization is felt differently in these ten largest cities (see Table 4.7). Cities with a higher concentration of pre-1965 immigrants—such as Philadelphia and Detroit— have a lower share of noncitizens among their immigrant populations.

Table 4.6. Naturalization Rates for Regions and Selected Countries, 1990

Region	Foreign Born 1990	Raw Naturalization Rate	Naturalization Rate among 1980 and Later Immigrants
Europe	4,016,678	64.7%	13.6%
Asia	4,979,037	40.8%	17.4%
North America	8,124,257	29.3%	12.5%
Caribbean	1,938,348	39.7%	15.1%
Central America	1,133,978	20.7%	9.8%
South America	1,037,497	30.8%	11.7%
Africa	363,819	34.1%	15.4%
Oceania	104,145	34.0%	12.6%

Table 4.6. *continued*

Country	Foreign Born 1990	Raw Naturalization Rate	Naturalization Rate among 1980 and Later Immigrants
China	529,837	44.1%	15.7%
Colombia	286,124	29.0%	11.2%
Cuba	736,971	51.0%	14.8%
Dominican Republican	347,858	27.6%	14.0%
El Salvador	465,433	15.4%	10.1%
India	450,406	34.9%	13.4%
Jamaica	334,140	38.4%	17.2%
Japan	290,128	28.2%	3.2%
Korea	568,397	40.6%	14.9%
Mexico	4,298,014	22.6%	12.7%
Philippines	912,674	53.9%	25.9%
Vietnam	543,262	42.7%	26.6%
Total	19,767,316	40.5%	14.4%

Note: The countries of origin listed are those with 250,000 or more of their former nationals residing in the United States in 1990 and who sent most of their immigrants after 1965.
Source: U.S. Bureau of the Census, 1993.

   Each of these large cities has a sizable noncitizen population. New York's numbers more than one million, Los Angeles' almost one million, and Chicago's nearly 300,000. This creates a dilemma in governance in these cities. These noncitizen populations are often concentrated and create areas of each of these cities where officials are elected from districts with few citizens (de la Garza, Menchaca, & DeSipio, 1994). Equally problematic, city bureaucracies may be less responsive in these areas that cannot so easily seek needed services. Where some of these elected officials and municipal bureaucracies are very conscientious in their efforts to reach out to noncitizen constituents and to speak to their needs, others neglect them. In the recent past, this neglect has spurred violence when these populations come to feel that their needs are not being met. The

Table 4.7. Naturalization Rates in the Ten Largest Cities, 1990

City	Foreign Born	Naturalized	% Non-Naturalized	Naturalized 1995
New York	2,082,931	865,416	58.4	58,766
Los Angeles	1,336,665	339,922	74.6	59,709
Chicago	469,187	177,444	62.2	19,302
Houston	290,374	78,276	73.0	13,906
Philadelphia	104,814	54,884	47.6	7,906
San Diego	232,138	84,336	63.7	4,443[a]
Detroit	34,490	15,520	55.0	6,130
Dallas	125,862	35,394	71.9	5,208
Phoenix	84,672	30,634	63.8	2,349
San Antonio	87,549	37,319	57.4	2,491

Notes: The foreign-born and naturalized populations reported here are not limited to post-1965 immigrants.
[a]FY 1994. The INS did not report on naturalizations in San Diego in FY 1995.
Sources: U.S. Bureau of the Census, 1993; U.S. Immigration and Naturalization Service, 1997a, pp. 150–151.

riots after the Rodney King verdict reflected immigrant–native tensions, as did the Washington Heights riots in New York (Baldassare, 1994). Washington's 1991 Mount Pleasant riots grew from tensions between police and Salvadoran residents. While riots such as these are very much the exception, they demonstrate the inherent tension in a situation where a noncitizen population is concentrated and comes to perceive that it is not receiving its needed share of municipal services. A trigger, such as a case of police brutality, can bring these simmering tensions to the surface.

The 1990 noncitizen share of urban population is somewhat misleading because political events of the past five years have fueled a dramatic increase in the number of naturalization applications. There are several reasons for this: In California, anti-immigrant rhetoric surrounding Proposition 187 (the 1994 initiative to deny state social welfare benefits to undocumented immigrants and their children) was a stimulus to action. More generally, increases in naturalization applications have come from a desire to protect eligibility for federal social welfare programs (a result of the 1996 Personal Responsibility and Work Opportunity Act that reformed federal welfare programs), a surge in the number of naturalization-eligible immigrants resulting from the Immigration Reform and Control Act of 1986, a response to an INS administrative requirement to replace aging green cards (that cost almost as much as and required comparable bureaucratic interaction to naturalization), and concerns about changes in criminal law relating to the deportation of permanent residents convicted of crimes (DeSipio, 1996b). Though slow to respond initially, the INS has naturalized a record number of immigrants in 1996. This number, however, will slow in the coming years as the INS responds to criticism of its rush to naturalize more than one million immigrants before the 1996 elections. As a result, backlogs in application processing are currently at record levels (Ojito, 1998).

Nevertheless, immigrants are naturalizing at higher rates than in previous years. In an effort to indicate the impact of current naturalization levels, Table 4.7 provides the number of naturalization applications approved in each of the ten largest cities in 1995, the first year in which the current surge of applications resulted in a high number of newly naturalized citizens. In most of these cities, the number of naturalizing citizens exceeds the number of new immigrants, a first in many cases. Despite this increase in applications, it will take many years to naturalize the current pool of noncitizens, let alone immigrants who arrive in the future. Thus, a continuing dimension of urban immigrant populations will be large clusters of noncitizens.

Conclusions

This discussion of the demographics of immigration and urban areas suggests several important characteristics of contemporary immigration for the study of urban politics. First, immigrants overwhelmingly migrate to urban areas, concentrating in a few of the largest cities. Second, when immigrants move in large numbers to these cities, they are overwhelmingly responsible for the cities' population growth, though each of the nation's largest cities has a sizable foreign-born population. Third, the majority of these urban immigrants are not naturalized. By their presence, then, they build the cities' population numbers—and offer the benefits that accompany numbers—but they also add to the demands on city services. These demands include those typical for all residents, as well as specialized needs that emerge from their immigrant status, particularly for educational services. These immigrants also create a dilemma in representation because of their high numbers of noncitizens.

Finally, these "immigrant populations" should not be viewed as homogeneous. In each of the cities receiving large numbers of immigrants, the nations and regions of origin are quite diverse. Thus, while immigrants provide the engine of urban growth, they do not make up a single population. Their public policy needs may have many similarities, but it is unlikely that any large city's immigrant populations will regularly act in concert to meet these needs.

ISSUE FOCUS AND POLITICAL ORIENTATIONS OF URBAN IMMIGRANT POPULATIONS

The study of the political orientations of U.S. immigrant populations has often been based as much on scholarly conjecture as on the actual beliefs of the immigrants themselves. Lack of empirical data is partially a result of academic bias, and partially a failure of survey research to identify and survey immigrant populations successfully. Immigrants are difficult to reach for a number of reasons: many do not speak English; some, such as the undocumented and recent immigrants, may not want to be reached; and survey questions are frequently not targeted to the experiences of immigrant populations. Based on what is known, I suggest a series of issues that immigrants, particularly Latino immigrants, perceive as important. As these populations grow and naturalize, they will likely bring these issues to municipal agendas in cities with large immigrant populations.

One of the legacies of past scholarship on immigrant attitudes is a continuing myth that immigrants are sojourners and, hence, more focused on the politics of their home countries than on politics in the United States (Burma, 1954, pp. 35–71; Madsen, 1964; Butler, 1986; Barrera, 1988). One consequence of this bias is that immigrants are presented as disengaged from U.S. politics. Several surveys of Latino populations demonstrate that this approach is false. Overwhelmingly, Latino immigrants—naturalized and non-naturalized—indicate that they are planning to reside for the rest of their lives in the United States, have a strong attachment to the United States, and, among a plurality, have a stronger national identification with the United States than with their countries of origin (de la Garza et al., 1992; Pachon & DeSipio, 1994). When probed, they demonstrate a knowledge of the issues in U.S. politics and have strong opinions about their public policy needs and the responsibility of governments in the United States to meet these needs.

There is no comparable national survey data on Asian immigrants or immigrants from other parts of the world, but there is no reason to believe that these immigrants are any more likely to manifest the attitudes of sojourners. For Asian immigrants, particularly those from China, Korea, the Philippines, and Vietnam, there is a formal measure of attachment to the United States in high naturalization rates (U.S. Immigration and Naturalization Service, 1997b, p. 137). While this myth of the immigrant as sojourner can be quickly disproved, it continues to appear in analysis of immigrants and U.S. politics

What, then, is the issue focus of immigrants in the United States? This question can only tentatively be answered because of the absence of survey data on most immigrant populations. Several recent surveys of Latino immigrant communities indicate that their public policy agenda does not differ considerably from the agendas of the population as a whole. This pattern appears both in surveys of attitudes toward national issues and surveys of attitudes toward local issues. Concerning both national and local issues, Latino immigrants were most likely to mention social issues, such as crime and drug control, as the most pressing issue for the nation as a whole and for their city (de la Garza et al., 1992, pp. 166–167). Economic issues were mentioned relatively less often than they would be by U.S.-born populations, distinguishing Latino immigrants somewhat from the population as a whole. Neither ethnic issues nor immigration policy were regarded by many Latinos as the most important issues either for the nation as a whole or for their cities.

At another level, though, Latino immigrants differ more dramatically from the population as a whole. Specifically, Latino immigrants advocate a larger role for government in their lives than does the population as a whole. This pattern is particularly evident around policies that will assist in their incorporation into U.S. society. Unlike the population as a whole, Latino immigrants call for an expansion of the role and responsibilities of government in a number of areas, including education, control of crime and drugs, health care, and child services. They are willing to increase their taxes in order to provide these new services (de la Garza et al., 1992, p. 170). Immigrants, more than U.S.-born Latinos, looked to government for solutions in such areas as housing and employment. This expectation that government would serve their interests arises in part from higher levels of trust in government found among Latino immigrants than U.S.-born Latinos. More than 80 percent of immigrant Latinos believe that government serves "for the benefit of all" compared to just 49 percent of U.S. citizen Latinos (de la Garza et al., 1992, pp. 81,

163). While these findings indicate that Latino immigrants have high expectations for government, there are no measures available to determine their sense of political efficacy.

Distinct policy needs also appear in the areas of language and education policy. The majority oppose the proposition that English should be the official language of the United States and believe that services should be provided in Spanish. Yet, they also believe that citizens and residents should learn English (de la Garza et al., 1992, pp. 176–177). They oppose current levels of immigration and support stronger measures to control undocumented immigrants. They do not, however, support proposals, such as California's Proposition 187, to deny social welfare and public education services to permanent residents and to the undocumented (de la Garza & DeSipio, 1998).

Latino immigrants report largely positive contacts with government. Although they perceive that their co-ethnics are subject to discrimination, several studies find that individuals do not report that they or their families have been subject to discrimination (de la Garza et al., 1992, p. 171; Pachon & DeSipio, 1994, p. 81; NALEO Educational Fund & Tomás Rivera Policy Institute, 1998, pp. 26–30).

Although there is less research to substantiate these findings, there also appears to be a disjuncture between elite and mass opinion, at least in Latino immigrant communities in Southern California and the New York/New Jersey metropolitan area. Studies of elites find higher levels of concern about the quality of delivery of municipal services, particularly police services. Community elites are more likely to report discrimination. Elites also report more concern about neglect of immigrant communities by city governments and the inability of immigrant-ethnic populations to organize (NALEO Educational Fund & Tomás Rivera Policy Institute, 1997; 1998; Tomás Rivera Policy Institute & NALEO Educational Fund, 1997). This finding may also apply outside of these two areas, but there has not been research that disaggregates Latino immigrant elite and mass opinion in other cities.

A final question that needs to be addressed in considering the political orientations of immigrants is the degree to which immigrants see a common "immigrant" agenda regardless of national origin. Here, again, survey data is of only moderate utility because not all immigrant populations are surveyed. Anecdotal evidence certainly suggests that issues *can* bring immigrant communities together. One of the better examples is the campaign to oppose Proposition 187. Issues of this magnitude are rare, however. On a more routine basis, immigrant communities often have little contact with each other and bring stereotypes from their homelands to the table when they encounter non-co-ethnic immigrants. Even within pan-ethnic communities, such as Latinos and Asian Americans, there is little contact across national origin groups and, initially, distrust (de la Garza et al., 1992, p. 195; Espiritu, 1992). The absence of survey data on the policy needs of immigrant populations other than Latinos makes it impossible to say whether issue-based coalitions can form to create an urban immigrant political agenda.

Thus, the policy world of immigrants has broad similarities to the population as a whole in terms of what issues are considered salient. Yet, Latino immigrants also call for more activist government to target the needs of the population. Immigrant opinions are especially strong on language and immigrant policies, which are issues of particular resonance for foreign-born Latinos. Where they are most distinct from the U.S.-born population is in the area of taxation. They are willing to pay to expand the size of government. For cities chronically short of funds, however, this may mean little as immigrant households generally have lower than average incomes and higher numbers of children, considerably reducing the possibility that they will come to be the source of many new taxes at least in the short term.

While conventional, these demands will present a challenge for urban governments. In times of tight municipal budgets, the provision of services to new immigrants may come at the cost of reduced services to other urban populations, including African Americans, who are much better organized. While there is evidence of multiracial, multiethnic coalitions in urban politics, there are also an increasing number of cases where immigrant, particularly Latino, populations ally with whites against African American–supported candidates.

POLITICAL OPPORTUNITIES OF IMMIGRANT POPULATIONS

Urban immigrant populations have a range of opportunities to influence the outcome of politics. To avoid excessive detail, I briefly suggest three models for immigrant political incorporation. Each builds on existing urban immigrant political activity, but also identifies a pattern that can begin to develop in other cities. These three models are: a transformation of community-based cultural, social service, and home-town focused organization to promote district-based electoral competition; the creation of linkages between U.S.-born and immigrant interests to create a common and more influential political voice that raises the salience of the immigrant/ethnic community in urban coalitions and spurs influence that transcends individual electoral districts; and the dominance of urban politics by a single immigrant/ethnic group.

As will become evident, these models are not mutually exclusive. All can operate simultaneously. Equally important, these models of urban immigrant political activity present a challenge to the study of urban politics because many of the activities may appear at a level where a traditional focus on electoral politics, coalitional politics, and group-based demand making would not see them. That is not to say that scholars are not studying the process of immigrant politicization. Scholars are, but they are often studying the groups themselves and are not examining these populations in the context of the immigrant and native populations of the cities. Thus, there is a greater need for urban politics to tap the emerging scholarship on Latino and Asian American politics to understand better the types and forms of immigrant politicization.

As a reminder, I want to emphasize that when I speak of immigrants, I am speaking of national-origin groups that either began to immigrate in large numbers after 1965 (such as most Asian immigrant populations and non-Mexican and non-Cuban Latinos) or, if they were part of earlier migration streams, that began to be viewed more regularly as potentially influential political actors in the past thirty years (such as Mexican, Cuban, and Filipino immigrants).

From Community-Based Organizing to District-Level Victories: The First Step from Immigrant Politics to Ethnic Politics

High rates of noncitizenship in many immigrant communities preclude regular influence by these groups on electoral politics. In these communities, political activity focuses on community-based organizations, the schools, and, among the citizens, targeted efforts at winning district-based elections for co-ethnics. These efforts occur both within specific immigrant-ethnic communities and, less regularly, as part of pan-ethnic Latino or Asian American coalitions.

Community-based organizing is often the first step in immigrant politicization. Often this organizing focuses not on the United States, but on the country or, more likely, city or village of origin. While a collective effort to celebrate a sending country holiday or to provide emergency relief or a clinic for the village of origin may not seem to connect to U.S. politics, it provides an organizational structure, perhaps a leader or group of leaders, and a network of participants that can be tapped when a

U.S.-focused need appears. This pattern of hometown organizing is not new to the current waves of immigrants; it can also be found among turn-of-the-century European immigrant communities. With the advent of modern communication and transportation, it has become more frequent and its impact more easily observed. This pattern of routinized connection to sending communities can be found among all Latino immigrant communities (except Cuban immigrants) (Massey et al., 1987; Georges, 1990; Pessar, 1995; NALEO Educational Fund & Tomás Rivera Policy Institute, 1997; Tomás Rivera Policy Institute & NALEO Educational Fund, 1997).

Often this transition from home country to U.S. focus is very subtle. An incident in the schools or between the police and the community refocuses immigrants' attentions in such a way that their interests expand and the pre-existing organizations come to serve multiple needs. Or, an organization forms to meet a special social welfare need that is not being met by native public or private institutions. Over time, these community-based organizations (CBOs) expand, diversify, come into conflict with each other, and specialize. While simplified, this pattern of organizational development appears in most concentrated immigrant populations. Usually, the initial focus is solely on co-nationals, or even more specifically, immigrants from the same city or region of the country of origin, though these ethnic boundaries tend to expand as immigrants focus more on issues in their U.S. political environment.

These national origin–based CBOs are supplemented by nonethnic organizations such as parent-based organizations in the schools and church-based organizations. These types of organizations are consistent across cities, though their longevity seems to vary considerably. These groups hold the potential for organization that transcends a single national-origin group and offer, for many immigrants, their first exposure to pan-ethnic Latino or Asian American politics.

A number of urban immigrant organizations across the country fit this pattern of political evolution. In Los Angeles, for example, the Mothers of East Los Angeles built on school and church-based organization to seek to influence city and state policies toward the environment (trash dumping) and prisons (Pardo, 1990). In South Texas, a network of city-specific CBOs organized under the coordination of the Industrial Areas Foundation addressed a range of local issues from schools to water and sewage to trash collection. Again, these organizations built on community-based institutions, particularly Catholic parishes (Márquez, 1997; Rogers, 1990). In New York, Dominican community hometown associations and direct service organizations provided the foundation for electoral competition that has led to the election of Dominicans to the New York City Council and the New York legislature (Hernández & Torres-Saillant, 1996, pp. 34–35). These examples are not unique and indicate a national pattern in which CBOs and nonethnic organizations offer an organizational bridge between organizing to meet the cultural and communitarian needs of immigrants and the political needs of immigrant-ethnics.

Some cities, particularly those that were also home to turn-of-the-century immigrants such as New York and Chicago, allocate some city resources directly to some of these CBOs. In this way, immigrants, or at least those in these organizations' networks, can be said to be a part of municipal politics. Other cities keep the CBOs at arm's length, at least until their organizing can include delivering votes and providing leadership on contentious issues.

As increasing numbers of a national-origin group naturalize, the focus of community elite politics often shifts to the election of a co-national to office. Various political environments structure opportunities differently. New York and Chicago, for example, have many school board offices that allow for many national-origin populations to have at least some electoral representation. Miami, Los Angeles, and Houston, on the other hand, have relatively few elective offices, so national-origin groups with few citizens and weak organization are less able to move into elective office.

This focus on gaining office, even with a single co-national, can lead to a new incentive for mobilization, but it can often divide ethnic-immigrant communities just as the CBOs are gaining the institutional strength to routinely contest for municipal services. In this latter case, the opportunity for elective office creates an incentive that may interrupt the slow development of community-based politics. Organizations that could become stronger and more concretely tied to the needs of their communities refocus their energies on gaining elective office, often for an organizational leader, and lose the incentive to organize around community issues. CBOs that already have conflicts over turf and issues add personalistic conflicts. Alliances necessary with other national-origin groups or mainstream political actors to seek office and win elections are used within the national-origin group as evidence of lack of authenticity. This pattern has been seen among Mexican immigrant/Mexican American organizations in Chicago and, to a lesser degree, among Dominican and Colombian immigrant organizations in New York. These examples of shifting focus from community organization to competition for elective office are not meant to undervalue the achievement of election to office. Instead, it is to suggest that the process of seeking election often begins the separation of the political worlds of immigrants from U.S. citizens. Thus, the non-naturalized may lose access to the CBOs that had developed in immigrant-ethnic communities.

Overall, CBOs and nonethnic organizations in these communities are a sign of political health, particularly for populations that include a large number of noncitizens. They offer the opportunity for individuals denied access to the ballot box to organize their demand making. As such, they need to be studied as a way to understand the process of political socialization in these populations. At the same time, the connections among home-country/home-town associations, community-based politics, and electoral politics needs to be analyzed in the context of the political environments of each of the major immigrant-receiving cities. While this phenomenon has been examined to the degree that it influences the outcomes of citywide politics and coalitions, it also needs to be examined in terms of the process of political incorporation of immigrant populations.

Ethnic Solidarity, Immigrant Issues, and the Los Angeles Mayoral Elections of 1997

Mexican Americans have long been a part of the Los Angeles political environment (Acuña, 1996). Over the past sixty years, they have organized at all levels—from CBOs to statewide campaigns—and have been excluded, manipulated, and part of winning coalitions at various points in the city's political history. They were an integral component of the early years of the Bradley coalition (Sonenshein, 1990; 1997). Immigrants and the recently naturalized have undoubtedly contributed to Mexican American political successes, but the U.S.-born have traditionally been wary of the immigrants and not traditionally organized around their interests (Gutiérrez, 1995).

Beginning in the early 1970s, other Latino populations began to immigrate to Los Angeles in large numbers, such as Salvadorans and Guatemalans. While they have added to the size of the Latino population and the expectations for Latino political influence, these new Latino populations have high numbers of noncitizens and see Mexican Americans not only as potential allies, but also as competitors who may be unwilling to share their hard-won gains (Tomás Rivera Policy Institute & NALEO Educational Fund, 1997). Thus, while outside analysts often viewed Los

Angeles' Mexican American, and later Latino, communities as one, they have always been divided by nativity and by national origin.

Traditional voting patterns changed Los Angeles in two ways in 1997—Latino voters outnumbered African American voters, and the majority of Latinos supported the Republican incumbent over the Democratic challenger; these changes may reflect that immigrant and native interests joined in a way that they have not traditionally done before. This statement is necessarily tentative because it is based not on hard numbers, which are not available, but instead on the relative strength of Latino turnout to black turnout and exit polls on voting in the mayoral race and a school bond proposition. What can be said more conclusively is that the consequence of the Latino vote was to ensure the passage of a school bond initiative that drew new participants to the polls and spurred support from four of five Latino voters. Thus, the two changes in Latino voting patterns resulted from mobilization around a community-driven issue that had particular resonance among the newly naturalized which linked their needs to those of the U.S. born: public education. The 1997 vote demonstrated that unity and a salient issue can bring Latinos—U.S. born and naturalized—to the polls and that they can determine the outcome when the rest of the electorate is divided or, even, slightly opposed to the position held by the Latino community.

For the first time in Los Angeles' modern history, more Latinos than African Americans voted in 1997. Latinos increased their share of the citywide electorate from 8 percent in 1993 to 15 percent in 1997, while African Americans dropped from 18 percent to 13 percent in the same two elections (Pinkus, 1997). Second, the Latino vote went more strongly to the mayoral candidate, incumbent Richard Riordan, than to his liberal opponent, state Senator Tom Hayden. Although the office is nonpartisan, Riordan's Republican partisanship and Hayden's Democratic partisanship were well known.

Despite his Republican roots, Riordan took pains to separate himself from the nativist tone of California's Republican leadership. This separation appeared in both his rhetoric and his use of the powers of appointment. He was able to supplement these symbolic and patronage appeals with an incumbent's greater name recognition and a campaign finance advantage.

During his first term, Riordan appointed Latinos to numerous posts (often at the expense of African Americans). These appointees may not have swayed many votes but demonstrated to community elites that Riordan was sensitive to Latino community needs and unlike other California

Republicans. Certainly, there was division among these elites, with many advocating loyalty to the Democratic Party, but Riordan created a space where his greater name recognition and financial advantages could work to his advantage at the mass level without generating strong opposition from community elites. In addition, Riordan spoke out on issues of concern to Latino communities, particularly Latino immigrant communities, including backlogs in naturalization processing at the Los Angeles INS Office and the school bond initiative that was also on the city ballot (McDonnell, 1997). Hayden, on the other hand, made no particular outreach to Latinos during the campaign and seemed to take their votes for granted. Riordan also outspent his opponent and was the frontrunner throughout the race. Undoubtedly, this strengthened his bid among Latinos, many of whom were new voters who had not been socialized in partisan politics.

On the surface, these results may look like the traditional pattern with the U.S.-born joining the few naturalized in a vote that differentiates them from noncitizens. Instead, however, the vote may well reflect a new level of ethnic solidarity that allowed the voices of immigrants to be heard through the votes of their citizen co-ethnics. This appears in two characteristics of the results. First, the surge in naturalization that began in 1993 began to bear fruit in terms of increasing Latino turnout. The surge in naturalization did not dramatically increase turnout in either the 1994 or 1996 statewide races (which included Propositions 187 and 209, respectively), although there was a slow increase in Latino turnout in 1994. Instead, however, these elections saw the replacement of longer-term Latino voters with new registrants, including many newly naturalized citizens (Rohrlich, 1997). By 1997, however, many new Latino voters joined the existing city electorate to spur Latino voting at record rates.

Second, what propelled Latinos to the polls was not the mayoral race, but instead the school bond initiative which received overwhelming (80 percent) support from Latinos, a rate higher than for any other racial or ethnic group (Pinkus, 1997). Thus, Riordan was the beneficiary of a vote on an issue of key importance to Latinos, regardless of nativity. Exit polling is not sufficiently specific to determine whether non-Mexican American Latinos were a part of this solidarity as well.

The legacy of 1997 has yet to be determined. It is relatively easy to say what it is not—a movement of Mexican Americans to the Republican party. Whether it is, however, a beginning of greater Mexican American political influence in Los Angeles in which they, and not African Americans, are the dominant minority population and whether the anti-immigrant rhetoric has galvanized ethnic unity will only be determined in future elections. Whether or not this is the case in Los Angeles, this scenario offers a second model for urban-immigrant political activity— a common cause with co-ethnic citizens who have sufficient political influence to shape the outcomes of municipal elections and, consequently, assure the immigrant/ethnic population a new prominence. In the Los Angeles case, the spur to ethnic unity was also a spur to naturalization, which laid the foundation for the growth in the overall vote.

Immigrant Dominance of Local Politics

A final case is quite unique, at least among large U.S. cities, but may become less so in the coming years. This is where immigrants and their children have come to dominate municipal politics. The best contemporary example of this model among large U.S. cities is Miami (Moreno, 1996). A second, though less clear example of this model, for smaller cities, is Monterey Park, California (Fong, 1994; Horton, 1995).[4] Monterey Park differs in that it is a pan-ethnic Asian alliance that shapes municipal politics which has had to work with non-Asians to maintain control of city government.

The Miami case offers a possibly unique case of immigrant/ethnic— specifically Cuban immigrant and Cuban American—dominance of local politics. This model does not offer any added opportunities for immigrant populations other than the dominant one. As I indicate later, the rise of Cuban American electoral influence in Miami may well work to the disadvantage of non-Cuban immigrants in south Florida.

Over the past fifteen years, Cuban Americans have been able to become the dominant political actors in Miami and Dade County politics. The origins of their dominance in Miami politics have been examined by Portes and Stepik (1993). After a series of political shocks in 1980 when their powerlessness in local politics became evident to community elites, the Cuban American community organized to translate their numerical strength into political advantage. Beginning with naturalization campaigns in the early 1980s and the steady capture of local electoral offices in the late 1980s and early 1990s, Cuban Americans are now in an enviable position in terms of local politics. From a position of holding virtually no political offices in 1980 and having little involvement or influence in local electoral politics, Cuban Americans now hold Dade County's mayoralty, a majority on the county commission, two congressional seats, thirteen state legislative seats, and have political influence in the cities within Dade County where Cuban Americans are concentrated.

One local office continues to elude Cuban Americans—judicial posts. Analysts of Dade County politics, however, predict that they will dominate this level of office, as well, by the end of the decade.

The example of Cuban Americans in Miami is unique, for now, and may continue to be in the coming years. They had several advantages that are not available to other immigrant-ethnic populations in other cities. These include the concentration of elites in the initial Cuban migration, its heavily politicized nature, the formation of the enclave that allowed Cuban Americans to build on the capital and technical expertise that some of their members brought on migration, considerable financial assistance ($2 to $4 billion) in direct and indirect aid from the U.S. government, the foundation of involvement in national politics at the time community elites began to be concerned about the need to influence local politics, the ability to demand resources from national political actors, and the Voting Rights Act (VRA) (Croucher, 1997; Grenier & Stepik, 1992; Moreno, 1996; Portes & Stepik, 1993).

The final three of these characteristics need some explanation. Part of the Cuban success after 1980 in local politics must be attributed to their position in national politics before 1980. The early post-1959 Cuban American immigration experience was different from that of other immigrant populations in that they entered the United States as refugees and received assistance from the U.S. government as ideological compatriots. This exile allowed Cuban immigrant leaders to establish connections to Washington long before they established similar connections to Miami or Tallahassee. By 1980, this meant that the Cuban immigrant community had both experience at working with governments in the United States and personal contacts. They quickly tapped these resources. When naturalization became a priority for the community, the leadership was able to guarantee a response from the otherwise lethargic INS. This effort reached its peak in what was then the largest naturalization ceremony ever, with Ronald Reagan as guest speaker, conveniently days before the voter registration deadline for the 1984 presidential race. This connection to national politics had another important consequence for the empowerment of the Cuban American community. Individual Cubans were mobilized around national as well as local issues. The naturalization effort and then local political campaigns always spoke of foreign policy, as well as the nitty-gritty of municipal issues (Moreno & Rae, 1992; Grenier et al., 1994).

The VRA also aided Cuban Americans in their rise to dominance in Miami politics. The Act covered Cuban Americans when it was extended to Latinos in 1975. Specifically, it offered procedural guarantees of access to registration and voting without fear of intimidation and bilingual election materials. The 1982 amendments, requiring that where possible majority-minority districts be drawn, also covered Cuban Americans (de la Garza & DeSipio, 1993). They must, at best, be seen as unintentional beneficiaries of the Act (Issacharoff, 1995); there were few Cubans in the United States prior to 1965 and the discrimination that they experienced was comparable to that of many new immigrant populations. Whether the act was intended to protect their interests, the courts have been sympathetic to their claims and the VRA has been instrumental in their rapid dominance of local political offices (*Johnson v. DeGrandy*, 114 S.Ct. 2647 [1994]). They particularly benefited from the minority district requirement. Originally, the Cuban American population was geographically compact. Equally importantly, Cuban Americans were overwhelmingly Republican and the incumbents were just as likely to be Democrats, so unlike other areas of the country, as soon as the post-VRA redistricting occurred, Cubans were likely to be able to win the seat.

While the VRA sped Cuban American political dominance in Dade County, it may not be a resource that immigrant-ethnic populations will be able to rely on in the future. Recent judicial challenges and changes in Supreme Court thinking about the constitutionality of majority-minority districting make it likely that courts and legislatures will not be as diligent (some would argue excessively diligent) in creating new minority districts after the 2000 census as they were after 1990.

Finally, it is important to note that the success of Cuban Americans in Miami has not necessarily sped the process of the political incorporation of other Miami immigrant populations and, in fact, has put some at a disadvantage in gaining political power (Warren, 1997). In fact, the political empowerment of Miami's Cuban Americans has come at the expense of African American populations, including Afro-Caribbean populations. When Cuban immigrants began to arrive in Miami in the early 1960s, few other immigrants moved to Miami. Today, Miami is continually among the top five immigrant destinations and Cuban immigrants no longer make up of the majority of these populations. While the model of Cuban Americans may energize these other immigrant populations, the combination of conditions that advantaged Cuban immigrants and their children is unlikely to be repeated in Miami.

These three factors make the rise of Cuban American influence in Miami unique. Although this model will undoubtedly repeat itself; it is much more likely to appear in smaller cities, such as Monterrey Park, where immigrant-ethnic populations can gain demographic and economic dominance. Like Monterrey Park, also, the heterogeneity of immigrant origins will make pan-ethnic coalitions rather than specific national-origin groups the likely beneficiaries of this process.

CONCLUSIONS

The volume of immigration since 1965 has begun a demographic transformation of the United States. That this large-scale immigration is concentrated not only in cities, but primarily in the larger cities, means these changes have been and will continue to be felt in these areas. Since the beginning of the 1990s, these post-1965 immigrants have begun to reach the point where they can have a political voice. I identify three models for this new political activity, recognizing that all three, and particularly the first two, operate simultaneously.

With the surge in naturalization that began in 1993, immigrants and their U.S.-born co-ethnics have laid the foundation to exercise their political voice. Yet, this influence is only beginning to be felt on a regular basis. For the reasons that I outlined, Miami is a unique case. The possible influence of immigrants of Mexican and other Latino origin in Los Angeles was only able to be felt at the ballot box because there was a large population of U.S.-born Mexicans and Latinos whose ancestry in the United States predates 1965. The 1997 election provided an issue—the school bond initiative—that united immigrants and natives. While issues such as this will be increasingly common in the future, the experience of success will also serve to build a longer-lasting coalition between immigrants and natives. Thus, the second model is not an all-or-nothing proposition. Instead, immigrants will build coalitions with their U.S.-born co-ethnics, but not all will succeed from issue to issue.

Over the coming years, however, more and more of these post-1965 immigrants will reach the point where they are able to win more than a single district-based election in a district with a high concentration of co-ethnics. This growing influence will force cities to adapt to new policy needs and to develop strategies to incorporate greater numbers of noncitizen immigrants. Just as immigration is a recurring phenomenon in American political life, so is this process of urban political change based on new immigration. The challenge, of course, is not just for cities to incorporate these new members, but also for urban politics to capture and understand the changing foundation of urban populations and, over time, of urban governance.

REFERENCES

Acuña, R. (1996). *Anything but Mexican: Chicanos in contemporary Los Angeles.* New York: Verso.

Allswang, J.M. (1971). *A house for all peoples: Ethnic politics in Chicago 1890–1936.* Lexington: University of Kentucky Press.

Baldassare, M., ed. (1994). *The Los Angeles riots: Lessons for the urban future.* Boulder, CO: Westview Press.

Barrera, M. (1988). *Beyond Aztlan: Ethnic autonomy in comparative perspective.* Notre Dame, IN: University of Notre Dame Press.

Burma, J.H. (1954). *Spanish-speaking groups in the United States.* Durham, NC: Duke University Press.

Butler, R.E. (1986). *On creating a Hispanic America: A nation within a nation?* Washington, DC: Council for Inter-American Security.

Cohen, L. (1990). *Making a new deal: Industrial workers in Chicago 1919–1939.* New York: Cambridge University Press.

Croucher, S.L. (1997). *Imagining Miami: Ethnic politics in a postmodern world.* Charlottesville: University Press of Virginia.

de la Garza, R.O., & DeSipio, L. (1993). Save the baby, change the bathwater, and scrub the tub: Latino electoral participation after twenty years of voting rights act coverage. *Texas Law Review* 71, 7: 1479–1539.

de la Garza, R.O., & DeSipio, L. (1998). Interests not passions: Mexican American attitudes toward Mexico, immigration from Mexico, and other issues shaping U.S.–Mexico relations. *International Migration Review* 32, 2: 401–422.

de la Garza, R.O., DeSipio, L., García, F.C., García, J.A., & Falcón, A. (1992). *Latino voices: Mexican, Puerto Rican, and Cuban perspectives on American politics.* Boulder, CO: Westview Press.

de la Garza, R.O., Menchaca, M., and DeSipio, L. (1994). *Barrio ballots: Latino politics in the 1990 elections.* Boulder, CO: Westview Press.

DeSipio, L. (1996a). *Counting on the Latino vote: Latinos as a new electorate.* Charlottesville: University Press of Virginia.

DeSipio, L. (1996b). After Proposition 187, the deluge: Reforming naturalization administration while making good citizens. *Harvard Journal of Hispanic Policy* 9: 7–24.

DeSipio, L., & de la Garza, R.O. (1998). *Making Americans/remaking America: Immigration and immigrant policy.* Boulder, CO: Westview Press.

Erie, S.P. (1988). *Rainbow's end: Irish-Americans and the dilemmas of urban machine politics, 1840–1985.* Berkeley: University of California Press.

Espiritu, Y.L. (1992). *Asian American panethnicity: Bridging institutions and identities.* Philadelphia: Temple University Press.

Fong, T. (1994). *The first suburban Chinatown: The remaking of Monterey Park, California.* Philadelphia: Temple University Press.

Gamm, G.H. (1986). *The making of the New Deal Democrats: Voting behavior and realignment in Boston, 1920–1940.* Chicago: University of Chicago Press.

Georges, E. (1990). *The making of a transnational community: Migration, development, and cultural change in the Dominican Republic.* New York: Columbia University Press.

Gómez-Quiñones, J. (1994). *Roots of Chicano politics, 1600–1940.* Albuquerque: University of New Mexico Press.

Grenier, G.J., & Stepik, A., eds. (1992). *Miami now! Immigration, ethnicity, and social change.* Gainesville: University Press of Florida.

Grenier, G.J., with Invernizzi, F., Salup, L., & Schmidt, J. (1994). Los bravos de la política: Politics and Cubans in Miami. In R.O. de la Garza, M. Menchaca, & L. DeSipio, eds. *Barrio ballots: Latino politics in the 1990 elections,* pp. 161–196. Boulder, CO: Westview Press.

Gutiérrez, D.G. (1995). *Walls and mirrors: Mexican Americans, Mexican immigrants and the politics of ethnicity.* Berkeley: University of California Press.

Heer, D.M. (1990). *Undocumented Mexicans in the United States.* New York: Cambridge University Press.

Hernández, R., & Torres-Saillant, S. (1996). Dominicans in New York: Men, women, and prospects. In G. Haslip-Viera & S.L. Baver, eds. *Latinos in New York: Communities in transition,* pp. 30–56. Notre Dame, IN: University of Notre Dame Press.

Horton, J. (1995). *The politics of diversity: Immigration, resistance, and change in Monterey Park, CA.* Philadelphia: Temple University Press.

Issacharoff, S. (1995). Groups and the right to vote. *Emory Law Journal* 44, 3.

Madsen, W. (1964). *The Mexican Americans of South Texas.* New York: Holt, Rinehart, and Wilson.

Márquez, B. (1997). The Industrial Areas Foundation and the Mexican American community in Texas: The politics of issue mobilization. In F.C. García, ed., *Pursuing Power: Latinos and the Political System,* pp. 127–150. Notre Dame, IN: University of Notre Dame Press.

Massey, D., Alarcón, R., Durand, J., & González, H. (1987). *Return to Aztlan: The social process of international migration from Western Mexico.* Berkeley: University of California Press.

McDonnell, P. (1997, September 18). Riordan assails citizenship backlog. *Los Angeles Times.*

Moreno, D. (1996). Cuban Americans in Miami politics: Understanding the Cuban model. In W.C. Rich, ed. *The politics of minority coalitions: Race, ethnicity, and shared uncertainties,* pp. 145–162. Westport, CT: Praeger.

Moreno, D., & Rae, N. (1992). Ethnicity and partnership: The Eighteenth Congressional District in Miami. In G.J. Grenier & A. Stepik III, eds. *Miami now! Immigration, ethnicity, and social change,* pp. 186–204. Gainesville: University Press of Florida.

Muller, T. (1993). *Immigrants and the American city.* New York: New York University Press.

NALEO Educational Fund & Tomás Rivera Policy Institute. (1997). *Diversifying the New York area Hispanic mosaic: Colombian and Dominican leaders' assessments of community public policy needs.* Los Angeles: NALEO Educational Fund & Tomás Rivera Policy Institute.

NALEO Educational Fund & Tomás Rivera Policy Institute. (1998). *America's newest voices: Colombians, Dominicans, Guatemalans, and Salvadorans in the United States examine their public policy needs.* Los Angeles: NALEO Educational Fund & Tomás Rivera Policy Institute.

Ojito, M. (1998, April 20). A record backlog to get citizenship stymies 2 million. *New York Times*: A-1.

Pachon, H., & DeSipio, L. (1994). *New Americans by choice: Political perspectives of Latino immigrants.* Boulder, CO: Westview Press.

Pardo, M. (1990). Mexican American women grassroots community activists: "Mothers of East Los Angeles." *Frontiers* II: 1–7.

Pessar, P. (1995). *A visa for a dream: Dominicans in the United States.* Boston: Allyn and Bacon.

Pinkus, S.H. (1997, August–September). GOP wins Los Angeles by a landslide. *The Public Perspective:* 44–45.

Portes, A., & Stepik, A. (1993). *City on the edge: The transformation of Miami.* Berkeley: University of California Press.

Rogers, M.B. (1990). *Cold anger: A story of faith and power politics.* Denton: University of North Texas Press.

Rohrlich, T. (1997, December 31). Latino voting in state surged in 1996 election. *Los Angeles Times.*

Sonenshein, R.J. (1990). Biracial coalition politics in Los Angeles. In R.P. Browning, D.R. Marshall, & D.H. Tabb, eds. *Racial politics in American cities,* pp. 33–48, 2nd ed. New York: Longman.

Sonenshein, R.J. (1997). Post-incorporation politics in Los Angeles. In R.P. Browning, D.R. Marshall, & D.H. Tabb, eds. *Racial Politics in American Cities,* pp. 41–64. 2nd ed. New York: Longman.

Tomás Rivera Policy Institute & NALEO Educational Fund. (1997). *Diversifying the Los Angeles Area Latino mosaic: Salvadoran and Guatemalan leaders' assessments of community public policy needs.* Claremont, CA: Tomás Rivera Policy Institute & NALEO Educational Fund.

U.S. Bureau of the Census. (1993). *The Foreign-Born Population in the United States. 1990 Census of Population.* 1990 CP-3–1. Washington, DC: U.S. Government Printing Office.

U.S. Immigration and Naturalization Service. (1997a). *1995 Statistical Yearbook of the Immigration and Naturalization Service.* Springfield, VA: National Technical Information Service.

U.S. Immigration and Naturalization Service. (1997b). *1996 Statistical Yearbook of the Immigration and Naturalization Service.* Springfield, VA: National Technical Information Service.

Warren, C.L. (1997). Hispanic incorporation and structural reform in Miami. In R.P. Browning, D.R. Marshall, & D.H. Tabb, eds. *Racial politics in American cities.* pp. 223–258. 2nd ed. New York: Longman.

NOTES

[1] I would like to thank John Mollenkopf, Katherine Underwood, and Rich Keiser for helpful comments on an earlier draft of this article.

[2] I use the term Latino to refer to residents of the United States who can trace their origin or ancestry to the Spanish-speaking nations of Latin America and the Caribbean. I use Asian American, similarly, to identify residents of the United States who trace their origin or ancestry to Asia. I do not assume that there is a heterogeneity of political values, attitudes, or behaviors among or within the pan-ethnic populations, but find them a convenient tool to categorize origins of immigrants and U.S. ethnic populations.

[3] The immigration data for the 1980s include recipients of legalization under the Immigration Reform and Control Act of 1986. Many of these legalization recipients had been resident in the United States since at least 1982 and some had migrated in the 1970s. Also, the INS records immigrants by metropolitan statistical area of intended residence. As a result, they overestimate the population intending to reside in the city itself.

[4] It should be noted that the politics of many other cities, though not large cities, nationally are dominated by an ethnic population, such as Mexican American in smaller cities in the Southwest. These ethnic populations are not made up of large numbers of naturalized immigrants, however, and are outside of the scope of this model.

CHAPTER 5

Can Cities Be Elastic and Democratic, Too?[1]

ARNOLD FLEISCHMANN

Controversy has swirled throughout the 1990s about the future of urban America. These debates have taken several often disparate turns. Perhaps the most provocative participant in this exchange has been David Rusk, the author of *Cities Without Suburbs* (1993). Rusk's primary message is that the separation of central cities from their suburbs has exacerbated "the racial and economic segregation that has created an underclass in many of America's urban areas" (Rusk, 1993, p. 1). In contrast to such "inelastic" cities, "elastic" cities—those capable of extending their boundaries to keep pace with suburban development—are characterized by better economic and social conditions.

Rusk is often associated with "the new metropolitanism," which focuses on metropolitan areas as economic entities, each competing with other regions, often on a global scale (see Downs, 1994; Orfield, 1997; and Peirce, 1993; among others). Advocates of this perspective promote regional approaches to problems, often arguing that metropolitan government should replace the large number of municipalities found in most urban areas. Just as quickly as Rusk and others promote "elastic" cities, minority political leaders often attack the idea of merging central cities and suburbs on the ground that the process would dilute the political power of blacks, Latinos, and other groups.

As this debate rages on, it often ignores at least two fundamental political questions. First, to what extent can coalitions be built to provide metropolitan areas with elastic governments? Second, will minorities or others considered disadvantaged under inelastic local governments fare any better under elastic ones? The bottom line here is not that Rusk is wrong, but incomplete. The same might be said of his critics. Still, he has raised critical issues for the nation's urban areas and their minority residents.

THE GOSPEL ACCORDING TO RUSK

Rusk has discerned twenty-four "lessons" and four "laws" from his review of urban development patterns in the United States. The lessons can be grouped to highlight some key themes. The first ten lessons (pp. 5–20) describe urban development after World War II. These patterns include low-density development, a concentration of minorities in metropolitan areas, growth in virtually all metropolitan areas, and the need for central cities to expand their boundaries in order to increase their population. Linked to these lessons are the eleventh and twelfth (pp. 20–23), which indicate that state annexation laws and suburban incorporations leave inelastic cities unable to expand and thus surrounded in metropolitan areas fragmented into numerous municipalities. In lesson 13, Rusk (pp. 23–28) also argues that elastic and inelastic cities have had different types of leaders, with older, inelastic cities generally characterized by "complacent" leadership that did not pursue annexation or consolidation effectively as postwar suburbanization took off.

The above trends, Rusk (lesson 20, pp. 38–40) adds, occurred as the economy became more global, which forced metropolitan areas to compete more vigorously for jobs and investment. Inelastic cities, however, were increasingly segregated by race and class from their suburbs (lessons 14–19 and 21–23, pp. 28–38, 40–44), which adversely affected education, economic growth, and the financial health of inelastic cities. Moreover, there was little evidence that inelastic cities could promote growth through redevelopment efforts alone (lesson 24, pp. 44–47).

What "laws" does Rusk infer from the lessons he sketches? The first is that "only elastic cities grow" (p. 10). The second law posits that "fragmentation divides; unification unites" (p. 38). Rusk means this in terms of mixing groups that otherwise would exist within separate local governments, as with the possibility of greater integration in larger school systems. The third law is similar: "ties do bind" (p. 41), which Rusk tries to demonstrate by linking job growth to the degree of elasticity in metropolitan areas. The final law is "ghettos can only become bigger ghettos" (p. 47). This means that inelastic cities reach a point where their population decline and disadvantages relative to their suburbs accelerate.

Taken together, Rusk's lessons and laws lead him to a seemingly inexorable conclusion: policies must be adopted to permit cities to be elastic if American urban areas hope to avoid widespread segregation and its accompanying problems. Cities, Rusk argues (p. 85), "must be redefined to reunify city and suburb. Ideally, such reunification is achieved through metropolitan government." Because this is not possible in many cases, Rusk offers three other "strategies for stretching cities" (pp. 85–130): ending fiscal imbalance through revenue sharing between rich and poor cities, using housing policies to reduce racial and economic segregation, and promoting metropolitan-wide economic development.

Rusk is not alone in his assessments. Not surprisingly, there are critics as well. Even if one accepts Rusk's description of the problems facing urban America and his proposed remedies, there are still a number of questions that he ignores, including how minorities fare politically in elastic cities.

A CLOSER LOOK AT SUPPORT FOR ELASTICITY

The Diagnosis

Early debates about fragmented (i.e., inelastic) metropolitan areas focused on efficiency and responsiveness in providing services. In many ways, such discussions ignored how governmental boundaries are drawn, which is a process that is far from benign. In fact, they often are drawn for motives related to race, class, and political power (see Fleischmann, 1986). For instance, Gary Miller (1981) has demonstrated that the much ballyhooed "Lakewood Plan" for providing services in suburban Los Angeles was not a model of efficiency, but a pattern of well-off residents using the political process of incorporating municipalities to insulate themselves from the less affluent. Nancy Burns (1994) has done a solid national analysis of the creation of municipalities and special districts after World War II. She concluded (p. 5):

> Businesses—developers and manufacturers—have led many of these efforts within the incentive structures defined by state and federal governments. In so doing, these businesses have created congenial regulatory climates, congenial tax climates, and mechanisms for increasing the value of land at slim cost to developers. In the process, these businesses have enabled middle- and upper-middle-class citizens to acquire services, to keep their taxes low, to wall out the poor, and to indulge their taste for racial exclusion.

Thus, research suggests that Rusk may even understate problems associated with suburban incorporation and autonomy.

The Remedies

Others have tried to specify how Rusk's calls for metropolitan-wide action might work, although there is little to suggest that easier annexation or consolidation procedures are in the offing. Thus, efforts to promote elasticity may be played out under existing rules, which generally seem biased in favor of the kind of suburban autonomy that leaves poor and minority residents concentrated in central cities.

An approach that would not disturb existing boundaries is the redistribution of resources within regions. Nunn and Rosentraub (1996) analyzed fiscal equalization plans in four metropolitan areas in different states. Their results suggest that tax-base and revenue sharing within metropolitan areas can reduce the competition decried by Rusk. Such programs are not necessarily easy to adopt or implement, as Orfield (1997) makes clear in his account of efforts to attack what he describes as older communities continually subsidizing development on the fringes of metropolitan Minneapolis-St. Paul. Ameliorating such inequities, Orfield argues, requires the building of coalitions among central cities and older suburbs. Efforts to promote such an agenda are underway in a number of areas (Garland 1997), but they can be fragile and must be active both locally and at the state capitol, where important laws are crafted that affect urban development.

Less radical are regional cooperation and planning, which often include a formal role for nongovernmental actors. Neal Peirce (1993) is among those trying to promote the institutionalization of such processes, which he sees as community-wide endeavors. Nunn and Rosentraub (1997) have analyzed several types of areawide mechanisms that might address a metropolitan area's development. Building on the track record in Denver, Pittsburgh, Toledo, and Portland, they consider several combinations of institutions and tactics involving the public, private, and nonprofit sectors. These arrangements could be used to promote a variety of outcomes related to economic development, municipal services, the physical environment, or social conditions. Such initiatives presume voluntary cooperation among leaders of major political and nongovernmental institutions, which makes them less encompassing than Rusk's recommendations. They also are built on bargaining among executives and other leaders of such organizations, who have few incentives to address economic and racial disparities, especially compared to central city mayors or governments covering a large share of an urban area (see Lewis, 1998)

CRITICISMS OF THE NEW METROPOLITANISM

Public choice theorists have long criticized metropolitan government as analogous to a monopoly that performs poorly (e.g., Ostrom et al., 1961; Parks & Oakerson, 1989). Instead, they argue that fragmented urban areas are like a market in which communities use tax and service levels to compete with one another for residents. Under such conditions, residents can use the "exit" option to express their dissatisfaction with a local government, which they could not do in a highly elastic city. Public choice theorists also contend that smaller governments can be more efficient, responsive, and accountable than larger ones. Research on these claims is equivocal, however (see Lyons et al., 1992).

Critics outside public choice theory also have focused on Rusk's policy recommendations. One claim is that efforts to promote greater elasticity are simply impractical, primarily for legal and political reasons. As Rusk readily admits, "in all of the Northeast and a great deal of the Midwest, these kinds of formal restructurings aren't possible" ("Debate on Theories of David Rusk," 1997, p. 17). Anthony Downs (1994) argues that Rusk's notion of metropolitan government is extremely unlikely to be adopted. Nevertheless, he argues that regional issues must be addressed in order to promote more efficient local economies, which require an alternative to the prevailing pattern of sprawl. To do so, Downs proposes cooperative planning efforts, aid programs, federal and state bureaucratic changes, and federal incentives to promote regionalism.

Perhaps a more telling criticism of Rusk's recommendations is that they may produce limited benefits for America's urban areas. Economist John Blair contends that Rusk's view of causality between elasticity and the economic well-being of metropolitan areas is overly simplistic. Indeed, it may leave out a host of factors influencing the local economy. Moreover, Blair's effort to test Rusk's claims statistically indicates that, when controlling for state trends, elasticity had at best a moderate effect on changes in metropolitan areas' population, employment, income, and poverty during the 1980s (Blair et al., 1996). These criticisms have not gone unchallenged, however. Rusk is quick to point out the crucial role of race in the fiscal and social disadvantages generally found in inelastic communities but less common among elastic urban areas ("Debate on Theories of David Rusk," 1997, pp. 12–17).

A final concern is whether Rusk's assessment might be somewhat time-bound. One might understand Rusk's pessimistic tone, but by the late 1990s, some observers saw central cities' dense development, labor markets, and amenities as advantages when compared to suburban development patterns (Farrell, 1998). This could bode well for minority residents of central cities. Rusk's analysis also may be time-bound because metropolitan areas may be at different stages in their development. As Orum (1995) argues, older cities commonly annexed or consolidated early in their development, but eventually encountered suburban resistance that could not be overcome. The same may hold true for newer cities, which means that Rusk's elastic cities will someday face the same racial and economic segregation found in today's inelastic areas.

KEY ISSUES

Rusk contends that minorities and the poor will benefit from living in more elastic cities. The rationale seems to be that elasticity provides them with political access to a larger economic pie, as opposed to the situation where the affluent may isolate themselves in suburban enclaves. Determining whether minorities fare any differently in elastic and inelastic cities can be addressed in part by examining two key issues: minority electoral power and the formation of policy of special interest to minority communities.

In many ways, Rusk ignores questions of political participation, particularly the brand of politics that shaped many elastic cities in the West and Southwest. These cities have a long history of elite domination associated with prodevelopment policies and limited minority involvement. Those patterns were challenged beginning in the 1970s, although the rise of minority political power may not have been possible without intervention by the federal government and fissures within long-dominant, middle-class coalitions (see Bridges, 1997; Orum, 1995; Mollenkopf, 1983).

Abandoning at-large elections for district representation may have been a necessary condition for change, but it is unclear if districts yielded major policy changes or merely increased minority membership on city councils (see Heilig and Mundt, 1984; Welch, 1990; Bridges, 1997). In a comparison of a consolidated (Lexington) and fragmented metropolitan area (Louisville) in the same state, Lyons et al. (1992, p. 187) concluded that "minority residents are provided more comprehensive services, are less dissatisfied and disaffected, and participate at least as much in consolidated systems as in fragmented systems featuring independent cities in which they are a majority."

Inelastic cities may be different because their larger minority populations seem to translate into electoral and policy successes. In particular, larger minority populations are associated with more favorable policies in areas such as employment, contracting, and public safety (see Saltzstein, 1989; Santoro, 1995). Increased minority membership on governing bodies and in public sector work forces may reduce disparities in government services (Meier, Stewart & England, 1991), although declining white populations may lead to conflict among minority groups for government jobs (McClain, 1993).

There could be a downside when minorities become a large share of a city's population. Rusk (1993, pp. 63–78) argues that economic and fiscal conditions are worse in inelastic cities, which tend to have higher minority populations and often severe city–suburban disparities. Thus, as minority residents and their influence increase, the inelastic cities over which they gain control may represent an ever-diminishing share of their metropolitan areas. Indeed, they may preside over a city's downward economic spiral and be desperate to secure private sector investment.

The alternatives to metropolitan government in older cities generally center around creation of regional institutions, a greater role for the states, or both. These strategies offer mixed blessings and opportunities to minority residents. Regional institutions may be heavily geared to supporting growth to the detriment of central cities and older suburbs (Orfield, 1997). In addition, regional special districts in areas such as transportation may be beyond the political reach of minorities in inelastic cities.

Inelastic cities are not completely opposite their elastic counterparts, though. They, too, can adopt development policies that impose substantial burdens on minority residents and neighborhoods, as Jones and Bachelor (1993) demonstrate with the automobile industry in Detroit. They also may be governed by pro-growth coalitions that include minority politicians, as in Atlanta (Stone, 1989). Suburbanites can still influence city politics, as evidenced by the significant share of suburban campaign contributions in Atlanta and St. Louis elections (Fleischmann & Stein, 1998).

As Orum (1995, p. 205) concludes, increased elasticity can rid "a metropolitan area of the inequalities that exist when suburbs and city lie side by side." Rusk addresses this point with various economic and social data. Yet, he tends to ignore local politics and policy. Conversely, critics often focus on the negative political effects of metropolitan and regional governments on minorities. As a preliminary way to gauge the effects of elasticity on minorities in urban America, our discussion examines elections and policymaking in the seven pairs of elastic and inelastic cities Rusk analyzes in great detail.

POLITICS IN RUSK'S MATCHED PAIRS OF CITIES

Electoral Politics

One way to examine minority influence in these fourteen cities is to examine their success at the ballot box. Table 5.1 measures the degree to which blacks and Latinos hold elective office. The ratio is calculated by dividing each group's percentage of offices held by its percentage of the jurisdiction's 1990 population. This ratio is slightly different than others in that it includes governing bodies, elected presiding officers such as city council presidents, and executives such as mayors.[2] The data are for 1993, the most recent year for which complete data were available and the publication date of *Cities Without Suburbs*. Ratios were calculated when blacks or Latinos constituted at least 5 percent of a jurisdiction's population (4.1 percent in almost all-white Madison). The table also reports ratios for the city's overlapping county, except in Indianapolis, Nashville, and Richmond. Data were not available for suburban municipalities, so county data are only suggestive of how minorities might fare under more elastic conditions. In most of these cases, the metropolitan area extends to include additional counties. These data also ignore differences in the functional assignment of services between cities and counties in the same urban area and among the metropolitan areas in Rusk's matched pairs.

Obviously, the data offer no stark contrasts between elastic and inelastic areas, cities in each matched pair, or cities and their overlapping counties. If anything, minorities are overrepresented at the county level (with the exception of Harris County, Texas, which was 18.2 percent Hispanic). Thus, there is no reason to assume that minority candidates will necessarily fare poorly in elastic local governments. This may be true for several reasons, though. One may be the effects of the voting rights revolution, which has made those who draw district boundaries conscious of minority representation. Whether this continues is questionable, however, in light of recent U.S. Supreme Court rulings (e.g., *Miller v. Johnson,* 1995).

Another reason that minorities approximate parity in elected office may be the growing willingness of Anglo voters to cast ballots for black and Hispanic candidates. An example here is the 1997 election of Lee

Table 5.1. Minority Representation in Selected Cities and Their Overlapping Counties, 1990

	Inelastic			Elastic	
City	Black[a]	Hispanic[a]	City	Black[a]	Hispanic[a]
Detroit	.881	N/A	Houston	.949	.735
(Wayne)[n]	1.23	N/A	(Harris)	1.10	0
Cleveland	1.78	N/A	Columbus	1.90	N/A
(Cuyahoga)	0	N/A	(Franklin)	0	N/A
Louisville	.962	N/A	Nashville	.588	N/A
(Jefferson)	1.48	N/A	(Davidson)[c]	—	—
Milwaukee	.863	N/A	Indianapolis	.889	N/A
(Milwaukee)	.750	N/A	(Marion)	—	—
Syracuse	.449	N/A	Albuquerque	N/A	1.17
(Onondaga)	1.01	N/A	(Bernalillo)	N/A	1.62
Harrisburg	.847	N/A	Madison	2.03	N/A
(Dauphin)	0	N/A	(Dane)	N/A	N/A
Richmond[d]	1.20	N/A	Raleigh	.455	N/A
			(Wake)	1.95	N/A

[a]The figure in the column is the ratio of the group's percentage of elected positions (governing body and executive) divided by its percentage of the jurisdiction's population in 1990.
[b]The name in parentheses is the overlapping county.
[c]The city and county governments are consolidated; data are reported for the city.
[d]Cities and counties do not overlap in Virginia.
Sources: Municipal/County Executive Directory; Black Elected Officials: A National Roster; The National Roster of Elected and Appointed Hispanic Officials; and the *1994 County and City Data Book.*

Brown as Houston's first African American mayor. Such success in city-wide races may depend, however, on the ability to field moderate black and Latino candidates who can raise campaign money, the ability of minority elites to settle on a single candidate for major offices, and the degree to which minority voters can be mobilized. Brown, for instance, faced no other black candidates, raised almost $2.7 million, and

had support from national Democratic officials. Moreover, blacks constituted 35 percent of the November 1997 turnout, compared to their 27 percent of Houston's population (Benjaminson, 1997; Bernstein & Mason,
1998; Rodriguez, 1998).

Having Latinos and blacks elected to local offices does not guarantee that the interests of their respective groups will be addressed. In their
analysis of ten cities abandoning at-large elections, Heilig and Mundt
(1984) found that minority council members were of similar occupa-
tional backgrounds as their Anglo counterparts, but assumed more of an
ombudsman role in which they became advocates for services in their
districts and purveyors of casework for their constituents.

There is no guarantee that minority representation will be more effective in either type of city. In elastic Columbus, poverty has continued
to grow in the central city as black and white middle-class residents
move to newer neighborhoods. Moreover, the city's white mayor has enjoyed favorable ratings, except among blacks: only 42 percent approved
of his job performance in a 1997 survey, compared to 69 percent of
whites. Much of the disparity has been linked to the mayor's investigation of administrative wrongdoing by the city's black police chief (Miller,
1996; Futty, 1997). In Houston, voters surprised many in November
1997 when they defeated a ballot proposition that would have ended the
city's affirmative action program. At the time, 44 percent of the respondents in a poll indicated that the city's race relations were fair, 38 percent
labeled them good, and 3 percent described them as excellent. Fifty-
three percent, however, indicated that relations were not changing, and
14 percent said they were getting better (Dyer, 1997). This was at a time
that Lee Brown was campaigning for mayor and the white incumbent,
who was not seeking reelection, strongly supported the existing system
of voluntary subcontracting goals, as did other leaders, such as the editors of the *Houston Chronicle* ("Affirmative Action," 1997).

Minority mayors in inelastic cities may be in an especially difficult
position. The pressures to cultivate business interests to promote development can often lead to criticism for not doing enough for their own community. Indeed, Detroit's mayor Dennis Archer was reported to have asked
Atlanta mayor Bill Campbell, "Are you catching it from people who think
you should be beating up on white folks?" (quoted in Fears, 1995).

Perhaps a more troubling aspect of race and representation is revealed in survey data from metropolitan Milwaukee. In Milwaukee
County, which is 21 percent black and includes the city, 48 percent identified race relations as a serious problem and 38 percent saw it as a minor

problem. To the west, in virtually lily-white Waukesha County, 10 percent saw race relations as a serious problem, 47 percent thought it a minor problem, and 40 percent saw it as no problem at all (Abdul, 1997). Rusk (1993, pp. 28–31) reminds his readers of how segregated metropolitan Milwaukee is. Yet, views on race seem to follow an "out sight, out of mind" mentality in which those living in affluent suburban areas do not see race as a matter of major importance. Getting these suburbanites to spend their tax dollars on issues that they have not defined would be a difficult task for metropolitan leaders.

Public Policy

If advocates of the new metropolitanism are correct, identifying and addressing regional issues are fundamental to the future of America's urban areas. For minorities, these include, at a minimum, economic development and the jobs–housing mismatch. The key question is, are such policies different in elastic and inelastic cities?

Economic development policy in the two types of cities has similarities. The greatest commonality during the 1990s has been the promotion of downtowns as amenities centers for tourism, the arts, and even residential construction. Such projects may bring outlying residents downtown on an occasional basis. They also may displace the poor and increase the political clout of a returning white middle class. Cleveland was a pacesetter here, with a new downtown stadium and arena, and attractions such as the Rock 'n Roll Hall of Fame. Columbus, on the other hand, struggles with a downtown that has experienced limited private investment and offers few attractions. Some places have only recently built coalitions to support downtown development, and it is too early to tell whether the groundwork they are laying will prove successful. Houston broke ground for a downtown stadium in 1997 and is enhancing mass transit. The private sector is adding condominiums and townhouses. Houston officials leave much in the hands of developers, however, and take a minimal approach to regulation. Detroit's tourism strategy has revolved around the controversial use of casinos, with approval of plans in 1998 (Keating et al., 1995; Williams, 1997; King & Howes, 1998). As Grunwald (1998) points out, a troubling aspect of comparing development is that data for elastic cities can be so highly aggregated that they mask problems for areas within such jurisdictions, as with schools, crime, and housing in Indianapolis.

Noticeable differences between the two types of areas also exist. Elastic cities, which tend to be newer, must contend with problems of growth, including traffic, air and water pollution, overcrowded schools, and similar public service pressures. In their zeal for growth, however, such places often ignore or delay action on such matters; their provision of services can also follow new development while ignoring older neighborhoods. Inelastic cities are left out of the growth in the suburbs, but within their borders, they contend with aging infrastructure, older housing, and changes in their economic base.

Among elastic cities, a regional growth conference in the Raleigh area tried to develop strategies that would lessen the continuing pressures to provide new roads and schools in fringe areas (Hicks, 1996). In Houston, there are complaints that the taxes that Houston residents pay to Harris County go to support fringe-area development (Sablatura, 1998). Elastic cities endure ongoing battles over annexation, which are sometimes fought in state legislatures, but almost always seem to engender hostility from their recently annexed residents. This has occurred in Raleigh and Houston, where the press has staunchly defended aggressive annexation both as fundamental to regional growth and the prevention of decay and as an equitable way to keep suburbanites from enjoying the benefits of the central city without paying taxes to support them ("Narrow Escape," 1997; "Key to Cities' Health," 1998). As the editors of the *News and Observer* argued in their defense of Raleigh's practices, "cities hemmed in by independent suburbs incur the huge costs of shrinking tax bases, higher crime and poverty" ("Attack on Annexation," 1996), while "suburbs that should be a vibrant part of the metropolitan whole instead become smugly isolated, ignoring—to their peril—the withering of the bigger, older city next door" ("Way to Grow," 1996).

In elastic cities, race often can be a subtext to regional issues. For instance, a Raleigh newspaper editorial warned that the failure to annex would mean that the city "loses the civic participation of many who might otherwise be among its most energetic leaders" ("Way to Grow," 1996). This is not necessarily an alarm regarding black leadership, but at least a recognition of what can happen when the affluent live in autonomous suburbs. Similarly, annexation in Columbus was more palatable because it supplied services to developers with minimum threats to suburban school districts (Cox & Jonas, 1993). The same is true of consolidation in Indianapolis, where school systems were not consolidated and the former city schools became the center of desegregation battles (D'Amico & Lenkowsky, 1995; Grunwald, 1998). Thus, elastic cities may not be all they are advocated to be by Rusk if public schools remain as segregated and troubled as in inelastic cities.

Elastic cities, in many ways, seem the epitome of development regimes. One concern here is that elected officials will be heavily influenced by developers whose interests include not only downtown, but outlying residential areas. In Raleigh, critics have focused on the large amount of campaign money the city's incumbent mayor raised from developers for his 1997 re-election bid (Eisley, 1998). Similarly, Houston has generally been regarded as a city where developers are largely left alone in terms of regulation, but subsidized in terms of infrastructure (Parker & Feagin, 1991; Williams, 1997).

There are variations, of course. Madison's progressive coalition is beginning to be pressured by those eager to promote development in an already vibrant downtown (Mosiman, 1996). Albuquerque's growth-oriented coalition, which had steered services toward middle-class Anglo areas for much of the postwar period, was eventually challenged by forces that criticized the city's annexation strategy and wanted to manage growth and promote greater equity (Bridges, 1997, pp. 158–159, 203–204).

Addressing spatial mismatch in both elastic and inelastic areas requires attention to housing affordability and quality, along with access to low-wage jobs. Both types of cities rely heavily on the automobile, but public transit may not make the suburbs accessible in inelastic cities. Such housing and transit dilemmas are linked, of course, to the exclusionary zoning practices found in many suburbs. In metropolitan Milwaukee, low-wage workers are concentrated in the city, but many entry-level jobs are concentrated in neighboring Waukesha County, where the median house value in 1996 was nearly $122,000, as opposed to $84,000 in Milwaukee County. During the current economic boom, some firms have used van pools to transport workers to the suburbs, while a few have actually moved to Milwaukee to gain better access to its labor pool (Daykin, 1997; Derus, 1997). How this strategy dovetails with welfare reform is unclear, and its effectiveness may not be felt fully until the next recession affects the less skilled. Still unresolved is how to provide transportation across governmental boundaries to deal with this spatial mismatch of jobs and affordable housing. Detroit, with its industrial past, has used various grants and incentives to revive some areas with manufacturing jobs (Meredith, 1997).

The other extreme may be Portland, Oregon, where regional government has used growth controls and public transit to steer jobs and housing inside the city limits, particularly downtown (Lewis, 1998, pp. 162–207). In elastic cities such as Columbus, regional housing agencies confront NIMBYism (Not In My Back Yard), although having a broader geographical scope may give them more ability to confront residential segregation in such a way as to lessen the spatial mismatch (Mayhood, 1998).

Regional issues are among the most difficult to solve because their resolution requires the cooperation of many independent political jurisdictions. While specific issues will vary from place to place, bargaining is the common process needed to address thorny regional problems in both inelastic and elastic areas. In inelastic cities, regional decision making requires cooperation among officials who represent not only substantially different constituencies, but autonomous governments. To accomplish anything, then, may require two types of bargaining. One involves the central city and perhaps some of its older suburbs sitting across the table from the affluent and rapidly growing suburbs. The second form of bargaining is between public officials and the private sector actors who shape development. The only real players operating on a metropolitan level in this process are large-scale economic organizations, such as chambers of commerce and major firms, and the state government.

In metropolitan Milwaukee, regionalism had its start when the city was able to shift some functions to Milwaukee County. The metropolitan area has expanded, however, and existing authorities for sewers and the baseball stadium to be completed by the year 2000 were not easily adopted. Indeed, suburban litigation over sewers lasted thirteen years, and the adoption by the governor and state legislature of a regional sales tax to pay for the stadium generated great hostility in most of the counties where it is paid (Romell, 1997). Transportation may be the next service to be addressed regionally in the Milwaukee area, in part because of the mayor's strong advocacy of light rail and the state's efforts to improve highways and roads (Parks, 1997; Sandler 1998). This kind of episodic regionalism has also occurred in Syracuse, which recently addressed the consolidation of police services with Onondaga County (Weibezahl, 1998).

In inelastic areas, experience thus suggests that regionalism may spread piecemeal, particularly for unthreatening services that suburbanites use. Survey data indicate that 41 percent of Milwaukee County respondents but less than a quarter of those in suburban Waukesha County favored a metropolitan government as a replacement to their counties. Majorities in both counties, however, favored regional authorities for transportation and the arts (Holly, 1997a, 1997b). Schools may be off the agenda, in part because Milwaukee mayor John Norquist (1998, pp. 83–98) is a strong backer of school choice. Bargaining among officials in inelastic areas may depend, as Orfield (1997) argues, on leaders of older suburbs working with central cities. This has occurred to a limited degree in Milwaukee on sewers and economic development (Thatcher, 1997). In metropolitan Detroit, however, some older suburbs have recognized their situation but have decided to compete with outer suburbs by avoiding tax increases while emphasizing schools, safety, and well-kept housing ("The Inner Ring," 1998).

How do minorities fare in such bargaining? Because minorities constitute a large share of the population in inelastic cities, one would assume that they would have some leverage in the major issues shaping central city development. Critics contend, however, that Cleveland's downtown resurgence resulted from a plan developed between city hall and economic elites that relied heavily on federal grants and tax breaks. These gains, they add, come at a substantial price to the city's residential neighborhoods (Keating et al., 1995). In Detroit, Mayor Dennis Archer's strategy of riverfront development and casinos is linked inextricably to satisfying General Motors (King & Howes, 1998).

At the regional level, one would expect minorities' influence to be more diluted than in central city policymaking. Moreover, in bargaining with suburbs, central cities can become identified with the interests of minorities, which can inject race into the process. In Milwaukee, efforts to overcome city–suburban conflict have been spearheaded by the region's daily newspaper and elite business organizations, which sponsored a fall 1997 conference on metropolitan problems. Milwaukee mayor John Norquist complained, however, that the process lacked minority representatives (Romell, 1997; Holly, 1997b).

Bargaining over regional issues can be substantially different in elastic areas. In such cases, minorities would constitute a smaller percentage of a city's population and city council seats, even though they might be represented proportionately (see Table 1). Elite economic actors operating on a metropolitan scale would remain the same as if the area were inelastic. There is a crucial difference in this calculus, though: the bargaining would be centralized, which means that a single jurisdiction could have substantial ability to address regional transportation, exclusionary zoning, and affordable housing. Moreover, as Paul Lewis (1998) concludes in his recent study of suburbanization, developers in elastic cities are forced to deal with politicians who have the capacity and incentive to act on a metropolitan scale. In inelastic cities, however, developers can play jurisdictions off against one another, and officials (with the possible exception of those in central cities) have almost no incentive to address regional issues. He is careful to add, though, that "an extensive central city ... may be a *necessary* condition for shaping suburban growth and alleviating regionwide problems and growth disparities. But unitary government is not a *sufficient* condition for such policy action" (p. 212).

CONCLUSION: ELASTICITY, DEMOCRACY, AND MINORITIES IN URBAN AMERICA

How, then, should minorities view Rusk's argument about elasticity? Unfortunately, the answer must be equivocal. At one level, there are few differences between elastic and inelastic cities in their emphasis on downtown development and the extent to which they elect minority officeholders. Moreover, major policy decisions, especially regarding development, seem to be the province of any community's economic elite or even outside actors.

Inelastic jurisdictions seem to offer minorities a chance to constitute a larger percentage of a city's electorate, which can translate into political control and enhanced public sector benefits. If current development patterns favor a resurgence of central cities, that might have a nice payoff. If not, the road to regionalism may be bleak indeed. Plus, the existence of many autonomous suburbs in inelastic areas allows an institutional means to promote residential segregation through exclusionary zoning and exacerbate the jobs–housing mismatch.

The dilemma here is to craft institutions and processes, as Rusk (1993, p. 85) argues, to "end fiscal imbalance through revenue sharing between rich and poor jurisdictions; diminish racial and economic segregation through affordable housing requirements and housing assistance metrowide; and, finally, promote metrowide economic development." This will require careful coalition building (Orfield, 1997) and probably a piecemeal approach, as in Milwaukee.

Elastic cities may offer several benefits to minorities. As Jones and Bachelor (1993, p. 240) suggest, a larger jurisdiction may be in a stronger bargaining position with external organizations such as large corporations. Some service costs can be shifted over a wider area, and dispersing affordable housing may be easier. That is consistent with Rusk's claim that elasticity forces Anglos and minorities to the same bargaining table to deal with issues affecting an area's development. An increased role for state governments in regional issues may bring mixed results for minorities. Given the growing differences between Democratic cities and Republican suburbs, turning to the states as Rusk suggests may involve not only racial, but partisan, disputes. In elastic cities, Republican legislators in outlying areas would seemingly need to represent the interests of their metropolitan government, as opposed to promoting suburbs in competition with their neighboring central city in inelastic areas.

If minorities support elasticity, is it a brilliant expansion of the scope of conflict that would make Schattschneider (1975) proud, or is it a Faustian bargain? Perhaps neither, but there seems little reason to dismiss Rusk out of hand. In deciding whether to support or oppose proposals leading to more "elasticity" local governments would do well to consider several questions: How will the change affect the ability to elect candidates and hire officials who address important concerns? What effect will the new government have on access to political institutions and policy-making? What will happen to political accountability? What could happen to the distribution of services and their costs under the new government? How might a more elastic city influence the crucial mix of land use, housing, jobs, and transportation? How will the state government influence the work and priorities of the new government? For blacks, Latinos, and other minorities, grappling with these questions will require vigilance and hard work, especially at a time when the national government is devolving more responsibilities to the state and local levels.

REFERENCES

Abdul, A.J. (1997, September 25). More jobs could attract minorities. *Milwaukee Journal Sentinel.* Internet (available http://www.jsonline.com).

Affirmative action: Voters recognized importance of everyone's having a stake (1997, November 5). *Houston Chronicle* (editorial). Internet (available http://www.chron.com).

Attack on annexation (1996, May 24). *Raleigh News and Observer* (editorial). Internet (available http://search.news-observer.com).

Benjaminson, W. (1997, December 7). Brown says his mayoral victory sends message. *Houston Chronicle.* Internet (available: http://www.chron.com).

Bernstein, A., & Mason, J. (1998, January 15). Houston mayoral candidates hit campaign spending record. *Houston Chronicle.* Internet (available: http://www.chron.com).

Blair, J.P., Staley, S.R., & Zhang, Z. (1996). The central city elasticity hypothesis: a critical appraisal of Rusk's theory of urban development. *Journal of the American Planning Association, 62,* 345–353.

Bridges, A. (1997). *Morning glories: Municipal reform in the Southwest.* Princeton: Princeton University Press.

Burns, N. (1994). *The Formation of American local governments: Private values in public institutions.* New York: Oxford University Press.

Carroll Publishing. (1994). *Municipal/county executive directory.* Washington, DC: Carroll Publishing.

Cox, K.R., & Jonas, A.E.G. (1993). Urban development, collective consumption and the politics of metropolitan fragmentation. *Political Geography,* 12, 8–37.

D'Amico, C., & Lenkowsky, L. (1993). Education. In W.H. Hudnut III, *The Hudnut years in Indianapolis,* 1976–1991 (pp. 190–205). Bloomington: Indiana University Press.

Daykin, T. (1997, September 24). Labor shortage may grow worse. *Milwaukee Journal Sentinel.* Internet (available http://www.jsonline.com).

Debate on Theories of David Rusk [edited transcript of proceedings] (1997). *The Regionalist,* 2, 11–29.

Derus, M. (1997, September 25). Workers face tough job finding homes in Waukesha County. *Milwaukee Journal Sentinel.* Internet (available http://www.jsonline.com).

Downs, A. (1994). *New visions for metropolitan America.* Washington, DC: Brookings Institution and the Lincoln Institute of Land Policy.

Dyer, R.A. (1997, July 18). Affirmative action receives nod in poll. *Houston Chronicle.* Internet (available http://www.chron.com).

Eisley, M. (1998, February 5). Fetzer's reelection cost record $500,000. *Raleigh News and Observer.* Internet (available http://search.news-observer.com).

Farrell, C. (1998, May 4). Brighter lights for big cities. *Business Week,* pp. 88–95.

Fears, D. (1995, June 25). Young black mayors must walk a fine line. *Atlanta Journal and Constitution,* p. A8.

Fleischmann, A. (1987). The goals and strategies of local boundary changes: Government organization or private gain? *Journal of Urban Affairs,* 8, 63–76.

Fleischmann, A., & Stein, L. (1998). Campaign contributions in local elections. *Political Research Quarterly,* 51, 673–689.

Futty, J. (1997, February 10). Mayor's job rating favorable. *Columbus Dispatch.* Internet (available http://www.dispatch.com).

Garland, S.B. (1997, June 2). The burbs fight back. *Business Week,* pp. 147–148.

Grunwald, M. (1998, September-October). The myth of the supermayor. *The American Prospect,* pp. 20–27.

Heilig, P., & Mundt, R.J. (1984). *Your voice at City Hall: The politics, procedures and policies of district representation.* Albany: SUNY Press.

Hicks, S. (1996, March 14). Triangle warned on growth. *Raleigh News and Observer.* Internet (available http://search.news-observer.com).

Holly, L. (1997a, September 22). Regional efforts succeeding in some communities. *Milwaukee Journal Sentinel.* Internet (available http://www.jsonline. com).

Holly, L. (1997b, September 28). Task force to study cooperation models. *Milwaukee Journal Sentinel.* Internet (available http://www.jsonline.com).

The inner ring: Fighting decline (1998, March 15). *Detroit News.* Internet (available http://detnews.com).

Joint Center for Political Studies. (1994). *Black elected officials: A national roster.* Washington, DC: Joint Center for Political Studies.

Jones, B.D., & Bachelor, L.W. (1993). *The sustaining hand: Community leadership and corporate power,* 2nd ed. Lawrence: University Press of Kansas.

Keating, W. D., Krumholz, N., & Metzger, J. (1995). Postpopulist public–private partnerships. In W. Dennis Keating, Norman Krumholz, and David C. Perry (eds.), *Cleveland: A metropolitan reader* (pp. 332–350). Kent, OH: Kent State University Press.

Key to cities' health (1998, February 17). *Raleigh News and Observer* (editorial). Internet (available http://search.news-observer.com).

King, R.J., & Howes, D. (1998, March 25). AGM, Archer, negotiate casino plans. *Detroit News.* Internet (available http://detnews.com).

Lewis, P.G. (1998). *Shaping suburbia: How political institutions organize urban development.* Pittsburgh: University of Pittsburgh Press.

Lyons, W.E., Lowery, D., & DeHoog, R.H. (1992). *The Politics of Dissatisfaction: Citizens, Services, and Urban Institutions.* Armonk, NY: M.E. Sharpe.

Mayhood, K. (1998, March 4). County 'no' won't stop housing plan. *Columbus Dispatch.* Internet (available http://www.dispatch.com).

McClain, P.D. (1993). The changing dynamics of urban politics: Black and Hispanic municipal employment—is there competition? *Journal of Politics, 55,* 399–414.

Meier, K.J., Stewart, Jr., J., & England, R.E. (1991). The politics of bureaucratic discretion: Educational access as an urban service. *American Journal of Political Science, 35,* 155–177.

Meredith, R. (1997, April 11). Motown enters the zone. *New York Times,* pp. C1, C3.

Miller, A.D. (1996, September 10). A polarization of people. *Columbus Dispatch.* Internet (available http://www.dispatch.com).

Miller, G.J. (1981). *Cities by contract: The politics of municipal incorporation.* Cambridge: MIT Press.

Miller v. Johnson (1995). 515 U.S. 900.

Mollenkopf, J.H. (1983). *The contested city.* Princeton: Princeton University Press.

Mosiman, D. (1996). Face of downtown at stake. (Madison) *Wisconsin State Journal.* Internet (available http://www.madison.com).

Narrow escape: City and suburbs both fortunate annexation not limited (1997, May 20). *Houston Chronicle* (editorial). Internet (available http://www. chron.com).

National Association of Latino Elected and Appointed Officials. (1994). *National roster of elected and appointed Latino officials.* Washington, DC: National Association of Latino Elected and Appointed Officials, Educational Fund.

Norquist, J.O. (1998). *The wealth of cities: Revitalizing the centers of American life.* Reading, MA: Addison-Wesley.

Nunn, S., & Rosentraub, M.S. (1996). Metropolitan fiscal equalization: Distilling lessons from four U.S. programs. *State and Local Government Review,* 28, 90–102.

Nunn, S., & Rosentraub, M.S. (1997). Dimensions of interjurisdictional cooperation. *Journal of the American Planning Association,* 63, 205–219.

Orfield, M. (1997). *Metropolitics: A regional agenda for community and stability.* Washington: Brookings Institution and Lincoln Institute of Land Policy.

Orum, A.M. (1995). *City-building in America.* Boulder, CO: Westview Press.

Ostrom, V., Tiebout, C.M., & Warren, R. (1961). The organization of government in metropolitan areas: A theoretical inquiry. *American Political Science Review,* 55, 831–842.

Parker, R.E., & Feagin, J.R. (1991). Houston: Administration by economic elites. In H.V. Savitch & John Clayton Thomas (eds.), *Big City Politics in Transition* (pp. 169–188). Newbury Park, CA: Sage.

Parks, D. (1997, September 22). Norquist central to regional issues. *Milwaukee Journal Sentinel.* Internet (available http://www.jsonline.com).

Parks, R.B., & Oakerson, R.J. (1989). Metropolitan organization and governance: A local public economy approach. *Urban Affairs Quarterly,* 25, 18–29.

Pierce, N.R. with C.W. Johnson & J.S. Hall. (1993). *Citistates: How urban America can prosper in a competitive world.* Wasington, DC: Seven Locks Press.

Rodriguez, L. (1998, January 30). Houston's black leaders pave new path to power. *Houston Chronicle.* Internet (available: http://www.chron.com).

Romell, R. (1997, September 21). Politics, growth collide. *Milwaukee Journal Sentinel.* Internet (available http://www.jsonline.com).

Rusk, D. (1993). *Cities without suburbs.* Washington, DC: Woodrow Wilson Center Press.

Sablatura, B. (1998, March 20). Clamoring for city's fair share. *Houston Chronicle.* Internet (available http://www.chron.com).

Saltzstein, G.H. (1989). Black mayors and police policies. *Journal of Politics,* 51, 525–544.

Sandler, L. (1998, March 22). State bid to solve stalemate on transportation hits a rut. *Milwaukee Journal Sentinel.* Internet (available http://www.jsonline.com).

Santoro, W.A. (1995). Black politics and employment policies: The determinants of local government affirmative action. *Social Science Quarterly,* 76, 794–806.

Schattschneider, E.E. (1975 [1960]). *The semisovereign people: A realist's view of democracy in America.* Fort Worth: Harcourt Brace Jovanovich.

Stone, C.N. (1989). *Regime politics: Governing Atlanta, 1946–1988.* Lawrence: University Press of Kansas.

Thatcher, B. (1997, December 28). Greco part salesman and part negotiator. *Milwaukee Journal Sentinel,* p. B1.

U.S. Bureau of the Census. (1994). *County and city data book.* Washington: Government Printing Office.

Way to Grow (1996, April 1). *Raleigh News and Observer* (editorial). Internet (available http://search.news-observer.com).

Weibezahl, S. (1998, March 26). Merger vote on police sought. *Syracuse Post-Standard.* Internet (available http://www.syracuse.com).

Welch, S. (1990). The impact of at-large elections on the representation of blacks and Hispanics. *Journal of Politics,* 52, 1050–1076.

Williams, J. (1997, September 24). Dangling carrots is the Houston way. *Houston Chronicle.* Internet (available http://www.chron.com).

NOTES

[1]My thanks to Mark Smith for his valuable research assistance on this project.

[2]This ratio is generally limited to members of legislative bodies. An alternative to the ratio measure is a subtractive one: a group's percentage of seats on an elected governing body minus its share of the jurisdiction's population. Research using this measure yields results comparable to use of the ratio measure. On the advantages and disadvantages of each measure, see Welch, 1990.

CHAPTER 6

Taken In or Just Taken?
Political Incorporation of
African Americans in Cities

RUFUS P. BROWNING*
DALE ROGERS MARSHALL
DAVID TABB

In this chapter we assess changes in the political incorporation of African Americans between 1990 and 1997, with special attention to the defeat of African American mayors in the four largest cities in the country: New York, Los Angeles, Chicago, and Philadelphia. Our work is based in part on research reported in *Racial Politics in American Cities* (Browning, Marshall & Tabb, 1997). In that book, authors of chapters assessed the political incorporation of African Americans and Latinos in major U.S. cities and changes since 1990.

WHAT IS POLITICAL INCORPORATION?

Our research on black political incorporation has been motivated by a question—Could a tremendous effort to overcome the barriers of racial exclusion from government and politics succeed? Could the election of black officeholders make city governments more responsive to the demands and interests of the previously excluded groups? "Political incorporation" is the label we applied to a variable—the extent to which a group is effectively represented in policymaking. As a variable, the term refers to the whole range of possibilities, from *exclusion*—little or no incorporation—to the *formal representation* of a group by members of that group (officeholding), to *substantial authority and influence* as well (Browning, Marshall & Tabb, 1984, 1985, p. 25).

The main concerns of our research were to understand the conditions in which strong political incorporation arose, if it arose at all, and to determine the extent to which a group's political incorporation had an

131

impact on the *responsiveness* of city governments to their demands and interests. Our aim was to describe the political relationships previously excluded groups enter into, and the effects on government and policy that emerged from these relationships. In particular, we wanted to identify political relationships that groups expected or that we expect to result in responsiveness; and to identify the actual effects of those relationships on governmental responsiveness. It was important for students of democracy—don't we all belong to that group?—to know whether political mobilization on the scale of the civil rights movement could overcome racial exclusion.

In our earlier research on ten northern California cities in the period 1960–1979, we measured the political incorporation of a group as *the extent to which it is represented in a coalition that dominates city policy-making on issues of greatest concern to the group.*[1] Dominant-coalition representation was a new relationship for African Americans and for Latinos in the United States, and many of them clearly expected it to change city governments for the better.

SUMMARY OF EARLIER FINDINGS

We showed in our earlier work that in ten northern California cities, biracial coalitions followed directly on the presence of substantial black populations (about 20 percent of city electorates) *and* substantial support from liberal whites (20–45 percent), during the 1960s and 1970s—that is, during and as a central drama of the tremendous political mobilization of African Americans that followed the civil rights movement (Browning, Marshall & Tabb, 1984, 1985, ch. 3).

Nationwide, in cities where blacks constituted a majority, they could and did build mostly-black political organizations and took over city government. (Examples described in *Racial Politics* are Atlanta, Baltimore, Birmingham, and New Orleans.) Where they were not a majority, biracial (black–white) or occasionally multiracial coalitions (black, white, Latino) were the strongest manifestation of dominant-coalition political incorporation.[2] Frequently, such coalitions were led by African American mayors.

In the ten California cities, the black–white biracial coalition was by far the most productive relationship for the kinds of responsiveness studied. City governments controlled by biracial coalitions typically greatly accelerated employment of African Americans in city government (ending discrimination, recruiting and hiring affirmatively), increased appointments of African Americans to boards and commissions (representation, decision making, influence), instituted affirmative action in contracting (minority economic development), and established civilian police review boards (accountability, reducing police violence toward black citizens). The biracial coalition in office was much more productive in the long run than black protest that did not culminate in a biracial coalition (Browning, Marshall & Tabb, 1984, 1985, chs. 4, 5).

Biracial coalitions developed where African Americans were substantially the largest racial/ethnic minority group. In some cities, the presence of several groups of roughly equal size posed a barrier to coalition formation. Coalition formation is more difficult in multiracial cities for several reasons: because negotiations to form a coalition are much more complex if three or four groups are involved instead of two; because of real tensions, cultural differences, and competition between groups; and because opportunities for politicians to set groups at odds with each other are multiplied. Several black mayors have accomplished multiracial electoral coalitions in increasingly multiracial cities—Harold Washington in Chicago, Dinkins for one term in New York. Tom Bradley's initially strongly biracial coalition also received electoral support from Latinos and brought them into city government. Still, multiracial coalitions are typically difficult and unstable arrangements.[3]

Studies of the greater variety of cities nationwide reported in *Racial Politics* (Browning, Marshall & Tabb, 1990) showed that the model of incorporation set forth in *Protest Is Not Enough* (Browning, Marshall & Tabb, 1984, 1985) had to be expanded to reflect barriers to dominant-coalition representation that were common nationwide but not present or not problematic in the ten northern California cities. Machine politics, a major barrier to coalitions led by African Americans, often operated as pre-existing coalitions controlled by white leaders who co-opted blacks and blocked competing grassroots mobilization efforts. Whether machine politics itself produced significant benefits for minority groups varied from city to city.[4]

THE DEFEAT OF AFRICAN AMERICAN MAYORS IN BIG CITIES

The late 1980s and early 1990s saw the high-water mark of black incorporation in dominant coalitions in the largest U.S. cities. New York, Los Angeles, Chicago, and Philadelphia all had African American mayors by 1989. But by 1996, all of these cities had white mayors. In Philadelphia,

Edward Rendell, a white, defeated two black candidates in the Democratic primary and went on to win the general election against weak opposition; he still leads a biracial coalition in office. In New York, Rudolph Giuliani defeated David Dinkins. In Chicago, Richard M. Daley defeated two black candidates who split the black vote.[5] And in Los Angeles, Richard Riordan defeated councilman Michael Woo, who was trying to hold the old Bradley coalition together for still another election.[6]

To people who welcomed the growing political incorporation of African Americans as a solution to their unacceptable exclusion, these defeats have been sobering, to say the least. The defeats are real, and the potential for further losses is not insignificant.

While alarm is appropriate, the picture is more complex than the defeat of black mayors implies. The four largest cities are important, but they are still only four cities. Even though some other U.S. cities appear to be on similar paths, still other cities do not show any diminution in the strength of African American political incorporation, as Richard Keiser explains in Chapter 7. And as we shall argue in this chapter, the contemporary nature and context of political incorporation are more complex than the simple model of a biracial coalition with an African American mayor that emerged from the 1960s and 1970s; that complexity must be understood. The contemporary complexity of black political incorporation must include an appreciation of the extent to which policy gains and structural changes have been institutionalized at all levels of government even as African American mayors have come and gone.

We first seek to understand why so many coalitions headed by African Americans have gone down to defeat in the largest cities. Second, we ask, what does it mean?

UNDERSTANDING DEFEAT

Ideology, Interests, and Leadership

Raphael Sonenshein and John Mollenkopf give an interpretation of the decline of African American mayors in terms of ideology, interests, and leadership—the shifting ways in which ideology and interests are engaged by issues and by the ways leaders create and respond to issues (Sonenshein, 1997a, 1997b; Mollenkopf, 1997). The ideological element is racial liberalism among whites and other groups, expressed in the support for African American mayors that is a necessary ingredient of biracial and multiracial coalitions. Jews especially have demonstrated strong support for the civil rights movement and for African American candidates; Latinos have also done so. But in recent elections in Chicago, New York, and Los Angeles, white (and Latino) liberals have defected significantly from the candidates of the minority-liberal side. Mollenkopf (1997, pp. 105, 109) refers to "the traumas of racial succession in neighborhoods and labor markets" in New York that pushed liberal Jews to the right. The recession of 1989–1993 created fiscal pressures that "made it difficult for [Mayor Dinkins] to deliver benefits to his core constituencies." Racially polarizing events and Dinkins's handling of them also alienated white supporters, enough to deprive Dinkins of his margin of victory. Sonenshein describes similar ways in which the interests of supporters of the Bradley coalition were disappointed, including the 1992 civil disturbance in South Central L.A. Fear of crime and violence also presented a salient issue on which conservative challengers capitalized. Though partly a media-driven panic, anger about crime is not without a basis in reality. Repeated drive-by shootings engender real terror and revulsion.

When the Movement Fades

It is not only that interests asserted themselves to challenge the call of ideology; the ideological thrust of the civil rights movement also lost much of its mobilizing energy. The civil rights movement was an extraordinary political resource for the political mobilization of African Americans and their allies in the 1960s and 1970s that is not available in the 1990s. It was the movement and its fierce energy that impelled the tremendous activity of the earlier period, and its high moral purpose articulated and engaged ideological commitments of people of all colors. The power and clarity of that purpose understandably reduced the salience of narrower interests. With some goals of the movement achieved and new generations coming of age not knowing the exclusion and oppression of the pre-movement period and not understanding the continuing discrimination of the post–civil rights era, the ties of ideology weakened and the claims of interest re-asserted themselves. When almost no African Americans held government jobs in many areas and very few were admitted to universities, it was possible for affirmative action in employment and admissions to prevail with an ideological appeal to racial justice and an interest-based appeal for racial peace. If racial peace now does not seem to be threatened and it is no longer clear on which side justice lies, a white or Asian parent whose child can't get into the university of choice might indeed be persuaded that affirmative action should be eliminated and that voting for politicians who seem to be protecting a patronage operation for some groups over others is no longer a valid expression of racial liberalism.[7]

From Biracial to Multiracial Cities

Behind the news of issues, events, and leaders, the fundamental resources of population for biracial coalitions and black incorporation are shifting, too. How limited our ability to predict! In 1980, Oakland was nearly half black and seemed certain to remain solidly black, but by 1995 the black population had fallen to only slightly over 40 percent, and Latinos, less than 10 percent in 1980, had grown to 17 percent. Asians constituted 16 percent, also growing.[8] Since 1983, black representation on the city council, including the mayor, had been at least 50 percent, but by 1998 there were only three African Americans, including the mayor, on a council of eight. In June 1998, former governor Jerry Brown led a nonpartisan primary election for mayor of Oakland by a huge margin and won the general election in November, ending twenty-one years of African American mayors in Oakland.

Between 1980 and 1990, African American populations declined as percentages of total population in six of the ten northern California cities. Black migration to the suburbs combined with rapid growth of Latino and Asian populations is changing the face of cities where African Americans are used to holding the highest offices and playing dominant roles in dominant coalitions. Many of the new residents are immigrants who cannot or do not vote. Still, the direction and speed of population change, and the competition between the groups, do not bode well for the maintenance of black-dominated coalitions.

Not only has it become harder to form coalitions as a result of the rapid growth of Latino and Asian populations and declining black populations in some cities, but also the ratio of political resources to population has declined for minority groups as a whole because so few members of these groups are voters. Latinos and Asians, in contrast to African Americans, typically constitute much smaller proportions of the electorate than they do of the population, partly because these groups are typically younger on average (fewer have reached voting age) but mainly because so many are not citizens. Forty percent Latino population in Los Angeles looks like a potent political resource, yet Latinos comprised only 10 percent of the votes cast in the 1993 mayoral election (Sonenshein, 1997a, p. 52).

Obviously a group's share of total population is not a good guide to its coalition prospects when few can vote. Group share of the adult population is a better measure, share of actual turnout would be still better; even better, because it reflects near-term potential turnout, is the number of adult citizens of each group as a percentage of all adult citizens in a city. In short, to understand what is happening and what might happen with coalition formation, the important thing is to focus on realizable resources, not simply on population. The realizable electoral resources of these groups are smaller than their populations suggest.

But Asian and Latino electorates are growing rapidly. Many immigrants in the United States are frightened by the wave of anti-immigrant feeling expressed all too clearly in efforts to strip illegal immigrants and some groups of legal immigrants of various government benefits, at both federal and state levels. Where many were content to seek economic success and forego political conflict, now powerlessness is understood to be a serious problem. In New York, Los Angeles, the San Francisco Bay Area, and other places where immigrants are concentrated, their rates of application for citizenship and of voter registration have accelerated under the impetus of fear and of mobilization financed and carried out by foundations and ethnic civil rights and political organizations, and the number of adult citizens of these groups is rising rapidly. Delays in processing citizenship applications will slow this movement somewhat, but we should expect Asian and Latino voting to approach, and in some places exceed, their proportions of the adult population, and the network of organizations that shape and compete for their votes to be much more active.

Where quiescence and nonparticipation were once the rule, fear and the possibility of political authority are now potent motivators. They were also for African Americans in the 1960s and 1970s. In city after city, African American voters registered and turned out to vote in response to the prospect that black candidates might win high office. It was not uncommon in that period for turnout of African Americans to equal white turnout at the most critical elections where the victory of a black candidate or a biracial coalition depended on it. Even though black turnout is typically lower than white turnout, this history shows that black voters can be mobilized if the cause is urgent enough.

From the Movement Ocean to the Belly of the Management Whale

The sequelae of the movement still manifest themselves in many ways, to be sure. Some of its inheritors are ensconced in the institutions of government and interest-group liberalism, which impose their own protocols and interests, as Adolph Reed (1995) has eloquently argued. It may not be inevitable, but it is predictable: the struggle for access to government, if "successful," means adopting its logic. It is not only whites whose interests are shaped and stimulated by the agenda of racial liberalism—African Americans who occupy positions in the system have compelling reasons to acquiesce in the limits of institutionalized incorporation.[9]

Counter-Mobilization

The counter-mobilization was already in full vigor, of course, and had been for three centuries—it was not *caused* by the civil rights movement—but it found new and powerful expressions, driven by the manifestations and successes of the movement: the Nixon/Wallace Southern strategy, the Reagan administration, and the attack on affirmative action. One achievement of the counter-mobilization was to cut federal funding to cities just as African Americans were gaining control of city governments, reducing their resources and weakening their ability to carry out their policy agenda.

Sincere Imitations

If the civil rights movement was the vanguard of the struggle for racial justice and equality, it would have followers. Latinos, Asians, Native Americans, women—their concerns could reinforce the universalistic appeal of civil rights, but their mobilization competes with the interests of African Americans when attention shifts to the scarce resources of jobs, contracts, government funding, public housing units, and educational opportunities. The continuing struggle for political equality finds African Americans in the curious position of occupants of the establishment, "cast [in Oakland] as the moral equivalent of white people, hoarding power in the face of change." John Russo, a white member of Oakland's city council, was quoted as saying, "I don't want to overstate this, but it's as if African Americans now are the ones standing in the schoolhouse door" (Tilove, 1996).

Los Angeles may also be a case in which a biracial coalition is a barrier to the legitimate aspirations of Latino and Asian groups:

> To a remarkable degree, the city's political system has remained stable in the face of huge demographic changes. Once Los Angeles's politics was black and white; to a shocking degree, it still is. And that represents a serious problem for democratic governance. (Sonenshein, 1997a, p. 60)

Once the dream, biracial coalitions in multiracial cities now signify exclusion, not a triumph of democratic incorporation.

In this rapidly shifting ground we can see the enormous importance of the civil rights movement and the political mobilization that followed it. The partial success of that mobilization and the subsequent decline of the movement and the passage of generations that it energized weakened ideological commitment to black political incorporation, reduced the unity and vigor of black political participation, stimulated counter-mobilization and allowed opposing interests to re-assert themselves, and inspired other excluded groups to compete with African Americans.

With all these forces at work (and others described in Browning, Marshall & Tabb, 1997), we can understand why biracial coalitions fall and why African American mayors are defeated in some cities. But what does it mean?

END OF AN ERA?

Is this the end of an era of black political incorporation?—Political power wrested from racial exclusion with such struggle, and so quickly lost again? It may well be the end of a period in which the liberal biracial coalition, including control of the mayor's office, is the most common prospect and goal for African Americans in large cities. Are there other kinds of incorporation? Can they be sustained? Can they be effective? How else can the interests of African Americans be effectively represented in city governments?

Because of changing population patterns and the lack of a movement with the moral force of the civil rights movement, the biracial coalition with African Americans dominant is not likely to be such a common pattern in the future. It was already not a feasible option in many cities. The near future is likely to be more varied than the past, a period in which people in different localities, with different histories and leadership, attempt to create local agendas and relationships without the intense structure of commitment and direction generated by the civil rights movement. Different scenarios are likely to play themselves out in different settings.

Multiracial Coalitions

One possibility is that activists in some cities will seek broader coalitions. This is likely to be a period in which coalitions are more fluid. A biracial coalition out of power is likely to redefine itself as multiracial if it can—if other groups can and will contribute their electoral resources to it. This effort will not always be made and it will not always be successful, especially at first. Where biracial coalitions have been most successful, old leaders and their agendas and conflicts may have to drop out of the picture first because it is so hard to give up the ingredients that once produced political success. Yet, multiracial coalitions remain a possibility in the intermediate term. It is true that blacks and Latinos, for example, find themselves in real conflict in many settings; but we should not underestimate the salutary effect of several years out of office on the emergence of leaders and their ability to forge new agendas and understandings.

Multiracial coalitions will tend to draw their mayoral candidates from a larger pool of prospects, regardless of race. Of course, the offering of candidacy is a tool of coalition formation. African Americans will not have an enforceable prior claim to the top office. Candidates and mayors will be increasingly diverse.

The most effective and stable multiracial coalitions will be constructed in ways similar to the construction of successful biracial coalitions in cities where black and white-liberal groups came together—by a solemn pact among widely respected leaders who develop trust in each other. They will each have demonstrated the ability to control candidacies in their groups and to deploy the group's electoral resources effectively. They will be able to prevent multiple candidacies from their groups so as to avoid splitting the groups' vote among competitors. They will reach clear agreements about candidacies, priorities, and appointments. They will treat each other with great respect, and their forces will work together to support the electoral slate of the coalition.[10]

Multiracial Competition

This is a less optimistic scenario. As many cities evolve toward multiracial populations:

> People of color will typically find it difficult to form coalitions because of their cultural differences and different positions in a racially obsessed society, and therefore different interests. Unless leaders can develop agendas that are more successful in bringing groups together, this scenario has division, not coalition, as its typical state, and political weakness as its typical result. (Browning, Marshall & Tabb, 1997, p. 289)

Centrist Coalitions—Representation and Responsiveness

Centrist coalitions in some cities are likely to be successful in garnering the support of a substantial fraction of the minority vote in addition to a large part of the white vote. In cities where electorates are relatively liberal, progressive and traditional liberal coalitions may contend for control, with African Americans represented in both and beneficiaries of significant benefits from both. In Berkeley, black property owners, represented by a councilmember, aligned themselves with the more conservative whites on issues of rent control in favor of landlords, while another black council member aligned herself with the left-leaning progressive coalition in favor of tenants. Both coalitions took many actions for the benefit of Berkeley's black population and carefully preserved most of the benefits they inherited from the years of peak biracial policymaking. (Black employment in Berkeley city government stood in 1994 at more than twice parity with the percent black of the adult population in Berkeley.)

Mollenkopf describes the Koch administration in New York:

> Despite the electoral failure of biracial coalitions and the low degree of minority political incorporation, New York City government still produces policy outputs that favor minority interests. . . . Minority employees now make up over half the civil service in New York. Mayor Koch was proud of appointing blacks or Latinos to 18 percent of his managerial positions, including the offices of police commissioner and several deputy mayors. While he rejected an independent police review board, he added civilians to a departmental review board. . . . The Koch administration used community development funds, city capital funds, and other sources of creative financing to launch an ambitious $5.2 billion program to rehabilitate abandoned properties for use as subsidized housing. Though the Giuliani administration has reduced funding for this program, it continues to support it, as did the Dinkins administration. (Mollenkopf, 1997, p. 102)

This looks like pretty strong political incorporation and responsiveness to us, even if it was produced by an administration that thwarted the aspirations of minority candidates to hold the mayor's office. Centrist coalitions, even if a majority of African Americans supported other candidates and do not control the mayor's office, may effectively represent their interests—at least some of them.[11] And, of course, African Americans held many other positions in New York, both party and governmental; as Mollenkopf makes clear, they were certainly not excluded from the Koch administration or from the Democratic organization.

Measuring political incorporation by focusing solely on the mayor's office is not fruitful. Incorporation as representation in a dominant coalition allows for the possibility that a white political entrepreneur organizes a coalition that includes African Americans but is not, if an African American candidate is also running, supported by a majority of African Americans; the coalition nevertheless succeeds in winning the mayor's office and deliberately sets out to meet some of their interests. To call such a coalition "conservative" is misleading in the context of accounts of the biracial coalitions that defeated "conservative" coalitions of the 1950s and 1960s, coalitions that had completely excluded African Americans from all aspects of city government. "Centrist" is an apt term for the contemporary coalitions because it correctly places them between the racialized appeals and agenda of many African American candidates for mayor, on the one hand, and the anti-black, exclusionist impulses of segments of the white population who would still support a Yorty or a Rizzo.[12]

A centrist coalition may not be the first choice of most African American voters, and its leader may be sharply critical of some African American politicians, as Mayor Koch was. Nevertheless, its organization may include African Americans, and its program may include parts of an African American agenda.

Competing Biracial or Multiracial Coalitions

The New York experience illustrates the powerful pressure on centrist coalitions in relatively liberal cities to respond to the interests of large minority populations. A centrist coalition in that setting has an incentive to respond to important minority interests to stave off the accusation of unfairness, which would antagonize both the minority electorate and many whites and lead to intensified mobilization against the coalition. Such a coalition has already incorporated minority interests. Then the electoral competition might be between two biracial or multiracial coalitions that both represent minority interests, one of which is more racialized in its appeals and goals and intent on allocating more resources to the benefit of one or more groups. Or they might differentiate themselves on machine-reform lines. Richard Keiser describes just such a development in Philadelphia, where "it is clear that these two coalitions [reform and machine], with blacks in leadership positions of both, are likely to battle for the future control of the city" (Keiser, 1997, p. 91).

Even where it is not successful in winning the mayor's office very often, minority political effort outside the dominant coalition plays the absolutely essential role of making the dominant coalition insecure and from time to time actually turning it out of office.

The influence over city government achieved in this way may not be negligible. It is founded in part on the adoption of some minority interests even by centrist coalitions; in part on the dense network of associations and resources that African Americans in large cities can now draw upon; and in part on the threat of electoral mobilization and challenge.

Exclusion

Exclusion is also a possibility, and it does and will occur in some cities. It will occur (already occurs) where the white population constitutes a majority and is largely illiberal on racial issues, with few liberals of any color. The exclusionist impulse remains strong in many localities and will find continued expression.

Another kind of exclusion may occur where a Latino or Latino–white coalition controls city government; Miami is a case in point (Warren, 1997).

On the issues, African Americans may find themselves increasingly isolated. Richard DeLeon has shown that the issue positions of African Americans in San Francisco are significantly though not entirely different from the positions of whites, Latinos, and Asians; African Americans are the most different group, whose views and votes do not align well across the issues with the majority positions of any other group, and "the city's African Americans have felt increasingly isolated politically and forced to go it alone without partners or allies" (DeLeon, 1997, p. 154). Of course, this was before the election of Willie Brown as mayor in 1995. Brown's unusual skill and strong commitments make his administration the most inclusive in San Francisco's history, but a city with a population that is only 10 percent black is not likely to have many African American mayors, and it is not inconceivable that the flow of population and the dynamic of issues, leaders, and coalition formation could produce a kind of neglectful exclusion of African Americans in the future. If this is conceivable in San Francisco, it is likely in other, less liberal cities. Even if a rollback to the exclusion of the pre–civil rights era has not happened anywhere to our knowledge, we do not reject out of hand the proposition that it will be attempted somewhere, probably carefully concealed beneath a sham representation.

The reconstruction of exclusion is a frightening possibility; it must be avoided. How to avoid it should be the subject of very serious discussion among African Americans and among racially liberal people of all colors. Needed is a generation of leaders who can reach out effectively across racial and ethnic lines and who can shape their agendas to forge links across those lines. This will often mean giving up demands that some group activists will insist upon, so it will place leaders in a difficult position with respect to their own people. The claims of the group will partly conflict with the claims of an emerging coalition—but this may be greatly preferable to exclusion.

Resources

Though representation in dominant coalitions is a form of political incorporation much to be desired, African Americans (and other groups) may have substantial influence even if they do not hold the main offices in a governing coalition, especially where they have achieved strong political incorporation. In some cities, city councils are powerful, and representation there can be employed to mobilize significant policy and spending initiatives or to ward off policy rollbacks attempted by unsympathetic mayors. Where once black councilmembers were secure and powerful in the supportive structure of a dominant biracial coalition, now they will devise ways of finding support from representatives of other groups.

An effect of incorporation and the growth of the minority middle class is the tremendous growth in the skills and resources of minority people—the lawyers, social-service activists and administrators, media people, governmental professionals and administrators, and other professional, technical, and businesspeople, and their increased wealth and self-confidence. There is now a dense network of middle-class minority leadership, able to lobby and mobilize quickly around issues, and to draw on their associations with professional colleagues in business, the law, community-based organizations, and public administration. Minority organizations now have the willingness and ability to call upon the law, to go to court, or to enlist the aid of allies in state or federal government, which they typically did not have thirty-five years ago.

Lacking representation in a dominant coalition, a group, or several groups, can still maintain a constant threat of revived electoral mobilization by conducting well-timed and well-organized protest and electoral effort. The threat of revived mobilization itself creates an incentive for the dominant coalition to heed some minority interests.

Dominant-coalition representation also does not capture the acceptance of once-opposed policies by formerly resistant officeholders. In Philadelphia, Mayor Edward Rendell is not Frank Rizzo—Mayor Richard Riordan of Los Angeles, following the African American Tom Bradley in office, is not Sam Yorty, who preceded Bradley. The blatant rejection of the concerns of African Americans articulated by Rizzo and

Yorty in their mayoral administrations and campaigns is not reappearing in the white mayors who have succeeded biracial coalitions with African American mayors. The fact that the new big-city mayors are white does not mean they espouse the positions common in the last defenders of exclusionary politics before black mayors.

These many changes are all resources that were typically not available to African Americans thirty years ago but are commonly available to them now. Measures of the political strength of minority groups must now tap these resources because they comprise contemporary tools for the representation of interests in governmental decision making. For African Americans in particular, as their resources of population wane in the face of immigration and population growth of other groups, these resources will be increasingly important. These resources themselves, and more described in the following section, are the outgrowth of decades of political and economic development.

INCORPORATION AND SOME SUCCESSES
OF RESPONSIVENESS

In *Protest Is Not Enough* (1984), we showed that responsiveness of the governments of the ten cities to interests of African Americans, in the period 1960–1979, was closely related to their representation in dominant coalitions—in other words, that strong representation in dominant coalitions did change city governments and their policy responses to African Americans.

Subsequent work by researchers on other cities, reported in *Racial Politics in American Cities* in 1990 and 1997, confirmed that the achievement of strong dominant-coalition representation typically did lead to much greater responsiveness than African Americans had experienced before 1960, when they were almost totally excluded from government and politics in most cities.[13] Strong political incorporation was certainly not achieved in all cities, but it had significant benefits where it was achieved.

The broader range of cities reported in *Racial Politics* also revealed much variation around this pattern. As noted above, in New York, even coalitions in office that African Americans did not support, in which they did not hold the highest offices, were relatively responsive to important interests (Mollenkopf, 1990, 1997). At the other end of the spectrum, in Atlanta even black-dominated coalitions in office did not seem particularly responsive to the most critical needs of Atlanta's large low-income

African American population (Stone, 1990; Stone & Pierannunzi, 1997). In other majority-black cities, the effectiveness and responsiveness of city governments varied greatly depending on the goals and abilities of mayors and the political contexts in which they operated (Perry, 1997; Orr, 1997).

Multiple Access to Governmental Authority

Responsiveness was most closely related to dominant-coalition representation in the early years, when the conservative, exclusionary regimes still in place in most cities continued to oppose racially liberal policies already adopted in other cities where biracial coalitions were first successful. But at least some of those policies eventually diffused to most cities, even those with no coherent minority-oriented politics, as a result of federal and state requirements, changing professional standards and practices, demographic shift, and the succession of racially illiberal mayors with more moderate officeholders—blatant, official racism and discrimination became unacceptable in many settings, affirmative action became common. In the northern California cities, for example, personnel policies designed to open city government employment to minorities were very closely related to the strength of African American political incorporation in 1970. A mere eight years later, they were not related at all—federal and state pressure and the diffusion of responsiveness, and perhaps efforts to undermine mobilization, had led the initially lagging city governments to adopt the same policies (Browning, Marshall & Tabb, 1984, 1985, ch. 5). This does not mean that cities with strong black political incorporation were not different from cities where blacks were not clearly represented in a dominant coalition—they were different—but it does mean that some of the interests of African Americans were effectively represented in *many* ways in most cities. A web of legal requirements and institutional pressures was constructed precisely to combat discrimination in government employment even in cities where African Americans were politically weak.

Whether multiple access to governmental authority of this sort is generally effective in producing responsiveness remains an empirical question; in the California cities there is no question that it produced significant gains in black employment in city governments where black people were still effectively excluded from positions of power (Browning, Marshall & Tabb, 1984, 1985; and same authors, 1997, pp. 30–31).

Welcome to the wonderful world of pluralism! Multiple points of access to governmental authority have been constructed around some interests of African Americans.

Responsiveness When Black Mayors or Biracial Coalitions Are Defeated

The evidence so far is that defeat has *not* brought with it a rollback of city government to the status quo ante in which African Americans were routinely excluded from any benefits of city government and any allocations of public resources. The experience so far of the cities where black mayors or biracial-multiracial coalitions have been defeated parallels the experience at the national level with the determined effort of the Reagan administrations to roll back the gains of the 1960s. At the national level, a coalition of blacks, liberals, and centrist forces in both parties emerged on civil rights issues and was

> usually able to control policy on these issues in the face of the opposition of even a popular president and Supreme Court majority. . . . The Reagan administration lost every legislative battle on civil rights that came to a vote in Congress. (Smith, 1992, pp. 112, 124, fn. 48)

This result depended on Democratic control of at least one house of Congress through that period, a condition not readily duplicated at the local level. In general, the key to preventing rollback is maintenance of a renewed, perhaps reconstructed, vigorous opposition coalition even if your coalition does not control the most powerful offices.

However, there is no question that real losses to the interests of African Americans occur when black mayors or biracial coalitions are defeated. Black community organizations that have received city government funding receive less. African Americans are appointed in smaller numbers to serve on city boards and commissions and to head departments and divisions of city government. Black employment in city government might continue at high levels, or it might decline, especially where other groups have grown and are employed at lower levels than blacks. Special programs to allocate city government contracts to minority contractors are likely to be weakened.

An especially frightening prospect is exemplified by the alleged brutal beating and torture of a Haitian immigrant in a Brooklyn police station on August 9, 1997:

> Louima, 33, said police beat him, stripped off his pants, pilfered money from his wallet, shouted racial insults at him and ordered him into a bathroom in the station house, where he said one officer sodomized him with the wooden handle of a toilet plunger and then stuck it in his mouth breaking off several of his top front teeth.

He said, "Stupid nigger . . . know how to respect cops. This is Giuliani time. It is not Dinkins time," Louima said yesterday from his hos-
pital bed in Coney Island, where he is in intensive care with punctured
intestines and a damaged bladder—wounds doctors say were caused
by a "blunt instrument." (Harden, 1997)

Months later, Mr. Louima retracted the statement that officers
who tortured him had shouted, "This is Giuliani time" (Kifner, 1998).
But the original statement became a major issue in the fall 1997 mayoral
campaign, and the leading Democratic candidate, Ruth Messinger,
repeatedly referred to "Giuliani time." Giuliani won by a wide margin
nevertheless.

Even a well-intentioned centrist regime sits at the apex of a structure
that, like most American institutions, includes employees with racist
views. It is not only the intentions of the top elected officials that count.
Racist impulses will be expressed if they are not consistently, vigorously
suppressed (and sometimes even if they are), and it is predictable that
they will be expressed in violent ways by that portion of police who harbor racial animosities and have poor control of them.[14]

It was a partly successful project of liberal biracial coalitions that
were in power for a long time to remake police departments under their
authority so as to remove or suppress racist behavior, especially violence
directed against racial minorities. Nationwide, this project still has a long
way to go—it is very difficult to turn police forces around. The recent centrist regimes have come into power by promising to be tough on crime.
When a white defeats a black for mayor, racist elements on the police
force are likely to interpret the mayor's program of "tough on crime" as a
license for increased violence against black and other minority citizens.[15]

To Mayor Giuliani's credit, he took immediate and vigorous steps to
shake up the police station where the incident occurred. The commanding officers of the station and the sergeant in charge when the incident
occurred were quickly transferred, twelve officers were placed on restricted duty, and charges of aggravated sexual assault and first-degree
assault were filed against two officers (Cooper, 1997). Eventually assault
charges were filed against four officers and federal civil rights charges
against the four officers and a police sergeant (Fried, 1998). Giuliani also
appointed a task force to investigate and make recommendations, then
contemptuously dismissed them (Barry, 1998).

Centrist coalitions that wish to avoid such incidents should actively,
publicly, and repeatedly stress their determination to prevent them and

should institute programs designed to do so. Otherwise they will soon find themselves discredited among people of color and among fair-minded whites.

It is predictable that some centrist regimes will indeed quietly relax affirmative personnel practices and change governmental behavior and policies of various kinds to the disadvantage of African Americans, not because their elected leaders are overtly racist but because they oversee institutions in which racial animosity will be expressed in the absence of the heightened attentiveness and determination of a biracial or multiracial coalition.

The Institutionalization of Political Incorporation

Control of the mayor's office is still important, and we can expect some disadvantages for African Americans to flow from defeat of African American mayors. But if we look at the responsiveness of city governments across a broad range of policies, we find that multiple points of influence and institutionalization have been created at all levels of government that protect the interests of African Americans—not all of their interests, but some important ones nevertheless. Effective representation depended in the early years on control of city government via a dominant coalition. Now it rests also on a widely diffused set of laws and on norms of governance accepted even by white mayors of the largest cities. In this setting, the defeat of the black mayors of those cities has not rolled their governments back to the exclusion and nonresponsiveness of the pre–civil rights era.

If a rollback to exclusion has not occurred, still the issues and coalition possibilities are shifting in multiracial cities and states with large immigrant populations. In the June 1998 California primary election, all four major candidates for governor, including the Republican attorney general, Dan Lungren, opposed a ballot proposition to eliminate most bilingual education (Prop. 227), in spite of the fact that it was favored by a substantial majority of the electorate. (It passed with 61 percent of the vote, and 67 percent of whites favored it [*Los Angeles Times,* 1998].) By rejecting this racially divisive proposal, Mr. Lungren showed he appreciates the salience of the issue for California's growing Latino electorate, 63 percent of whom opposed it, and the necessity of not angering Latinos and other immigrants and mobilizing them against Republicans as the November general election approached. Where were black voters on the issue? A majority of them sided with Latinos, 52 percent opposing Prop. 227—a good sign for the multiracial coalition of the future.

IS POLITICAL INCORPORATION ENOUGH?

This examination of the changes in African American political incorporation over the last seven years shows that patterns of incorporation that were variable in the earlier period have become very diverse and complex. It also shows that there have been some successes of responsiveness, sometimes associated closely with dominant coalition representation and sometimes following from other sources and mechanisms of influence and governmental authority.

Political incorporation of the dominant-biracial-coalition sort was clearly not enough even where it occurred to secure the broad goal of equality for African Americans, and it did not occur in many cities with substantial black populations. In spite of its extent and successes, the political incorporation of African Americans and other minority groups has failed to make a perceptible dent in severe poverty, poor education, and high unemployment.

Many authors of *Racial Politics* criticize regimes with high levels of political incorporation for not bringing about greater redistribution in order to meet the needs of lower income minorities. In a separate work, Robert C. Smith, focusing mainly on the national picture, concludes that

> the black movement has been almost wholly encapsulated into main-
> stream institutions; coopted and marginalized. As a result it has be-
> come largely irrelevant in terms of a politics and policies that would
> address the multifaceted problems of race in the post–civil rights era.
> (Smith, 1996, p. xvi)

From this perspective, there has been a failure not only of black mayors and biracial coalitions but of the entire political-economic structure of the United States.

Nevertheless, from our perspective, minority political incorporation has not been a sham. It is an important step that should not be discounted just because it has not ended poverty and urban decay. We agree with Adolph Reed, Jr., that "the presence of a black mayor or regime has some, but less than dramatic, racially redistributive effect on allocation of public resources" (Reed, 1988). Following the evidence brought forth by the authors of *Racial Politics*, we would extend that modest and partial blessing to biracial and multiracial coalitions whether headed by an African American mayor or not and perhaps to some coalitions that were not the first choice of blacks. We would extend it also to a wide variety of other legal and institutional structures that are sometimes responsive to demands for fairness and nondiscrimination in the allocation of resources. African Americans have *not* been simply "taken" by political incorporation. It is in the nature of partly successful movements that their accomplishments, once taken as great victories, are more or less quickly taken for granted, especially when there is so much more to be accomplished.

Yet we acknowledge the limits of incorporation. The race-specific agenda of maintaining and extending the civil rights gains of the 1960s has achieved major successes in incorporating blacks into political systems, but the broader progressive policy agenda has not succeeded in achieving fundamental social and economic reform around full employment and ghetto reconstruction, which are especially salient for African Americans (Smith, 1996, pp. 24–25). In spite of black political incorporation and the growth of a black middle class, too many African Americans still live in high-poverty areas at unacceptably low levels of income and employment, isolated both from middle-class black people and from whites. Their continuing isolation after decades of political progress for African Americans is a disturbing reminder of the limits of incorporation in the post–civil rights era.

Many of the forces shaping the conditions under which the mass of low-income minority people live are not under the control of city governments, whether they are run by minority regimes or not. In a capitalist world and a capitalist society with a fragmented federal government, in which cities compete with each other for investment, it is entirely unrealistic to expect even the most strongly incorporated regime to achieve the elimination of poverty and urban decay.

On the other hand, it is not unrealistic to insist that city governments work on the quality of education, jurisdiction permitting or jurisdiction expanded to claim authority over education; and on community economic development; improved transportation access to employment; information systems to improve the efficiency of local and regional labor markets; one-stop centers for welfare, training, counseling, work preparedness, and job finding; the availability of housing for low-income households; effective job training; low-cost child care; and enforcement of nondiscrimination in housing, employment, and other areas. The agenda of typical black and biracial regimes and coalitions has been unsatisfactorily limited. These coalitions and the multiracial coalitions that form to take their place will have to develop a more imaginative, persuasive, and effective agenda than they have developed so far.

Vigorous programs in these areas, an "opportunity-expansion" regime in Clarence Stone's words, might indeed make a dent in poverty if leaders and voters can find the political agenda and craft the coalitions that will support them (Stone, 1993).

Even though multiracial coalitions are difficult to form, in "the post-incorporation world" of multiracial cities, it is essential to learn how to bring many groups together. What does not work is a single-minded focus on one's own race or ethnicity. "Using ethnicity as a bond for coalitions—rather than addressing the serious economic and social issues of community life—will have the paradoxical effect of exacerbating coalition tensions" (Sonenshein, 1997b, pp. 273–274). And multiracial coalitions and leaders must go beyond the electoral in the search for vehicles for equality, including community-based organizations (Herbert, 1997).

Potential leaders and activists of multiracial coalitions have often based their careers on cultivating their own groups—they will need to learn new strategies. They, and all of us, will have to learn to formulate issues and deal with each other in ways that respect the position and history of each group and the differences between them while nurturing and focusing on common values and common interests.

If African Americans have not been "taken" by political incorporation, neither have they been "taken in." They have insisted on coming in. Of course, insistence was not enough to achieve political incorporation—they carefully developed trust, they made artful use of issues, they envisioned that which seemed most unlikely, and they fostered coalitions that reduced the obstacles to equality, but not enough. That agenda remains unfinished.

NOTES

[1]Browning, Marshall & Tabb, 1984, 1985, p. 25. The cities were San Francisco, San Jose, Oakland, Sacramento, Berkeley, Stockton, Richmond, Hayward, Daly City, and Vallejo. These cities ring San Francisco Bay except for Sacramento and Stockton, which lie in the San Joaquin Valley, the agricultural interior between coastal hills and the Sierra Nevada.

[2]But African Americans continued to be largely excluded from city government and subject to substantial official discrimination in some cities; of the cities studied in Browning, Marshall & Tabb, 1990 and 1997, these were Miami (Florida) and Vallejo (California).

[3]Philip Isenberg (white) put together a multiracial coalition in Sacramento, California, that genuinely incorporated black and Latino leadership as well as electoral support. It survives still, now led by a Latino mayor.

[4]On machines and the trials of black incorporation in multiracial-multieth-nic cities, see chapters by Mollenkopf (New York), Keiser (Philadelphia), Orr (Baltimore), Pinderhughes (Chicago), and DeLeon (San Francisco) in Browning, Marshall & Tabb, 1997, and by Starks & Preston (Chicago) in Browning, Marshall & Tabb, 1990. Other barriers to dominant-coalition representation are summarized in Browning, Marshall & Tabb, 1997, pp. 284–285.

[5]Harold Washington (black) was elected mayor of Chicago in 1983 and re-elected in 1987, but died shortly after. His council-appointed successor, Eugene Sawyer, also black, lost to Richard M. Daley in a special election in 1989.

[6]See the chapters on these cities by Keiser, Mollenkopf, Pinderhughes, and Sonenshein in Browning, Marshall & Tabb, 1997.

[7]We mean by this language not a description of any particular politician, but an illustration of how perceptions can fall into place so as to weaken otherwise accessible liberal impulses.

[8]Tilove, 1996. Tilove writes: "Richard Zamora, who leads the Hispanic city employees' organization in Oakland known as Amigos: 'Oakland is a multicultural city. It just got stuck thinking it was a black city.' "

[9]"A fourth and related dimension of incorporation is the integration of private civil rights and uplift organizations into a regime of race relations management driven by incrementalist, insider negotiation" (Reed, 1995, p. 184).

[10]See Browning, Marshall & Tabb, 1984, 1985, pp. 48–53, for an account of the formation of the first biracial coalition in Berkeley in 1955.

[11]We do not mean to imply by the shorthand term "interests" that they are given. In the practice of city governments, however, a known set of interests has come to the fore at the intersection of what African Americans have demanded and what courts, state legislatures, the federal government, and other powerful entities are willing to accept.

[12]The last white mayors of Los Angeles and Philadelphia before biracial coalitions propelled African Americans into the mayor's office.

[13]The twenty-one cities reported in Browning, Marshall & Tabb, 1997, included seven of the largest twelve cities in the country, by the 1990 census. All of the twenty-one cities had populations greater than 87,400 in 1990, and the percentage of white non-Hispanic city population was less than 65 percent in every case. Ninety-seven other U.S. cities also met both those criteria in 1990. See Browning, Marshall & Tabb, 1997, Figure 1.1, p. 7.

[14]According to Harden, 1997, there has been a 56 percent increase in complaints about police misconduct in New York since Giuliani came into office.

[15]*The New York Times* quoted Mayor Giuliani's predecessor as mayor on August 17 (Barry, 1997):

> Dinkins said the Giuliani administration's aggressive approach to law
> enforcement, typified by its quality-of-life crackdown, encourages

officers to treat city residents in a brusque manner approaching harassment.

"What happens is the police officer who is good and honest and fair-minded, that won't be a problem for him or her," Dinkins said. "But for those police officers who are inclined to step over the line, it's real dangerous, because they think that it is sanctioned to behave as they wish."

REFERENCES

Barry, D. (1997, August 17). Second officer faces charges in torture case. *The New York Times.* <http://www.nytimes.com>

Barry, D. (1998, March 27). Giuliani dismisses police proposals by his task force. *The New York Times,* Metropolitan Desk. <http://www.nytimes.com>

Browning, R.P., Marshall, D.R., & Tabb, D.H. (1984, 1985). *Protest is not enough; The struggle of Blacks and Hispanics for equality in urban politics.* Berkeley: University of California Press.

Browning, R.P., Marshall, D.R., & Tabb, D. H. (eds.) (1990, 1997). *Racial politics in American cities.* White Plains, NY: Longman.

Cooper, M. (1997, August 18). 2nd officer gives account of sex assault of Haitian. *The New York Times.* <http://www.nytimes.com>

DeLeon, R.E. (1997). Progressive politics in the left coast city: San Francisco. In Browning, Marshall, & Tabb (eds.), *Racial politics in American cities* (2nd ed.), pp. 137–159.

Fried, J.P. (1998, February 27). U.S. takes over the Louima case; 5th suspect, a sergeant, is indicted. *The New York Times,* Metropolitan Desk. <http://www.nytimes.com>

Harden, B. (1997, August 15). Mayor shakes up N.Y. precinct after attack on immigrant. *San Francisco Chronicle,* p. A4.

Herbert, B. (1997, August 3). Brick by brick. *The New York Times,* sect. 4, p. 13.

Keiser, R.A. (1997). After the first black mayor: Fault lines in Philadelphia's biracial coalition. In Browning, Marshall, & Tabb (eds.), *Racial politics in American cities* (2nd ed.), pp. 65–93.

Kifner, J. (1998, January 15). Louima says his attackers did not yell "Giuliani time." *The New York Times,* Metropolitan Desk. <http://www.nytimes.com>

Los Angeles Times (1998, June 14). Profile of the electorate: CNN/*Los Angeles Times* exit poll conducted June 2, 1998. <http://www.latimes.com/HOME/NEWS/POLLS/>

Mollenkopf, J. (1990). New York: The great anomaly. In Browning, Marshall, & Tabb (eds.), *Racial politics in American cities* (1st ed.), pp. 75–87.

Mollenkopf, J. (1997). New York: The great anomaly. In Browning, Marshall, & Tabb (eds.), *Racial politics in American cities* (2nd ed.), pp. 95–117.

Orr, M. (1997). The struggle for black empowerment in Baltimore: Electoral control and governing coalitions. In Browning, Marshall, & Tabb (eds.), *Racial politics in American cities* (2nd ed.), pp. 201–219.

Perry, H.L. (1997). The evolution and impact of biracial coalitions and black mayors in Birmingham and New Orleans. In Browning, Marshall, & Tabb (eds.), *Racial politics in American cities* (2nd ed.), pp. 179–200.

Pinderhughes, D.M. (1997). An examination of Chicago politics for evidence of political incorporation and representation. In Browning, Marshall, & Tabb (eds.), *Racial politics in American cities* (2nd ed.), pp. 117–135.

Reed, A., Jr. (1988). The black urban regime: Structural origins and constraints. In M. P. Smith (ed.) *Power, community and the city* (1988). Quoted in Browning, Marshall, & Tabb, *Racial politics* (1997), p. 292.

Reed, A., Jr. (1995). Demobilization in the new black political regime: Ideological capitulation and radical failure in the postsegregation era. In M.P. Smith & J.R. Feagin, eds., *The bubbling cauldron: race, ethnicity, and the urban crisis.* Minneapolis: Minnesota University Press.

Smith, R.C. (1992). "Politics" is not enough: The institutionalization of the African American freedom movement. In R.C. Gomes & L.F. Williams (eds.), *From exclusion to inclusion: The long struggle for African American political power,* pp. 97–126. Westport, CT: Greenwood Press.

Smith, R.C. (1996). *We have no leaders: African Americans in the post-civil rights era.* Albany: State University of New York Press.

Sonenshein, R.J. (1997a). Post-incorporation politics in Los Angeles. In Browning, Marshall & Tabb (eds.), *Racial politics in American cities* (2nd ed.), pp. 39–63.

Sonenshein, R.J. (1997b). The prospects for multiracial coalitions: Lessons from America's three largest cities. In Browning, Marshall, & Tabb (eds.), *Racial politics in American cities* (2nd ed.), pp. 261–276.

Starks, R.T., & Preston, M. B. (1990). Harold Washington and the politics of reform in Chicago: 1983–1987. In Browning, Marshall, & Tabb (eds.), *Racial politics in American cities* (1st ed.), pp. 88–107.

Stone, C.N. (1990). Race and regime in Atlanta. In Browning, Marshall, & Tabb (eds.), *Racial politics in American cities* (1st ed.), pp. 125–139.

Stone, C.N. (1993). Urban regimes and the capacity to govern: A political economy approach. *Journal of Urban Affairs,* 15, 1, pp. 1–28.

Stone, C.N., & Pierannunzi, C. (1997). Atlanta and the limited reach of electoral control. In Browning, Marshall, & Tabb (eds.), *Racial politics in American cities* (2nd ed.), pp. 163–178.

Tilove, J. (1996, December 8). Minorities fighting each other for power; Many ready to abandon idea of rainbow coalitions. Newhouse News Service. In *The Times-Picayune*, p. A20.

Warren, C.L. (1997). Hispanic incorporation and structural reform in Miami. In Browning, Marshall, & Tabb (eds.), *Racial politics in American cities* (2nd ed.), pp. 223–246.

CHAPTER 7

Analyzing Urban Regime Change
Black Power, White Backlash,
and Shades of Gray[1]

RICHARD A. KEISER

For students of regime change, the 1990s have been a bountiful source of empirical data. In four of America's largest cities, elected white mayors have succeeded black mayors. In New York, Rudolph Giuliani defeated one-term mayor David Dinkins; in Los Angeles, Mayor Tom Bradley retired after serving from 1973 to 1993 and was succeeded by white Republican Richard Riordan; in Chicago, Richard M. Daley became mayor after defeating the city's second black mayor, Eugene Sawyer, in the Democratic primary; and in Philadelphia, Edward Rendell was elected mayor after Wilson Goode served the maximum two consecutive terms.

According to journalist Jim Sleeper, these election outcomes indicate that black mayors, who "cry racism," are being defeated by politically centrist white men who tout "a can-do pragmatism and a common civic identity that is more than the sum of skin tones, genders, sexual orientations and resentments" (Sleeper, 1993, pp. 20–25). Sleeper labels the two groups of leaders Rainbow I and Rainbow II mayors. He further elaborates that black Rainbow I mayors who headed multiracial coalitions were pro-choice and pro-gay rights left-liberals and were overly concerned with identity politics. They pursued redistributive policies that pitted identity groups against each other and were unwilling to take steps to rein in rampant fiscal profligacy. They are being replaced by Rainbow II mayors who are defined as businesslike reformers seeking tax relief, fiscal conservatism, and less generous union contracts. These mayors have gained the support of Latinos and blacks who are allegedly disillusioned with identity politics and no longer seek redistributive policies based on identity, particularly affirmative action, from government.

157

Sleeper's provocative presentation should prompt urban scholars to address, in a considerably more sober and less invidious manner, the following questions: Is the ascendance of these four white mayors linked? Is black political power in urban America being repudiated and rolled back? What has become of the coalitions that elected the four black mayors? Who are the winners and losers produced by the replacement of these black mayors? Have similar changes taken place in the executive office of other major cities? Have we seen similar changes in representation on the city councils of these cities? This chapter offers answers to some of these questions and proffers an analysis of the politics surrounding alleged regime change in two of the aforementioned cities, Philadelphia and New York.

FOUR CASES IN AN INHOSPITABLE UNIVERSE

These four cases certainly suggest there is a phenomenon to be explained; Sleeper's article explained the demise of black Rainbow I mayors as due to a growing disdain for identity politics among whites, Latinos, Asians, and even some African Americans. But in other large cities of 200,000 or more population, such as Detroit, New Orleans, Atlanta, and Washington, DC, black mayors continued to be elected. In the Motor City, Dennis Archer became the city's second black mayor when he succeeded the retiring Coleman Young. In the Big Easy, Marc Morial was the third black mayor to be elected, with each serving the maximum two consecutive terms. In the Big Peach, former city councilman Bill Campbell became Atlanta's third black mayor, continuing black control of this office that began in 1973. In Washington, DC, Marion Barry returned to the office he previously held when he was once again elected mayor. One might contrast the two sets of four cities and conclude that they do not offer robust support for the hypothesis that black political power in urban America is being repudiated.

But one might plausibly reject this conclusion and argue instead that Detroit, New Orleans, Atlanta, and Washington share a characteristic with salient electoral implications that distinguishes them from the cities in which white mayors were elected: In 1990 blacks were the overwhelming majority in each of the cities that elected black mayors, as Table 7.1 indicates, while in the cities in which white mayors succeeded black mayors, blacks remained a minority of the population.[2]

Cities with majority black populations are important to study for a variety of questions. But with respect to coalition formation, the dynamics that black leadership face in these cities (whether or not the leader-

Table 7.1. Percent Black in City Population, 1990

New York	28.7
Los Angeles	14.0
Chicago	39.1
Philadelphia	39.9
Detroit	75.7
Washington, DC	65.8
New Orleans	61.9
Atlanta	67.1

Source: U.S. Bureau of the Census. (1994). *County and City Data Book, 1994.*
Washington, DC: U.S. Government Printing Office.

ship is united or fragmented) is different than in cities where blacks are
not the majority and all black leaders are forced to build coalitions to win
citywide office.

Are there very large cities (greater than 200,000 population) in
which blacks are not the majority that have elected black mayors? Or do
we see electoral outcomes in other cities that bolster a hypothesis of rollback of black political power and dissolution of established biracial
coalitions? In seven other very large cities with minority black populations, black mayors have been newly elected or re-elected in the 1990s:
Cleveland (47 percent black) re-elected Mike White, Denver (13 percent
black) re-elected Wellington Webb, Minneapolis (13 percent black) re-
elected Sharon Sayles Belton, San Francisco (11 percent black) elected
Willie Brown, Dallas (30 percent black) elected Ron Kirk, Houston (28
percent black) elected Lee Daniels, and Seattle (10 percent black) re-
elected Norm Rice. The larger universe of cities that we have mentioned
in this discussion is inhospitable to the hypothesis that a rollback of
black political power has characterized the close of the twentieth century. The experiences of New York, Los Angeles, Chicago, and Philadelphia seem isolated and atypical rather than modal and a basis for
discussing trends. There may be no single set of phenomena that explain
the similar outcome of white mayors succeeding black mayors (e.g., the
death of identity politics).

Must the ascendance of white mayors represent a transformation
and rollback of political power in these cities? Is there no other perspective available for interpreting such events? To pursue this question, we need to go beyond a mere look at the race of the mayor and

systematically distinguish between regime change and mere personnel change that does not affect regime type.

TYPOLOGY OF REGIME CHANGE: STATUS QUO, TRANSFORMATION, AND REVERSION

In response to the query of whether there has been a regime change, there are three possibilities on which I will focus: maintenance of the *status quo; transformation* to some new type of regime with a different governing coalition and different answers to the questions of who governs and who benefits; and *reversion* to the previous status quo.[3]

The first regime change path, status quo maintenance, represents no significant change in regime although there may be changes in personnel or issues on the policy agenda. A mayor may win re-election and change members of his or her cabinet or some loyal members of city council may be replaced by other equally loyal members. Although there are changes in personnel, the character of the regime that exists does not change. This could be the case even if the person occupying the mayor's office changes; one need only think of how little change took place in ethnic political machines when the boss replaced one mayor with another to recognize that mayoral change is not synonymous with regime change. For illustrative purposes, a more recent example would be Mayor Jane Byrne (1979–1983) in Chicago. She was elected by a somewhat different coalition than her predecessor in Chicago and she ran on a platform that called for reform of the Democratic machine and promised new political opportunities for formerly subordinated groups. Yet it was quickly evident that this was nothing more than duplicity; Byrne fortified the ailing Chicago Democratic machine, she did not reform or dismantle it. As well, even though she benefited from an increased black turnout and overwhelming black support, her administration continued to politically subordinate blacks. The most important elected official in the political system changed, but the regime did not (Grimshaw, 1992; Keiser, 1997b).

A second possible outcome of regime change analysis is discovery of a clear and definite transformation from one kind of regime to another. In such a case the questions of who governs and who benefits point to a decidedly different set of interests than previously. For instance, the election of Republican Fiorello La Guardia as mayor of New York produced a genuine transformation in the city, crippling the Tammany machine that had survived so many challenges, and yielding considerable progress in the political incorporation of Jewish- and Italian-Americans (Kessner, 1989). The transformation of Oakland from a regime dominated by a conservative coalition that excluded blacks to a biracial coalition regime that advanced black incorporation would be another example (Browning, Marshall, & Tabb, 1984).

As these examples suggest, analyses of regime transformation typically would reveal a different set of public and private sector actors and a different policy agenda. Yet, this is not an imperative. A mayor and city council, for instance, may initially govern in a way that is responsive to particular private interests and certain community organizations and then may shift to governing more in accord with a different set of interests, for a number of reasons. These would include: elected officials taking their initial electoral constituency for granted; exogenous events making the pursuit of one set of policies no longer possible or another set of policies much more profitable, such as a sizable decrease in federal aid to a city; or a city leader seeking to nourish new informal alliances to facilitate his or her pursuit of a statewide office such as governor. For instance, scholars of Los Angeles politics typically argue that Mayor Tom Bradley (1973–1993) initially led a regime that was focused on achieving African American and Jewish political incorporation, generally liberal and pro-environment policies, and downtown development. But by the mid-1980s the regime Bradley headed was much more pro-growth than liberal environmentalist and the benefits of black political incorporation were not being expanded beyond the middle class (Jackson & Preston, 1994). In Bradley's case the regime transformation was due to a number of phenomena that produced the decay of the logic of one regime and the emergence of another; in other instances regime transformation might be caused by a single, dramatic event such as a fiscal crisis, a political scandal, or the death of a political leader.

The third broad category that regime change analysis may describe is what I label reversion to the previous status quo. This takes place when a regime transformation is short-lived and never fully consolidated. After a brief interregnum, the answers to the questions of who governs and who benefits are once again largely the same as they were prior to the aborted transformation. In regime reversions the events that seemed to presage regime transformation are subsequently understood to be ephemeral phenomenon. The potential for regime transformation did exist, and at a particular snapshot in time it may have appeared that regime transformation had taken place. But events did not pan out, opportunities were not taken advantage of, and a new regime did not stabilize. For activists and citizens, these short-lived administrations are significant, but from a diachronic perspective they are periods of turbulence caused by fleeting phenomena. The reform administrations that Plunkitt of Tammany Hall derided as "mornin' glories [that] looked lovely in the mornin' and withered up in a short time" are examples of regime reversions (Riordon, 1963). The reformers won some major city offices for one or perhaps two elections, but they were unsuccessful in forging anything more than a temporary coalition; the preferences of the electorate and the governing ethos of the city were not rewritten.

In the remainder of this chapter I will use this typology as a tool to explain the political events that produced the election of white mayors in two of the four cities that previously were led by black mayors. (Space limitations preclude a full discussion of all four cities.) These explanations represent alternative hypotheses in contradistinction to the view that the election of white mayors represented a rollback of black political power and a rejection of identity politics and redistributive policies.

STATUS QUO MAINTENANCE IN PHILADELPHIA

In 1991 Edward Rendell succeeded Wilson Goode as mayor of Philadelphia and the city went from having a black mayor to being governed by a white mayor. Is this an indicator of the rollback of black political power or disintegration of the biracial coalition that twice elected Goode? The answer offered here to this question is, no, as analysis that goes beyond the simplistic equation of white mayor succeeds black mayor, hence black politics is repudiated, will reveal. Philadelphia is an example of status quo maintenance in which a governing regime changes some personnel and some policy agenda items without altering its basic character. Ed Rendell did not defeat Wilson Goode; Goode was forced to quit the mayor's office after serving the maximum two consecutive terms. Rendell did defeat leading black candidates who aspired to the office; however, Rendell comes from the same moderate-to-liberal, biracial faction that produced Wilson Goode. Rendell previously had enjoyed the electoral support of the biracial, reformist faction of the Democratic party. Moreover, the substance of Rendell's governance is quite similar to Wilson Goode's, although their personal styles are very different. Finally, Philadelphia's powerful city council is at least as influenced by black leadership as it was during the Goode administration and there is little evidence that the mayor and city council have initiated any policies that have resulted in the rollback of black political power.

Goode and Rendell: Continuity of the Liberal, Biracial Regime

Ed Rendell broke into the city's politics in 1977 by defeating the incumbent Democratic district attorney who had been accused repeatedly of petty corruption, had made plea bargaining the default option of his office, and had taken no steps to investigate or prosecute the numerous charges of police brutality against Frank Rizzo's police force. The team that helped him run his campaign and construct his electoral coalition was a group of biracial reformers (including an umbrella black leadership organization and the leadership of the city's Americans for Democratic Action chapter) who had come together a year before to organize an effort to recall Mayor Frank Rizzo. One of Rendell's first actions as district attorney was to create a police brutality investigative unit, and the unit he created had teeth.

After his re-election romp, in which he won every ward in the city, it became clear that Rendell was one of the most popular candidates in the party among both blacks and whites. In 1986 Rendell sought the party's nomination for governor. He sought and received the endorsement of the Black Clergy of Philadelphia and Vicinity, a powerful organization with a proven record of influencing black voting behavior; but he ultimately did not win the primary. The clergy organization believed that Rendell had agreed not to run against Goode in 1987 in exchange for their endorsement; when Rendell did seek the Democratic party mayoral nomination in 1987 against incumbent Wilson Goode, the black ministers charged him with reneging on the promise. Rendell's claim that he never made such a promise earned the enmity of the black ministers.

Rendell entered the Democratic mayoral field in 1991 knowing that his only chance of winning was if the black vote was split (Paolantonio, 1991). Black voters were the majority of the party and white voters told pollsters that they were prepared to vote for another black candidate (even though they overwhelmingly disapproved of Goode's performance). Two very serious black mayoral candidates did emerge. With the black vote divided, Rendell easily won both the Democratic primary (gaining significant black support as he almost always had) and the mayoral election (Keiser, 1997a). No black candidate emerged to run as an independent mayoral candidate in 1991. Nor did Rendell face any black challengers in either the 1995 Democratic primary (uncontested) or general election. He won 77 percent of the vote in his 1995 re-election and won about 90 percent of the vote in predominantly black wards. These data provide a strong basis for rejecting the claim that

Rendell's mayoralty indicates a repudiation of the agenda of black leaders or voters.

Governance in the Rendell Administration

Rendell has become one of the most esteemed mayors in the nation because in his first year he produced a small budgetary surplus in a city that had a junk bond rating and a $250 million cumulative deficit. Not only is he a friend of President Bill Clinton, he is also a poster boy for the *Wall Street Journal, The Economist,* and the conservative Manhattan Institute because he rolled back union benefits and froze wages to save $78 million annually. But Wilson Goode had also instituted policies of fiscal retrenchment that had some negative impacts on traditional Democratic constituencies such as labor and blacks. For instance, Goode's efforts to restore fiscal discipline to the city led him to refuse the demands of the public employees union and withstand a twenty-day strike by predominantly black sanitation workers in the summer of 1986. Two years later Goode won another confrontation with the sanitation workers and reduced the size of trash collection crews from three or four to two. This decision eliminated the jobs of about 1,500 workers (Paolantonio, 1993). Goode's inability to avert a fiscal crisis had less to do with the liberal spending of the mayor and much more to do with the personal political ambitions of two black councilmembers who believed (one incorrectly, one correctly) that preventing stabilization during the Goode administration would give them a better chance to claim considerable credit for the accomplishment in the next administration. Councilman Lucien Blackwell saw himself as Mayor Lucien Blackwell presiding over a return to fiscal well-being, but he did not anticipate dividing the black vote with another black candidate and paving the way for Rendell. Councilman John Street would become city council president after the election (when the incumbent retired) and he saw himself as orchestrating the city's climb back to fiscal health along with the next mayor. Street's vision became reality and there is not a single knowledgeable observer of the city's politics who would not give at least half of the credit for the city's financial rebound to the city council president.

Sleeper's portrayal of Rainbow I black mayors as being obsessed with left-liberalism, identity politics, and racial divisiveness—crying racism as he so delicately phrased it—also does not ring true as a description of Wilson Goode. Rendell is no more centrist than Goode, nor is he any less inclined to support a woman's right to an abortion or gay rights. True to his background in public administration and management rather than politics, Goode was often quoted as saying there was no black or white way to deliver public services. Other politicians and mayoral wannabees in Philadelphia did play identity politics as if it was the only card in their hand, but not Goode. Lumping Goode together with such politicians is like pairing together Colin Powell and Louis Farrakhan.

Rendell and Goode are similar in another way; both espouse good government ideals at the same time that they do nothing to stop the machine-style politics that is alive and well in Philadelphia. After initial resistance, Goode learned how to "go along to get along"; Rendell seemed to need even less prodding (Keiser, 1997a).

The willingness to privatize municipal services is yet another thing that does not distinguish Rendell from his black predecessor, contrary to Sleeper. During Goode's two terms the city increased its overall spending on privatized contracts from 22 percent to 37 percent of the city's budget (Meyers & Paolantonio, 1991). Mayor Goode shifted all six public golf courses to private management and turned a $1 million a year loss into a $500,000 profit for the city. He also privatized the trolley service in Fairmount Park, all road resurfacing, and custodial services in certain buildings, including city hall (Hinds, 1991). Goode tried to inaugurate the privatization of the city's computer operation and its trash collection; both initiatives were blocked by a city council that did not want to balance the city's budget on the backs of the largely black municipal workforce. Goode's privatization efforts drew national attention before this policy approach became commonplace in cities ("Privatization Called 'Wave of Future,' Maybe Only Way to Pay," 1990). Mayor Rendell has taken only a few steps toward privatization and in some instances he has backed away from initial plans for privatization (Collins & Marder, 1997). During the mayoral campaign he would go no further than saying that his administration would privatize "if the unions could not perform more efficiently" (Meyers & Paolantonio, 1991, p. 1C). Rendell's administration has shifted about 800 workers from public sector status to the private sector; more than 27,000 still remain on the city payroll. In many instances the same person still holds the job but receives a less costly compensation package. Typically there are no pension plans and much less comprehensive health plans. Adding together the impact of privatization, unfilled vacancies, and new hires, Rendell in his first term reduced the city payroll by about 900. Mayor Bill Green (1980–1984) reduced the city payroll in his single term by almost 2,300 workers. Mayor Wilson Goode (1984–1992) reduced the city workforce by nearly 3,800 in his two terms in office. Reducing the clout of unions like the American Federation of State, County and Municipal Employees is not a new sport in American cities. The elimination of federal CETA funding in the early 1980s has pushed mayors throughout the country into this game (Loeb, 1994). Rendell's privatization initiatives are hardly the kind of public policy reorientation that could distinguish him from Mayor Goode or from black mayors in other cities.

Although the mayor is often a city's most prominent policymaker, regime change cannot be equated with mayoral change. The fact that power is shared with a city council represents a structural factor that can promote or obstruct regime change. In Philadelphia, black city councilmembers pull the strings of government quite effectively for their constituents. In a city in which about 40 percent of the population is black, seven of the seventeen city council members (41 percent) are black, including the president of the city council. Black city council members acted independently to protect constituent interests under the previous moderate white mayor and under Wilson Goode. There is no indication that they behave any differently in the Rendell era. Mayor Rendell and city council president John Street govern as a team. The two meet every week accompanied only by their most trusted advisor. Council president Street orchestrates an unusual degree of unanimous consent from the council by mixing quiet negotiations and compromise with threats. He waves a big stick that includes total control of all city council perks (e.g., office space, parking) and control of appointments to all committees and organization of the council's calendar of legislation. The operation runs quietly and efficiently, and Rendell and Street share the credit. As of May, 1999, Street had won the Democratic party mayoral nomination.

The election of Edward Rendell does not tell us much about the rollback of black political power. Rather, Rendell's election sheds light on the problems of factionalism and disunity that can emerge in the black community once the unifying impact of electing a first black mayor has been removed.[4] Rendell's election also reminds students of urban politics that moderate, growth-oriented biracial regimes were originally led by whites and can once again be headed by a white mayor. The continuing influence that black political leaders exercise on the city council also should remind journalists and other students of the politics of minorities in urban America that victories in the struggle for political incorporation are won not solely through control of the mayor's office, and that these victories, once institutionalized, prove resistant to corrosive forces.

REGIME REVERSION IN NEW YORK

At first blush, New York presents a sharp contrast to Philadelphia. If in Philadelphia we see significant continuity, in New York dramatic change seems apparent. The administration of Rudolph Giuliani represents a rejection of the liberal, biracial regime of David Dinkins that took significant steps forward on minority incorporation. New York appears to represent evidence in support of the hypothesis that the recent elections of white mayors are indicative of a repudiation and rollback of the gains won by blacks in biracial coalitions during the 1980s (and earlier in some cities where these coalitions were long-lived). However, I will argue that the Giuliani regime is an example of *regime reversion*, in this case to the conservative, nonminority incorporative, antiredistributive politics of Mayor Abraham Beame (1973–1977) and Mayor Edward I. Koch (1977–1989). The Giuliani regime cannot represent a repudiation of biracial regimes and black political incorporation because these phenomenon were *unconsolidated* in New York. Dinkins's election was a product of ephemeral circumstances (which I explain later). The Koch regime was the status quo and, after one term of David Dinkins, the Giuliani administration has returned New York to the status quo ante. The argument presented here is not deterministic and does not imply that Dinkins could not have installed and consolidated a regime that incorporated blacks and perhaps other subordinated groups. There are myriad possible outcomes in politics. But Dinkins and his allies were unsuccessful in consolidating power and transforming the city's politics; instead, there was a reversion to the status quo ante.

The Giuliani Administration as Reversion to the Koch Regime

In rejecting the liberalism of David Dinkins, New Yorkers were continuing down a path that they began more than two decades earlier. Brecher and Horton mark 1969 as a watershed in the city's political culture, with conservatives and liberals polarizing on race and the majority of the city's white majority supporting conservative candidates: "The most dramatic change in 1969 was the sharply increased role of race relations as a political issue. This had national as well as distinctly local origins. . . . The divisive campaign relating to a referendum over the creation of a civilian complaint review board for the Police Department in 1966 and the bitter struggle over school decentralization in 1968 divided New Yorkers over racial issues in enduring ways" (Brecher & Horton, 1993, pp. 89–90). New Yorkers turned away from the liberalism of John

Lindsay and elected Mayor Abraham Beame in 1973. In 1977, they again rejected liberalism and elected the pragmatic, moderate Edward Koch over Mario Cuomo. By Koch's third term, he had moved so far to the center that he won the endorsement of the Republican party as well. Yet Koch was still able to forge what Mollenkopf loosely labeled a "rainbow coalition" of most of the city's white voters, a majority of Latinos, and a significant minority of black voters (Mollenkopf, 1994). Giuliani's electoral coalition is quite similar except that the proportions of Latinos and black voters are still smaller. Giuliani's election should not be construed as a shift to the far right. Although a Republican, the mayor has described himself as "a moderate Democrat" (Pinkerton, 1997) and his platform includes a number of stances that Sleeper ascribes to Rainbow I mayors. Giuliani supports legal abortion, gun control, domestic partnership benefits for gay couples, and criticizes the GOP for threatening the rights of legal immigrants. He supported liberal Democrat Mario Cuomo against Republican George Pataki in the 1994 governor's race. John Mollenkopf noted that one important commonality between the Koch and Giuliani administrations is that both "view blacks as the opposition" (1997, 100).

Anti-crime policies that have produced claims of racism and discrimination have been a centerpiece of the urban agendas of both mayors. Both Koch and Giuliani have rejected independent police review in stark contrast to the Dinkins administration which created the Civilian Complaint Review Board (CCRB). The CCRB was created in late 1992 and was the first independent board charged with investigating public complaints of police brutality (not corruption) in the city's history. Candidate Giuliani was a vocal critic of the creation of the board and marched in a protest at City Hall with 10,000 off-duty officers. The CCRB has accomplished little and the Giuliani administration has worked to undercut it. The mayor tried to eliminate one-quarter of the investigatory staff in his 1998 budget, but the city council restored the positions. Similar cuts were submitted in Giuliani's previous budgets. The police commissioner (appointed by the mayor) has not treated the CCRB seriously and has not handed down serious punishments to officers who are found guilty of misconduct, according to officials from the New York Civil Liberties Union (Barry, 1997).

Giuliani's administration has gained national acclaim for cutting the city's murder rate by 60 percent and overall crime rate by 43 percent over three years (1993–1996). This was done through a policy of using computers to identify crime hot spots and then holding precinct commanders responsible for deploying additional officers and producing results. Those who produced results were promoted. Given this incentive system for results, it is perhaps not surprising that there has been a dramatic increase in the number of citizen complaints of police brutality and misconduct. From 1993 to 1996 (the year that police commissioner William Bratton left the New York Police Department in a dispute with Mayor Giuliani) citizen complaints rose 65 percent (Pray, 1997). Yet it was not until the brutal sodomization and beating of Haitian immigrant Abner Louima by police officers in the 70th Precinct station house became an issue in the 1997 mayoral race that Giuliani acted on the problem and added $1.5 million and twenty-five new staff members to the CCRB budget (Cooper, 1997).

In the public policy arena, both Koch and Giuliani also instituted policies of fiscal retrenchment that garnered the support of the city's financial elite. Both recognized that the city's labor unions have been backpedaling and accordingly developed alliances with the unions based on pragmatism and survival rather than liberalism and empowerment. Both mayors share the view that the city should not intervene in the housing market. Because of intense criticism of Koch for his lack of a housing program, he finally instituted a subsidized housing program in his final term; still, many more middle-income units were produced than low-income units and low-income rehabilitation was concentrated, in effect ghettoized, in the South Bronx and Harlem (Mollenkopf, 1994). Giuliani's market-driven policy of housing neglect is more straightforward and consequent de facto support for private sector–driven gentrification is unabashed; the city has begun selling housing formerly slated for rehab or taken over for tax-payment failure (Gurwitt, 1995). Both mayors have also tried to reduce the city's costly involvement in health care for the poor by selling the city's public hospitals. This was part of an overall attack on poorer beneficiaries of public services. In the early Koch years, according to Mollenkopf, "Those who depended on public assistance fared the worst. . . . In relative terms, the Koch administration reduced the budget shares going toward social services, property services and education" (1994, p. 138). In the Giuliani administration, the biggest cuts were inflicted on the Board of Education which absorbed the largest share of more than $1 billion in cuts during the mayor's first term (Traub, 1996). Cuts to public education are particularly damaging to minorities, who represent 83 percent of public school students. Other cuts that have disproportionately affected the poor and minorities include a $700 million reduction in the Medicaid budget, and elimination of more than 1,000 welfare caseworkers, 100 homelessness caseworkers, and 1,200 other social workers. As well, funding has been cut in foster care programs, day care services, youth programs, and tuition has been increased in the city university system (Minerbrook & Ipoco, 1995; Logan, 1994).

Finally, with respect to the redistributive potential of municipal employment, both mayors reject affirmative action and minority business enterprise programs as insupportable quota systems. Giuliani ended Dinkins's minority and female contracting initiative and has labeled such set-aside programs as "fronts for out-of-town whites" (Salaam, 1996, p. 16). As a Republican mayor in the 1990s Giuliani has jumped on the bandwagon of privatization, going beyond rhetoric to pare down the city's huge bureaucracy. Koch did not attack the city's unions when he was mayor; however, during his administration spending on contracts to third parties that performed services for local government grew dramatically (Mollenkopf, 1994).

Again, regime change cannot be analyzed solely through an examination of mayoral coalitions and policies. Unlike during the Koch administration, the city council has become a powerful institution due to charter reform. The city council is overwhelmingly Democratic (forty-five of fifty-one members) and has had a very contentious relationship with the mayor. In Giuliani's first term, the council overrode ten mayoral vetoes (Toy, 1997). Yet even after court ordered redistricting to increase the number of majority minority districts in 1991, the representation of blacks and Latinos remains below the parity level for these groups' proportion of the population. In the Koch years, blacks held about 20 percent of the seats and Latinos held about 9 percent; they were about 24 percent and 20 percent of the population, respectively, for a parity score of .66. In the Giuliani administration, blacks hold 29 percent of the seats on the city council and Latinos hold 16 percent. Their respective proportions of the city population have increased to 26 and 27 percent, producing a parity score of .85 (Moss, Townsend & Tobier, 1997). In terms of other powerful citywide positions, there has been little change since the Koch administration: there remains one black and one Latino borough president. Among both blacks and Latinos divisions remain between insurgents and regulars aligned with the conservative regime leadership. Mollenkopf's 1990 conclusion remains accurate at the close of the decade: "minority elected officials are not a powerful and independent force in the overall allocation of public benefits, although they do extract rewards from the white political establishment" (Mollenkopf, 1990, p. 78). Fewer rewards are distributed to minority groups and their leaders in the Giuliani administration than was the case under Koch, but the position of blacks and Latinos—outside of the governing regime—remains the same.

Explaining Regime Reversion: Scandal and Destabilization

As a datapoint, the Dinkins election is an outlier; the trendline before (the Koch administration) and after (the Giuliani administration) follows roughly the same trajectory and this dramatically differs from the Dinkins trajectory. How and why was David Dinkins elected in the interim? There are a number of factors that can destabilize a long-standing regime and create the conditions for either regime transformation or reversion. For example, the sudden death of a leader, an external fiscal crisis like a national depression, a critical election in the sense that V. O. Key used the term, or a huge political scandal all can deal a destabilizing shock to a regime; undoubtedly there are other such factors. The Dinkins triumph provides an example of the impact one such factor, scandal, can have on a previously stable regime.

In 1985, Edward Koch was elected to his third term as mayor of New York with 76 percent of the vote. His longevity and popularity had made him a best-selling author and the undisputed national spokesperson for New York City. A record-setting fourth term seemed inevitable given the persistent fragmentation that existed among his opponents. In previous elections, candidates representing black, Latino, and white liberal factions had emerged, and their multiple candidacies assured Koch of victory and sapped the strength of his opposition.

Days after Koch took the oath of office for the third time, his close friend and Queens borough president, Donald Manes, attempted suicide. As details emerged, it became apparent that the attempt was prompted by a widening investigation of the city Parking Violations Bureau (PVB) which revealed that Manes himself had accepted at least $285,000 in bribes. Manes succeeded in a second suicide attempt on March 12, 1986. He was later named as an "unindicted co-racketeer" by a team of prosecutors led by U.S. Attorney Rudolph Giuliani (Newfield & Barrett, 1988). Stanley Friedman, the Democratic party chief of the Bronx and another Koch friend, was indicted in connection with the broadening scandal, and a series of well-publicized prosecutions followed. In all, about a dozen top Koch appointees resigned in disgrace because of "indictment, conviction or scandal" (Green, 1989, p. 422).

Voters who had supported the agenda and policies of the Koch administrations felt betrayed by the man. The cumulative effects of the scandals manifested themselves as a decline in Koch's public and organizational support. By late 1988, Koch's approval ratings had fallen to around 35 percent (Klein, 1988); nearly three quarters of the city had approved of his performance in his heyday (McNickle, 1993, p. 299). In a January 31, 1989 poll which asked voters whether they thought Koch should run again, 73 percent of all voters—and 75 percent of Democrats—said no ("Voters More Than Bored . . . ," 1989). In mid-June polling, Koch stood thirteen percentage points behind both Dinkins and Giuliani (Logan, 1989b).

The repercussions of the scandals also splintered Koch's organizational base. In previous re-election campaigns, Koch received active and unanimous support from Democratic county chairmen. In this race, the political climate changed dramatically. The Manhattan and Bronx organizations endorsed Dinkins. Brooklyn's Democratic leaders endorsed city comptroller Harrison J. Goldin. The Queens organization, upon which Koch had long counted for support, was also the organization most affected by the scandals, and now endorsed chairman of New York's Charter Revision Committee Richard Ravitch. Only New York's smallest borough, Staten Island, provided full organizational support to the Koch effort (Klein, 1989). The mayor's commanding electoral and organizational base of, just five years before had crumbled. J. Phillip Thompson (Thompson, 1990) argued that the disintegration of the borough organizations enabled black politicians in Queens and the Bronx to support a black mayoral challenger to Koch, a move they could not take in previous elections when their behavior was circumscribed by the choices made by the borough leadership.

A poll taken in late January 1989 found that corruption and scandals were the largest single reason New Yorkers named for opposing Koch (Logan, 1989b). Yet there were other reasons for Koch's falling popularity, including the successful mobilization of the city's blacks and Latinos behind Jesse Jackson's 1988 presidential nomination bid and the events of winter 1986 in Howard Beach, Queens, that resulted in the death of one black man and the brutal beating of two others. But these, too, were exogenous events that offer no support for the claim that Dinkins represented the culmination of years of political toil that were suddenly and summarily repudiated by Giuliani.

Like the mornin' glory reformers of the Tammany era, once the stench of the scandals had passed, Dinkins's administration was in jeopardy. Dinkins theoretically could have consolidated his political power and expanded his electoral coalition beyond the razor thin majority that gave him 48 percent of the vote to Giuliani's 46 percent. Much ink has been spilled discussing what Dinkins could have done and how events conspired against him. But for our purposes what is crucial is that enough voters switched allegiance from Dinkins to Giuliani (and some changes took place in turnout levels among supporters of each) so that Dinkins's victory margin of less than 50,000, the smallest in the city's history, was replaced by a slightly larger margin for Giuliani. Mollenkopf concluded: "the conditions that enabled a biracial coalition to elect an African American mayor proved to be short-lived in New York City. Once again, regular Democrats showed a surprising ability to restore their organizations in the wake of the scandals of 1986 and 1987; by 1993, a number of Democratic political clubs in white ethnic areas declared for Rudolph Giuliani's candidacy" (1997, p. 110). Giuliani's decisive 1997 mayoral election, with a coalition of a majority of whites, and sizable minorities of Latinos and blacks that looks much like the old Koch coalition, seems to have reconsolidated the conservative, minority cooptative regime.

Regime Reversion and the Rainbow II Hypothesis

If Giuliani's administration represents a reversion to the Koch regime type, then what conclusions can we draw with respect to the large questions with which this chapter began? Does the defeat of New York's first black mayor by a moderate white Republican represent a rollback of black political power and a repudiation of the liberal, biracial coalitions that have elected black and white mayors during the 1970s and 1980s? Have Rainbow I black mayors who emphasize divisive identity politics and who "cry racism" been replaced by Rainbow II centrists who promote a common civic identity and a new emphasis on fiscal efficiency? The foregoing analysis suggests that black political leadership, rather than being rolled back, was not very developed. During the Koch era, black leaders (and Latino leaders) repeatedly failed in efforts to unite the natural constituencies of an anti-Koch coalition behind one candidate; at times the black communities could not even persuade the strongest black candidate to run against Koch. The absence (or delegitimacy) of black leaders who were capable of forming such a coalition left a leadership vacuum that was filled by Al Sharpton, Alton Maddox, and C. Vernon Mason. It was these men who preached racial divisiveness and cried racism. Dinkins clearly was not a Rainbow I mayor who cried racism and practiced identity politics; as in Philadelphia, this description better fits blacks who failed in their efforts to be citywide leaders. David Dinkins was drafted for a mayoral run and catapulted to a position of citywide legitimacy (beyond Manhattan) by virtue of the unusual circumstances of scandals that felled the Koch administration. The "gorgeous mosaic" that elected him was as fragile as a newborn baby; it was not a mature coalition that had been nourished in successive electoral iterations. Hence, the defeat of Dinkins was not the rollback of established black political power nor was it a repudiation of a movement with deep roots. With respect to the usefulness of the Rainbow II designation, although Giuliani fits the description of this type, I have shown that Ed Koch fits at least as well. And if this is the case, then we are hardly talking about some new phenomenon in urban politics.

The More Things Change, the More They Stay the Same

New York (as well as the unexamined cases of Chicago and Los Angeles) does highlight one important piece of data, the tendency for a sizable but by no means wholesale shift of Latino voters from their previous coalition with black leaders to alliance with the new white mayors. This topic merits separate exploration that cannot be pursued here. Considerable skepticism is, however, advised regarding broad statements about the end of Latino–African American alliances such as the following: "In city after city, state after state, the two groups [Latinos and Jews] vote the same way. What they do not do—to the great surprise of leaders in both communities—is vote like African Americans" (Beinart, 1997). Data from elections in Denver, San Francisco, Minneapolis, Houston, and Dallas would not support this claim. What journalists do is one thing, but scholars should not forget the lessons of history; Italians sometimes voted with the Irish and other times voted with Jews and against the Irish. When elections were noncompetitive and the Irish were certain victors, Italians often jumped on the bandwagon and were willing to take whatever jobs, status, and other benefits the Irish would part with. But when elections were more competitive a bidding war might ensue; if Jews were seeking a different set of rewards than Italians or were more willing than the Irish to carve out a greater share for Italians, they could be more successful at wooing the Italian vote than were the Irish. Just how surprising is it that Latino voters have supported Richard M. Daley in Chicago? Latinos had supported the senior Daley and Jane Byrne when they ran the city, they shifted to Harold Washington only after he won the 1983 Democratic mayoral primary, and they shifted back to Daley once it became obvious that he would be the benefactor of divisions within his black opposition. Finally, should we be surprised that Latino support for

Giuliani grew in his two races against Dinkins and his recent victory over Ruth Messinger? No, because a mobilized Latino electorate gave Mayor Koch about 62 percent of their vote in the 1985 mayoral election. Mollenkopf (1994, pp. 184–185) wrote that Giuliani's "largest strategic blunder" in his 1989 loss to Dinkins was to not make a greater effort among Latinos because all evidence suggested that they were predisposed to vote for a conservative white candidate. Party label is not irrelevant to Latinos. But in 1997 white Republicans Giuliani and Riordan (as well as Daley) shared one thing with black Democrats Webb, Brown, and Sayles Belton: they all faced opponents who were longshots. Latino support over the long haul has appeared to be much more pragmatic than ideological.

With respect to blacks, there is little evidence to support the claim that black political power is being rolled back at the mayoral level. In cities where it has been underdeveloped and precarious, such as New York and Chicago, black incorporation still has a long way to go. In other cities where black political power has developed incrementally, such as Philadelphia, rollback of incorporation would require the defeat of minorities and their allies on the city council and in the mayor's office as well as a reorientation among private sector elites.

NOTES

[1] I would like to thank John Mollenkopf and Katherine Underwood for comments on an earlier draft of this chapter that was presented at the 1997 American Political Science Association meetings. I would also like to thank Susannah Gallin for research assistance.

[2] Birmingham, Baltimore, and Newark are three additional cities of at least 200,000 population that are majority black and that re-elected black mayors in the 1990s.

[3] Here I use regime in the way Clarence Stone has redefined the term. I mean the governing coalition of elected and unelected actors and their formal and informal means of exercising power. See Stone (1989).

[4] For a fuller discussion of this theme in Philadelphia politics, see Keiser, 1997b.

REFERENCES

Barry, D. (1997, July 13). Independent agency fails to police the police, critics charge, *New York Times,* p. 19.

Beinart, P. (1997, August 11). New bedfellows, *New Republic*, p. 23.

Brecher, C., & Horton, R., with R.A. Cropf & D.M. Mead. (1993). *Power failure: New York City politics and policy since 1960.* New York: Oxford University Press.

Browning, R., Marshall, D.R., & Tabb, D. (1984). *Protest is not enough.* Berkeley: University of California Press.

Collins, H., & Marder, D. (1997, June 13). Mental health unit run by city gets a reprieve, *Philadelphia Inquirer,* p. 1-B.

Cooper, M. (1997, September 17). Mayor to help police monitor he had fought, *New York Times,* p. 1-B.

Green, M. (1989, March 27). With Malice toward all: The N.Y.C. scandals of Ed Koch, *Nation,* p. 422.

Grimshaw, W. (1992). *Bitter fruit: Black politics and the Chicago machine, 1931–1991.* Chicago: University of Chicago Press.

Gurwitt, R. (1995). The trials of Rudolph Giuliani, *Governing,* 8:25.

Hinds, M. de. (1991, May 14). Cash-strapped cities turn to companies to do what government once did, *New York Times,* p. 8.

Jackson, B.O., & Preston, M.B. (1994). Race and ethnicity in Los Angeles Politics. In G. E. Peterson (ed.), *Big city governance and fiscal constraints.* Washington, DC: Urban Institute Press, pp. 85–104.

Keiser, R.A. (1990). The politics of a biracial coalition in Philadelphia. In R.P. Browning, D.R. Marshall, & D. Tabb (eds.), *Racial politics in American cities.* New York: Longman, pp. 49–72.

Keiser, R.A. (1997a). After the first black mayor: Fault lines in Philadelphia's biracial coalition. In R.P. Browning, D.R. Marshall, & D. Tabb (eds.), *Racial politics in American cities,* 2nd ed. New York: Longman, pp. 65–93.

Keiser, R.A. (1997b). *Subordination or empowerment? African American leadership and the struggle for urban political power.* New York: Oxford University Press.

Kessner, T. (1989). *Fiorello H. La Guardia and the making of modern New York.* New York: McGraw-Hill.

Klein, J. (1988, December 5). Koch's last stand? But don't bet on his pulling a Custer, *New York,* p. 56.

Klein, J. (1989, June 12). Enough already? Koch and the dropout talk, *New York,* p. 14.

Loeb, V. (1994, October 6). City privatization lowers costs while raising eyebrows, *Philadelphia Inquirer,* p. 1.

Logan, A. (1989a, June 19). Going . . . , *New Yorker,* 65:82.

Logan, A. (1989b, August 21). Upstairs, downstairs, *New Yorker,* 65:82.

Logan, A. (1994, 2 May). Rudy's people. *New Yorker,* 70:46.

McNickle, C. (1993). *To be mayor of New York: Ethnic politics in the city.* New York: Columbia University Press.

Meyers, D., & Paolantonio, S.A. (1991, March 17). City services debate goes public: Could private sector do it better, *Philadelphia Inquirer,* p. 1-C.

Minerbrook, S., & Ipoco, J. (1995, 29 May). A trial of two cities. *U.S. News and World Report,* 118:30.

Mollenkopf, J. (1990). The great anomaly. In R. Browning, D.R. Marshall, & D. Tabb, (eds.), *Racial politics in American cities.* New York: Longman, pp. 75–87.

Mollenkopf, J. (1994). *A phoenix in the ashes: The rise and fall of the Koch coalition in New York City politics.* Princeton: Princeton University Press.

Mollenkopf, J. (1997). The great anomaly. In R. Browning, D.R. Marshall, & D. Tabb, (eds). *Racial Politics in American Cities,* 2nd ed. New York: Longman, pp. 97–115.

Moss, M.L., Townsend, A., & Tobier, E. (1997). Immigration is transforming New York City, Taub Urban Research Center, New York University.

Newfield, J., & Barrett, W. (1988). *City for sale.* New York: Harper and Row.

Paolantonio, S.A. (1991, March 1). Rendell and Hearn: The outsiders? *Philadelphia Inquirer,* p. 1-B.

Paolantonio, S.A. (1993). *Frank Rizzo: The last big man in big city America.* Philadelphia: Camino Books.

Pinkerton, J.P. (1997, April 10). Mayors show GOP needs big tent, *Newsday,* p. 53.

Pray, R. (1997, December 16). ACLU warns of "Dark Side" of N.Y. police plan, *Philadelphia Inquirer,* p. 1.

Privatization called "wave of future," may be only way to pay. (1990, August). *Highway and Heavy Construction,* 8:13–14.

Riordon, W.L. (1963). *Plunkitt of Tammany Hall.* New York: E. P. Dutton.

Salaam, Y. (1996, April 20). Mayor Giuliani whitewashes city hall, *Amsterdam News,* 87(16):4–16.

Sleeper, J. (1993, November 1). The end of the rainbow, *The New Republic,* pp. 20–25.

Stone, C.N. (1989). *Regime politics: Governing Atlanta, 1946–1988.* Lawrence, KS: University Press of Kansas.

Thompson, J.P. (1990). David Dinkins' victory in New York City: The decline of the Democratic party organization and the strengthening of black politics, *PS: Political Science and Politics,* 6:145–148.

Toy, V.S. (1997, November 26). Veto of police review board overridden, *New York Times,* p. 3-B.

Traub, J. (1996, 14 October). Rudy awakening. *New Yorker,* 72:25.

Voters more than bored of Ed, poll shows. (1989, January 31). *Daily News,* p. 5.

CHAPTER 8

Context, Identity, and Incorporation
Are Latinos in the Midwest Different?

THOMAS LONGORIA, JR.

In the 1990s, 62 percent of all U.S. Latinos lived in the Southwestern states of Texas, New Mexico, Arizona, California, Colorado, Nevada, and Utah (Statistical Record of Hispanic Americans, 1995). Racism and discrimination are historically imbedded and remain pervasive in areas such as education, employment, housing, and income. Lynchings, illegal land seizures, disenfranchisement through the poll tax, and voter intimidation are part of the recent history of Mexican American–Anglo relations in Texas (see Moore & Pachon, 1985 for a discussion).

Reaction to these historical, economic, and social factors facilitated the formation of a particular Chicano/Latino politics in the Southwest. Prior to the 1960s, assimilation was seen by many Mexican Americans as a way to counteract discrimination, leading to the formation of the League of Latin American Citizens (LULAC) (Marquez, 1993). As times changed, the Chicano civil rights movement asserted a distinct racial and ethnic identity and initiated third-party efforts such as the Raza Unida Party (Garcia, 1989). Massive voter registration efforts and legal challenges to structures that limited the effectiveness of Latino voting such as at-large elections by the Southwest Voter Registration and Education Project and other organizations continued into the 1980s and 1990s. The articulation of an issue agenda for Mexican Americans that focuses on representation and gaining a fair share of public resources and jobs has a decades long history.

The long and rich political and cultural history has produced a substantial body of Southwest-based social science research, including classic studies (for example, Grebler et al., 1970; Moore & Pachon, 1985;

Acuna, 1988) as well as specialized research on issues such as political behavior, descriptive and substantive representation, community organization and coalition building, intra and intergroup attitudes, assimilation and acculturation (for a few recent examples see de la Garza et al., 1994; Garcia, 1988; Polinard et al., 1994; Welch & Siegalman, 1993; Tedin & Murray, 1994; Dyer et al., 1989; Anderson & Saenz, 1994). The majority of these studies are based on regional and state-level analyses, specifically the Southwest and Southwestern states and cities.

However, the focus on the Southwest detracts from a full understanding of the considerable variation in the historical and sociopolitical circumstances that exist across the United States. Scholars and journalists frequently make theoretical and empirical generalizations about Latinos living in all regions based on the considerable knowledge of the Southwest. An especially problematic version of this problem is when national-level studies ignore the Midwest. For example, Mladenka notes that the Latino population in the Midwest and Northeast is small and eliminates these regions from his analysis of local government employment equity (1989, p. 182). Welch and Sigelman (1993) examine Hispanic political ideology and partisanship using several major national surveys but do not take into account potential regional differences. A recent special issue of the *Hispanic Journal of Behavioral Sciences* using the 1989 Latino National Political Survey included studies of different national origin groups, but no studies examining regional differences (Garcia et al., 1996).

In 1990, there were 1,726,509 Latinos living in the Midwestern states of Illinois, Wisconsin, Michigan, Indiana, Ohio, Minnesota, Iowa, Missouri, and Kansas compared to 1,276,545 in 1980 (Statistical Record of Hispanic Americans, 1995). Of all U.S. Latinos, 9.0 percent lived in the Midwest in 1990, compared with 9.0 percent in 1980 and 4.4 percent in 1970. While Latinos in the Midwest remain a small percentage of the total U.S. Latino population, the growth and different regional context make a detailed examination necessary for a more complete understanding of U.S. Latino politics (Cardenas, 1976).

The literature on Latinos in the Midwest is underdeveloped in comparison to research on Latinos in the Southwest. Notable exceptions include historical studies of migration patterns, the process of migrant recruitment for work in agriculture, railroads, and industry, the struggles to foster community building through mutual-aid societies, and the pressures for acculturation and assimilation (Valdes, 1991; Garcia, 1996). The process of political community building in Chicago in light of

Latino diversity and economic restructuring in the Midwest has also been examined (Padilla, 1993). When socioeconomic conditions in the Southwest and the Midwest are examined, differences are often found. For example, there are more Latino children living in ghetto areas in the Southwestern metropolitan areas than in the Chicago metropolitan areas (St. John & Miller, 1995).

While potentially different Latino population characteristics in the Midwest are relevant factors in research that purports to study "Latino" politics, perhaps equally important is the potentially different sociopolitical context in the Midwest. This different context suggests that the social construction of racial identity, identity politics, and inter- and intra-ethnic coalition formation must be considered. These latter considerations are downplayed in research contexts where Latinos are relatively homogenous and in traditional contexts such as Mexican Americans in the Southwest, Puerto Ricans in the Northeast, and Cubans in South Florida.

For example, there are potentially regional differences in "political resources"—which include the percentage Latino population, levels of education, and Latino income relative to white income—that have been found to predict levels of Latino descriptive and substantive representation (see, for example, Meier & Stewart, 1991). Moving into the middle class and associated increases in political resources may be occurring at different rates and in different patterns in the Midwest and create a different political context. While the connection between political resources and descriptive and substantive representation makes a consideration of these factors in a comparative context necessary, other reasons include the consequences of diversity in small to mid-sized Midwestern cities and suburbs and the evolution of biracial cities into multiracial cities.

While Midwest Latinos are still a relatively small percentage of all Latinos and Midwest residents, the existing literature on Latinos in the Midwest makes a case for further research. A study specifically comparing demographic characteristics of Chicanos in the Midwest and Southwest in the 1970s found that, other than significant percentages of other Latinos, there were no "significant similarities and differentials" that required further investigation (Estrada, 1976, p. 232). A detailed profile of Chicago in 1970 found that there were no Latino alderpersons, state legislators, and few municipal employees (Salces & Colby, 1988). In addition, most Latinos were recent arrivals, 70 percent of Mexicans were not U.S. citizens, and Latinos were dispersed in many neighborhoods in the 1970s (Salces & Colby, 1988).

More than twenty years of population growth, migration and settlement, and formal and informal institutional development may have produced meaningful differences in the Midwest. Certainly, by the 1990s, many distinct Latino neighborhoods had been formed in Chicago (Padilla, 1985). Additionally, other factors such as suburbanization, national origin diversity, and the development and evolution of the nonprofit/community-based organization sector have potentially changed the social and political context of Latinos in the Midwest.

Levels of minority suburbanization have risen since the 1980s and fragmented metropolitan areas around major Midwestern cities increase the potential for minority suburbanization compared to the Southwest where cities have more commonly pursued annexation strategies (Rusk, 1993). Minorities are usually better off relative to whites in metro areas that are less fragmented (Rusk, 1993). From the perspective of the political resources model, Latinos in suburbs may have lower levels of political resources and thus be less able to gain political influence and power. On the other hand, Latinos in some suburbs may be better off than their neighbors and have enhanced ability to gain representation and political influence.

Latino national origin diversity is another factor that potentially makes the Latino experience in the Midwest distinctive. Salces and Colby (1988) argue that Latino diversity is an obstacle to Latino political mobilization in Chicago. However, Padilla (1985) has found the formation of coalitions between Mexican Americans and Puerto Ricans in Chicago. The emergence of a pan-ethnic Latino consciousness, where national origin takes on a lesser significance and political influence is enhanced, is one consequence of this social and political interaction (Padilla, 1985). Latino diversity may hinder the effectiveness of political resources when national origin remains a crucial voting cue and Latino candidates divide Latino votes and advantage white candidates. Research examining intragroup attitudes has found that Puerto Ricans and Mexican Americans have less favorable views of each other than they have of whites and other non-whites (Longoria & Espinosa, 1998), suggesting that future cooperation and pan-ethnic voting, when it does occur, may not be broad-based and long-lasting.

The nonprofit and community-based organization sector may take on different characteristics in the Midwest. One factor related to Latino diversity is that many organizations are established along national-origin lines (i.e., either Puerto Rican or Mexican) and are focused on cultural awareness and social functions rather than politics and the mobilization of Latinos (Salces & Colby, 1988). National membership organizations such as GI Forum, Mexican American Legal Defense and Education Fund (MALDEF), and the League of United Latin American Citizens (LULAC), and National Council of La Raza (NCLR), were founded and usually hold national meetings in the Southwest. Local chapters of these membership organizations may be fewer in number and weaker in terms of visibility and resources in the Midwest compared to other regions where these organizations have a longer history. A study of Chicano community-based organizations in the Midwest, conducted in the 1970s, found that parallel organizations (e.g., GI Forum, LULAC) and alternative organizations (e.g., United Farm Workers, Raza Unida, and Brown Berets) were active (Parra et al., 1976) but did not quantify or define what constituted "active."

However, community-based organization may hinder rather than advance the political empowerment of Latinos. Parra et al. (1976) assert that parallel—or mainstream/conventional—organizations can be captured by white elites who provide funds through government contracts to deliver social services. This concern about cooptation of community-based organizations has become more of a possibility since the 1970s with the emergence of the contracting state (Smith & Lipsky, 1993). Community-based organizations are dependent on local governments that provide grant money to fund projects and implement programs. Receipt of government grants is usually contingent on adherence to requirements and standards that may distance the organization from community residents. While the issues of cooptation and organizational change are beyond the scope of this study, regional differences in the nonprofit sector may influence the nature of political activism, agenda setting, and levels of descriptive representation.

The differences between the Midwest and other regions go beyond the size of the Latino community. Political resources and other contextual factors such as suburbanization, Latino diversity, and community-based organizational development affect the ability to translate these resources into descriptive representation. However, a lack of data leave questions such as the direction of causality and the explanatory power of these variables unexamined in this study. This chapter examines the resources that are available to Latinos in the Midwest and the potential for these resources to lead to enhanced Latino representation. Knowledge of the Latino political resources and other factors suggest the extent that the Midwest is different or similar to the Southwest. The chapter concludes with a discussion of the impact of the Midwest context on the social construction of identity and a consideration of future directions for research on Latino politics.

This study presents data for all Midwestern states and areas where Latinos make up more than 10 percent of the population and selectively makes comparisons with other regions and states to determine if the Latino political context is different (see, Hispanic Databook of U.S. Cities and Counties, 1994). The 10 percent cut-off point is used to select areas that have a large enough Latino population to influence elections. Zip codes with more than 10 percent Latino residents are also examined because they represent an area sufficiently large to draw a majority-Latino electoral district. The goal is to present a profile of important regional and local-level characteristics of Latino communities in the Midwest, rather than select either a macro-level regional approach or only compare local-level data.

POPULATION RESOURCES

The Latino population in the Midwest and in each of the Midwestern states is presented in Table 8.1. Much of the growth in the regional Latino population is accounted for by increases in Illinois. The Latino population in Illinois grew from 3.5 percent of the state population in 1970 to 7.9 percent of the state population in 1990. The Latino population in Illinois more than doubled from 393,204 to 904,446, or a 130 percent increase in the Latino population. The other Midwestern states had less than 4 percent Latino population in 1990. In most states, the absolute numbers have grown slightly and, as a result, the total percentage of the state population has not increased as dramatically as in Illinois. For example, Indiana experienced a decline in both total and percentage Latino from 1980. However, the growth in the population in several states is notable. For example, in Wisconsin, there was a 33 percent increase in the Latino population from 1980 to 1990.

Nationally, the percent Latino grew from 6.5 percent in 1980 to 9.0 percent in 1990. Growth of the Latino population in other regions has been considerable and greater than in the Midwest. In the Northeast, the percent Latino increased from 5.3 to 7.4 percent, in the South, 5.9 to 7.9 percent, and the in West, 14.4 to 19.1 percent (Aponte & Siles, 1994). Latinos in the Midwest remain a small percentage of the total Midwest population, increasing from 2 percent in 1980 to 3 percent in 1990. States in the Southwest, for example, have shown increases in the Latino

Table 8.1. Latino Population by State, 1980–1990

State	Total Latino 1990	Percent Latino	Total Latino 1980	Percent Latino
U.S. Total	22,354,059	9.0	14,608,673	6.5
Illinois	904,446	7.9	635,602	5.6
Indiana	98,778	1.8	87,047	1.6
Iowa	32,647	1.2	25,536	0.9
Kansas	98,670	3.8	63,339	2.8
Michigan	201,596	2.2	162,440	1.8
Minnesota	53,884	1.2	32,123	.8
Missouri	61,702	1.2	51,653	1.1
Nebraska	36,969	2.3	28,025	1.8
Ohio	139,696	1.3	119,883	1.1
Wisconsin	93,194	1.9	62,972	1.3
Midwest Latino Population	1,716,592	3.0	1,268,620	2.0
Texas	4,339,905	25.5	1,890,648	16.4

Source: U.S. Bureau of the Census, *1990 Census of Population and Housing,* Summary Tape File 1c, United States Summary, February 1992.

population comparable to Illinois but far greater than the other Midwestern states. For example, Texas' Latino population grew by 2,449,257 since 1970 and at a growth rate of 58 percent. The percentage of the Texas population that is Latino grew from 16.4 percent to 25.5 percent.

Individual areas of concentration are presented in Table 8.2. There were seventy-three counties, cities, towns, villages, or zip codes with greater than 10 percent Latino population in 1990. The mean population of these areas is 27,840 (standard deviation = 11,652; median = 5,220). The mean total population for the thirty-three cities with more than 10 percent Latino residents is 117,837; excluding Chicago, the mean is 34,528. The mean Latino population for the thirty-three cities is 22,318; excluding Chicago, the mean Latino population is 6,313. These descriptive statistics show that the typical Latino community in the Midwest is quite small.

Table 8.2. Latino Population, Income, and Education in the Midwest

Area	Percent Latino	Total Latino	Income Ratio	Education Ratio
Chicago, IL 60647	67.3	64,565	.77	.76
Chicago, IL 60608	62.7	52,853	.87	.74
Chicago, IL 60622	60.0	44,518	.66	.66
Chicago, IL 60623	56.0	62,814	1.00	.70
East Chicago, IN	46.9	15,895	.97	.90
Chicago, IL 60639	43.2	32,214	.79	.79
Kansas City, MO 64108	41.6	2,932	.66	.64
Milwaukee, WI 53204	40.4	16,939	.72	.70
Cicero, IL	35.8	24,142	.70	.70
Chicago, IL 60618	32.1	28,349	.69	.78
Detroit, MI 48209	30.7	11,927	.90	.83
Chicago, IL 60632	29.9	18,559	.72	.83
West Chicago, IL	29.8	4,409	.63	.41
Melrose Park, IL	29.7	6,195	.67	.63
Chicago, IL 60617	27.8	27,367	.68	.60
Chicago, IL 60609	27.6	24,798	1.05	.73
Detroit, MI 48216	27.4	2,275	.92	.79
Chicago, IL 60625	26.6	22,144	.68	.71
Chicago, IL 60651	25.4	19,833	.80	.61
Chicago, IL 60629	24.5	22,436	.79	.71
Blue Island, IL	24.5	5,220	.73	.67
Waukegan, IL	22.7	15,752	.61	.51
Aurora, IL	22.6	22,505	.60	.43
Chicago, IL 60640	22.1	17,020	.58	.63
St. Paul, MN 55107	20.9	3,283	.68	.82
Cleveland, OH 44113	20.7	4,144	.77	.62
Franklin Park, IL	20.6	3,808	.64	.44
Chicago, IL 60626	19.8	11,355	.58	.58
Chicago, IL	19.2	534,475	.58	.62

Table 8.2. *continued*

Area	Percent Latino	Total Latino	Income Ratio	Education Ratio
Chicago, IL 60613	19.2	9,427	.44	.59
Scottsbluff, NE	19.2	2,633	.01	.57
Bensenville, IL	19.0	3,376	.67	.62
Elgin, IL	18.4	14,170	.53	.47
Chicago, IL 60612	17.6	7,816	1.09	.69
Chicago, IL 60660	17.3	7,794	.62	.70
Lorain, OH	16.8	11,969	.68	.74
Carpentersville, IL	16.3	3,757	.72	.53
Northlake, IL	15.8	1,976	.70	.64
Chicago, IL 60641	15.4	9,190	.74	.82
Sterling, MI	15.4	2,330	.66	.74
Chicago Heights, IL	14.6	4,829	.69	.62
Scottsbluff Co., NE	14.4	5,188	.51	.58
Round Lake Beach, IL	14.1	2,317	.67	.59
Holland, MI	14.0	4,304	.54	.53
Prospect Heights, IL	14.0	2,133	.46	.35
Gary, IN 46405	14.0	1,713	.72	.92
Cook County, IL	13.3	678,974	.51	.59
Kane, IL	13.3	42,224	.57	.43
Omaha, NE 68107	13.3	3,173	.75	.69
Mundelein, IL	13.3	2,822	.58	.43
Lake Station, IN	13.3	1,836	.77	.90
Addison, IL	12.9	4,135	.51	.43
Adrian, IL	12.8	2,828	.62	.67
Chicago, IL 60657	12.7	8,305	.38	.66
Schiller Park, IL	12.5	1,399	.65	.71
Cleveland, OH 44109	12.4	5,854	.55	.75
Joliet, IL	12.3	9,451	.59	.51
Detroit, MI 48210	12.1	4,822	1.00	.80

Table 8.2. *continued*

Area	Percent Latino	Total Latino	Income Ratio	Education Ratio
Defiance, OH	11.9	1,995	.70	.69
Hammond, IN	11.7	9,856	.73	.83
Cleveland, OH 44102	11.7	6,223	.69	.77
Rolling Meadows, IL	11.2	2,530	.48	.51
Omaha, NE 68108	11.0	1,396	.66	.88
Lansing, MI 48906	10.7	3,056	.54	.62
Gary, IN 46406	10.7	1,627	1.03	.82
Milwaukee, WI 53215	10.6	5,121	.64	.72
Chicago, IL 60633	10.6	1,319	.79	.95
Hanover Park, IL	10.5	3,453	.60	.55
Kansas City, MO 64111	10.3	2,067	.75	.87
Romeoville, IL	10.2	1,436	.91	.83
Belvidere, IL	10.1	1,612	.63	.41
Saginaw, MI	10.0	6,951	.01	.85

Source: Hispanic Databook of U.S. Cities and Counties, 1994.

The mean percentage concentration in this selection is 21 percent (standard deviation = 1.5; median 16). The mean for the thirty-three cities is 17 percent. The largest single percentage concentration of Latinos is 67.3 percent in Chicago zip code 60647. The largest concentration in a Midwestern city is East Chicago, with 46.9 percent. Of the top twenty areas of concentration, twelve are Chicago zip codes, four are Chicago suburbs, and the remaining are zip codes in other major cities. There are twenty-seven areas with more than 20 percent concentration, and forty areas with more than 15 percent, including cities outside of the Chicago metropolitan area (e.g., Lorain, Ohio; Scottsbluff, Nebraska).

The concentration of Latinos in the Chicago metro area reflects settlement patterns in the Midwest. Latino immigrants, mostly Mexican, arrive in Chicago and then move to other cities in search of better jobs (Aponte & Siles, 1994, p. 35). Inner-ring suburbs in particular are undergoing demographic and social changes that make them more similar to central cities in terms of problems and needs than outer-ring suburbs (Orfield, 1997). The Latino population in cities outside of the Chicago metropolitan area will likely reach a critical mass in the near future. Researchers should begin examining these areas now to pick up the dynamic process of demographic change and political adjustment. The process of secondary migration from Chicago should also be examined in more detail. For example, if migrants from Chicago have higher levels of job skills and more stable immigration status, researchers on Latino political incorporation should take these factors into account.

INCOME AND EDUCATION RESOURCES

Income and education ratios are key political resources. Cities where Latinos have higher levels of income and education may be more able to enhance levels of descriptive representation. The extent that Latinos and non-Latinos have comparable income and education resources is relevant because these cities may be more favorable political and policy environments for Latinos (Meier & Stewart, 1991).

Table 8.2 reports how Latinos in the Midwest fare in terms of income and education resources. The mean per capita income for Latinos in the selected areas is $7,897, compared to $12,226 for all residents of the selected areas. When income is examined as a ratio to compare the relative status of Latinos to all residents—Latino income divided by overall income—there is no consistent pattern. The top twenty most favorable areas for Latinos include a wide variety of locations including city of Chicago zip codes, and inner-ring suburbs such as E. Chicago, outlying communities in the Chicago metropolitan area (e.g., Romoeoville), and other population centers such as Dayton, Cincinnati, Columbus, and St. Louis and relatively affluent suburbs such as Sterling Heights, Michigan. Eighteen areas of concentration include Latinos who have approximate parity with non-Latinos (greater than .75, where 1 = parity). The income ratios are not correlated with factors such as area size (r = -.12) or the percentage of the Latino community (r = .34). Latinos have levels of income comparable to other residents in a variety of settings including urban areas, suburbs, and rural areas, suggesting that the consequences of suburbanization, while widespread, are not consistent with the expectation that suburbanization necessarily brings affluence and greater political resources.

When education levels are compared, the mean percent of Latinos who have completed high school is 44 percent (standard deviation = 1.2; median 42.9) percent versus 66 percent (standard deviation = 1.4;

median = 68.2) for all residents. When education levels are examined in terms relative to education levels of all residents, favorable areas include zip codes in major cities, and less affluent Chicago metro area suburbs such as East Chicago, Lake Station, and Gary. The ten areas with the lowest levels of education equity include areas where Latinos are living in more affluent Chicago metro area suburbs, for example, Rockford, Carpentersville, Elgin, and Addison.

LATINO DIVERSITY

Another population characteristic relevant to enhancing Latino descriptive representation is national-origin diversity. The term "Latino community," which groups different national origin Latinos and assumes a common culture and interests should be used with caution. The formation of intra-ethnic coalitions depends on contact that is assumed to be more likely in the Midwest because of significant percentages of Mexicans, Puerto Ricans, and other Latinos. Coalitions are especially important because Puerto Ricans may be the majority of eligible and registered voters in areas where Mexicans are the majority of Latino residents.

Table 8.3 presents the percentage Mexican origin, Puerto Rican, and other Latinos in each area to illustrate how widespread intra-ethnic contact is on a subregional level. The mean percentage of Mexican Americans is 72 percent, 17 percent Puerto Rican, and 11 percent other Latino origin. Twenty-one of the 73 areas of concentration in the Midwest have more than 20 percent of two groups represented. However, only four have more than 40 percent of two groups represented. Diversity is found at the regional level, but diversity is not common at the subregional level.

However, Latino diversity in terms of eligible Latino voters is also important because Puerto Ricans are citizens by birth. In 1990, 33 percent of Latinos in the Midwest were noncitizens, compared to 32 percent in the Northeast, 7 percent in the South, and 48 percent in the West (Statistical Record of Hispanic Americans, 1995). Assuming that the 33 percent noncitizens is constant across all Midwest, the number of areas with a Mexican majority decreases from sixty-two to forty-four. Areas such as Gary zip code 46405 and Chicago zip codes 60641 and 60622 go from majority Mexican American to plurality Puerto Rican residents and become more diverse.

This result is a best case scenario from the perspective of Mexican American electoral strength because Mexican immigrants, even when naturalized, tend to vote at lower levels (DeSipio, 1996). The potential

Table 8.3. Latino Diversity

Area	Percentage Mexican	Percentage Puerto Rican	Percentage Other
West Chicago, IL	97.9	0.8	1.3
Blue Island, IL	95.0	1.5	3.5
Omaha, NE 68107	94.6	0.4	5.0
Kansas City, MO 64108	94.2	0.6	5.2
Chicago, IL 60608	93.9	3.7	2.4
Chicago, IL 60623	93.4	3.6	3.0
Omaha, NE 68108	92.9	0.4	6.7
Joliet, IL	92.8	3.0	4.2
Sterling, IL	92.4	3.3	4.3
Scottsbluff, NE	92.2	0.0	7.8
Chicago, IL 60633	90.6	6.7	2.7
Saginaw, MI	90.2	3.2	6.6
Chicago, IL 60617	90.1	6.4	3.5
Scottsbluff Co., NE	89.9	0.0	10.1
Chicago, IL 60609	89.1	5.5	5.4
Chicago, IL 60632	88.7	6.6	4.7
Belvidere, IL	88.4	3.3	8.3
Chicago Heights, IL	87.7	4.6	7.7
Prospect Heights, IL	87.4	7.7	4.9
Adrian, IL	86.5	5.0	8.5
Aurora, IL	86.3	8.9	4.8
Franklin Park, IL	86.2	7.1	6.7
Rolling Meadows, IL	85.7	1.8	12.5
St. Paul, MN 55107	83.8	7.9	8.3
Kane, IL	83.4	9.9	6.7
Kansas City, MO 64111	83.2	1.4	15.4
Bensenville, IL	83.1	2.7	14.2
Chicago, IL 60629	82.9	10.7	6.4
Gary, IN 46406	82.5	11.0	6.5

Table 8.3. *continued*

Area	Percentage Mexican	Percentage Puerto Rican	Percentage Other
Mundelein, OH	82.5	2.0	15.5
Hammond, IL	82.0	13.2	4.8
Melrose Park, IL	82.0	5.6	12.4
Holland, MI	81.9	8.8	9.3
Addison, IL	81.8	8.1	10.1
Lansing, MI 48906	81.8	0.7	17.5
Elgin, IL	81.3	12.4	6.3
Northlake, IL	80.8	5.1	14.1
Cicero, IL	79.2	6.6	14.2
Hanover Park, IL	78.7	7.1	14.2
Defiance, OH	78.1	11.6	10.3
East Chicago, IN	76.3	22.0	1.7
Romeoville, IL	75.4	16.2	8.4
Carpentersville, IL	75.1	7.9	17.0
Lake Station, IN	74.9	13.9	11.2
Chicago, IL 60612	74.4	21.1	4.5
Detroit, MI 48216	73.3	20.2	6.5
Waukegan, IL	73.1	16.3	10.6
Detroit, MI 48209	72.2	18.4	9.4
Schiller Park, IL	71.4	9.8	18.8
Chicago, IL 60626	70.4	7.2	22.4
Detroit, MI 48210	68.8	21.0	10.2
Cook County, IL	67.9	19.1	13.0
Milwaukee, WI 53204	65.2	30.7	4.1
Chicago, IL	65.0	22.6	12.4
Round Lake Beach, IL	60.9	12.7	26.4
Milwaukee, WI 53215	60.7	35.2	4.1
Chicago, IL 60613	55.1	22.9	22.0
Chicago, IL 60661	53.8	5.2	41.0

Table 8.3. *continued*

Area	Percentage Mexican	Percentage Puerto Rican	Percentage Other
Gary, IN 46405	51.6	44.6	3.8
Chicago, IL 60622	51.5	42.0	6.5
Chicago, IL 60657	50.9	21.9	27.2
Chicago, IL 60640	50.2	15.1	34.7
Chicago, IL 60618	47.8	30.6	21.6
Chicago, IL 60625	46.2	18.1	35.7
Chicago, IL 60641	45.8	37.5	16.7
Chicago, IL 60660	45.4	11.4	43.2
Chicago, IL 60639	41.6	47.1	11.3
Chicago, IL 60651	38.5	55.3	6.2
Chicago, IL 60647	38.3	50.3	11.4
Lorain, OH	18.4	78.9	2.7
Cleveland, OH 44102	9.5	80.8	9.7
Cleveland, OH 44109	3.8	82.9	13.3
Cleveland, OH 44113	2.2	91.6	6.2

Source:Hispanic Databook of U.S. Cities and Counties, 1994.

political clout of Mexicans is reduced in areas with higher percentages of noncitizens, and without pan-ethnic cooperation, the potential clout of the Latino "community" is also undermined.

COMMUNITY-BASED ORGANIZATIONS

The translation of political resources into descriptive representation is necessary for enhancing minority representation. Community-based organizations play an important role as community organizers and agenda setters. Because of historical factors, there may be fewer nonprofit and community-based organizations in the Midwest compared to other regions. On the other hand, local governments contract out when they do not have the expertise to reach target populations. There may be more contracting out in the Midwest because there are fewer Latino elected officials and bureaucrats. As a result, local governments in the Midwest may supply more resources and create incentives for the formation of community-based organizations.

Assumptions and hypotheses regarding possible differences in the Latino-serving nonprofit sector in the Midwest cannot be tested without an accurate census of organizations and a valid measure of the elements that constitute a "Latino" organization. However, as a preliminary analysis, the number of community-based organizations that serve Latino communities by providing, for example, job training, youth recreation and diversion programs, child care, and English and citizenship classes is presented in Table 8.4.

All of the Midwestern states have, on a per capita basis, more community-based organizations than Texas. The average per capita number of community-based organizations in the Midwest is .53, or one organization for every 2,000 residents (2 * .53), compared to .16 per capita in the Southwest, .06 per capita in Florida, and .20 per capita in New York. In Texas, there is one organization for every 10,000 residents (10 *.09). Besides these regional differences, there is no systematic pattern. Both Wisconsin and Illinois, for example, have around one organization for every 5,000 residents.

Table 8.4. Number of Community-Based Organizations, 1996

State	Number Community-Based Organizations	Per Capita
Illinois	142	.16
Indiana	37	.37
Iowa	23	.72
Kansas	32	.34
Michigan	171	1.18
Minnesota	63	1.18
Missouri	17	.27
Nebraska	27	.73
Ohio	33	.24
Wisconsin	17	.18
Texas	407	.09

Source: Hispanic Resource Directory, 3rd ed., 1996.

LATINO REPRESENTATION IN THE MIDWEST

As of 1996, only sixty-six Latinos served as elected officials in Midwestern states compared to twenty-one in 1973 and eighty-three in 1990 (Urban Affairs Institute, 1974; National Association of Latino Elected Officials, 1990, 1996). In addition, only seventeen Midwest cities, towns, or villages have at least one Latino elected official in 1990 (National Association of Latino Elected Officials, 1996).

Without more data and more cases, it is impractical to use the political resources model and quantitative analysis to test whether Midwest Latinos are underrepresented compared to Latinos in other regions. The impact of regional differences in the distribution of political resources and other contextual factors such as suburbanization, Latino diversity, and the activity of the nonprofit sector remain unexamined. However, making specific comparisons of similar metropolitan areas can shed light on the extent that Latinos are underrepresented in the Midwest.

As illustrated by the data presented earlier, Latinos are concentrated in the Chicago metropolitan area. The Chicago metro area includes a large central city, inner ring blue collar suburbs, and affluent suburbs. Latino representation levels in the Chicago metro area are compared with representation levels in the Dallas–Fort Worth and the Houston metro areas, which have similar characteristics as large metropolitan areas surrounded by less affluent inner-ring suburbs and more affluent outer-ring suburbs.

In the Chicago metro area (Cook, Lake, Du Page, Kane, and Lake, Indiana counties), there are twenty-three cities that have between 10 and 50 percent Latino population, 17.3 percent of which have at least one Latino elected official. In the Houston metro area (Harris, Fort Bend, Brazoria, and Galveston counties), there are sixteen cities that have between 10 and 50 percent Latino population, of which 50 percent have at least one Latino elected official. Of the eight cities in the Dallas–Fort Worth metro area (Dallas, Tarrant, Rockwall counties), 12.5 percent have at least one Latino elected official.

SUMMARY OF DESCRIPTIVE DATA

Aggregate data provides, at best, an indirect and incomplete measure of the political resources of Latinos and Latino communities in the Midwest. However, some relevant issues are raised by data presented in this chapter.

A majority of the Latino population in the Midwest lives in Illinois and most of the cities with significant percentages of Latino residents are located in the Chicago metropolitan area. A study of Latino representation in the Midwest using 1990 data is essentially a study of the Chicago metropolitan area. The next census may show enough growth in other areas to make intraregion and regional levels of analyses more meaningful. However, direct migration, rather than indirect migration, and residential patterns that range from inner-city barrios, to low-income inner-ring suburbs, to affluent outlying suburbs make the city of Chicago context different and limit the ability to make generalizations to the Midwest.

Latino population growth in the suburbs is important because it is possible that these areas might become majority Latino in population and become areas where conflict over political power emerges. Because of white flight, many inner-ring suburbs have changed from majority white to majority minority in less than a decade. However, the data illustrate that income and education resources do not vary systematically with type of area (e.g., suburb versus central city) and relatively weaker political resources in some areas suggests that Latino empowerment will not be a function of population and political resources alone. While Latinos are better off in absolute terms in some suburbs, this is not true in less affluent inner-ring suburbs. The more relevant consequence of Latino suburbanization is that these suburbs have at-large election structures and Latino residents have little recourse to change these structures in the current political and legal climate. Even if Latino political resources are more substantial in suburban areas, without single-member districts and grassroots mobilization by nonprofit and community-based organizations, which tend to be located in central cities, representation levels are not likely to increase.

The finding that Latinos are better represented in the Chicago metro area than in the Dallas–Fort Worth metro area is a reminder that appealing to context and local circumstances is important but not necessarily conducive to broad theoretical conclusions. Higher levels of Latino representation in Houston is largely the result of more extensive and aggressive challenges to at-large elections than occurred in the Dallas and Chicago metro areas. If history is destiny, Midwest Latinos, as well as other Latinos in areas that have not solidified past gains in minority representation, face an uphill battle.

Ultimately, the extent that the Midwest is distinctive and whether Latino political empowerment occurs, is partially a matter of political resources, but also what Latino community leaders do with these resources. Continued population growth in the Midwest will bring to light problems that require a local government solution and stimulate claims for descriptive and policy representation. Because the responsibility for community empowerment falls increasingly on those working at the grassroots level, future research on Latino politics and policy should examine the role and effectiveness of the nonprofit sector and the impact of these community-based organizations on Latino political activism and empowerment. It is conceivable that in the politics of transition, cooptation will occur as entrenched white interests try to delay political change. Conflict may increase incentives for assimilation or lead to increased activism based on ethnic identity. Whatever the outcome, these dynamics are likely to vary within the Midwest just as they have in the Southwest.

IMPLICATIONS: THE CONSTRUCTION OF A LATINO COMMUNITY

Census categories and macro-level data are, at best, indirect and incomplete measures of what is distinctive about Latinos and Latino communities in the Midwest. The patterns of political resource distribution in the Midwest, and factors such as suburbanization, diversity, and the development of the nonprofit sector help shape a different political context. Context can also be examined as something different than a set of environmental social characteristics because individual and collective reactions to context affect the "social construction" of ethnic identity and community.

The social construction perspective reminds us, at least for a moment, to put aside the variables of the political resources model that are commonly used in quantitative research. The social construction of Latino identity, especially in areas with different historical, social, and economic contexts, is potentially important because how Latinos perceive themselves and community influences the formation of a Latino public interest.

The question regarding the formation of a Latino public interest would seem overly academic in most cases. For example, in Mexican American barrios in Los Angeles issues such as representation in local government and the need to influence the policymaking process is an obvious and central concern. Tangible threats such as California's Propositions 187 and 209 that threatened to take benefits from undocumented workers and challenged bilingual education mobilized Latinos and fostered the creation of a more politically active Latino community. These threats simply do not exist at the same level of intensity in the Midwest.

Partially because of fewer tangible threats and a different history, demands for descriptive and policy representation in the Midwest may be less intense than in the Southwest, Northeast, and South Florida. These perceptions may lead to a new political space defined more by coalitions with whites than ethnic coalitions or coalitions with African Americans.

Ethnic labels and ethnic identity are also local and situated in a particular context. An individual's ethnicity—that is, membership to an ethnic group that remains constant—should be contrasted with a person's "ethnic identity in the context of different situations" (Saldana, 1995, p. 44). The relevance of situational identity is especially pronounced in the Midwest where population characteristics and history suggest a different discourse and construction of Latino identity. For example, the immigration patterns for many Midwest Latinos more closely resemble historical patterns of European immigration. For Midwest Latino immigrants, returning home is difficult and low-wage jobs are plentiful.

A good example of the relevance of social construction of identity is how Latino diversity is to be interpreted and how the influence of diversity manifests itself in the Midwest. For example, attitudinal differences between individuals who self-identify as Mexicans, Puerto Ricans, and Cuban Americans have been documented at the individual and population level. However, research that examines the statistical relationships between external ethnic labels and different attitudes, preferences, and behaviors usually does not take into account the distinction between ethnic labels, which is fixed, and ethnic identity, which varies based on context.

Case study research has shown that "Latinismo"—the notion that Latinos of all backgrounds are one pan-ethnic community—is situationally specific, suggesting that "the Latino-conscious person sees himself as a Latino sometimes and as Puerto Rican, Mexican American, Cuban and the like at other times" (Padilla, 1985, p. 13). Thus, even if there are statistically significant differences between those who choose one label over another, little can be said of individuals because "it is important to recognize that self-identification with and the use of a particular term also depends on the alternatives available in each context" (Oboler, 1995, p. 102).

If Latino consciousness is fluid and subject to the alternatives available in each context, then an examination of how context is shaped becomes necessary. For example, community-based organizations play an important role in mobilizing community and maintaining cultural traditions. In the Midwest, there are more Latino-oriented organizations per capita and these community-based organizations, according to one study, tend to be fragmented by national origin and more focused on cultural awareness and social functions than politics and Latino political empowerment (Salces & Colby, 1988). A comparative analysis would be necessary to determine whether community-based organizations in the Midwest are still fragmented and apolitical and whether these are characteristics more pronounced in the Midwest. However, before beginning such a study it is necessary to outline why Midwest community-based organizations might be different and whether there would be a significant impact on Latino politics.

Community-based organizations in the Midwest, and in other regions, are capable of enhancing political empowerment, providing social services, and engaging in community building cultural and social functions. However, preserving cultural traditions instills a belief in uniqueness and difference, not only from whites and African Americans, but also from other Latino origin communities. Celebrating cultural difference and trying to build a political community among Latinos is a difficult task, especially if rewards are still viewed as distributed along national-origin lines, for example, a Mexican American community-based organization, or a Puerto Rican elected official. Further, emphasizing difference from non-Latinos may lead to a rejection of mainstream politics and institutions. This tension between uniqueness and sameness potentially creates a context where Latino-oriented community-based organizations and community leaders may unintentionally—or intentionally in some cases—weaken the potential for cooperation among Latinos and political empowerment in the formal sector.

Without a consideration of the extant context and the priorities and attitudes of community leaders and organizations that reinforce existing dynamics or encourage other cultural, social, and political options, the models used to study Latino politics and representation will be incomplete. While the social construction framework suggests context matters, it also suggests that context is not destiny. Future research should seek out the different situations that enhance Latino consciousness and whether there is some connection between Latino consciousness and descriptive and policy representation. Thus, more research on Latinos in the Midwest, where these issues are more salient, is clearly necessary.

REFERENCES

Acuna, R. (1988). *Occupied america: A history of Chicanos.* New York: Harper & Row.

Aponte, R., & Siles, M. (1994). *Latinos in the heartland: The browning of the Midwest.* Lansing, MI: Julian Samora Research Institute.

Anderson, R.M., & Saenz, R. (1994). Structural determinates of Mexican American intermarriage, 1975–1980. *Social Science Quarterly, 75,* 414–430.

Cardenas, G. (1976). Who are the Midwest Chicanos: Implications for Chicano studies. *Aztlan, 7,* 141–152.

de la Garza, R.O., Menchaca, M., & DeSipio, L. (1994). *Barrio ballots: Latino politics in the 1990 elections.* Boulder, CO: Westview Press.

DeSipio, L. (1996). Making citizens or good citizens: Naturalization as a predictor of organizational and electoral behavior among Latino immigrants. *Hispanic Journal of Behavioral Sciences,* 18, 194–213.

Dyer, J.A., Vedlitz, A., & Worchel, S. (1989). Social distance among racial and ethnic groups in Texas: Some demographic correlates. *Social Science Quarterly,* 70, 607–616.

Estrada, L. F. (1976). A demographic comparison of the Mexican origin population in the Midwest and Southwest. *Aztlan,* 7, 235–254.

Garcia, F. C. (1988). *Latinos and the political system.* Notre Dame, IN: University of Notre Dame Press.

Garcia, F.C., Falcon, A., & de la Garza, R. (1996). Special issue: Ethnicity and politics: Evidence from the Latino national political survey. *Hispanic Journal of Behavioral Science,* 18, 91–103.

Garcia, I. M. (1989). *United we win: The rise and fall of La Raza Unida Party.* Tucson: MASRC, University of Arizona Press.

Garcia, J. R. (1996). *Mexicans in the Midwest, 1900–1932.* Tucson: University of Arizona Press.

Grebler, L., Moore, J.W., & Guzman, R.C. (1970). *The Mexican American people: The nation's second largest minority.* New York: Free Press.

Hispanic databook of U.S. cities and counties. (1994). Compiled By the Research Staff of Toucan Valley Publications, Inc. Milpitas, CA: Toucan Valley Publications.

Hispanic resource directory. (1996). A.E. Schorr (ed.). Juneau, AK: The Denali Press.

Longoria, T., & Espinosa, K. (1998). Social distance among Latinos. Unpublished manuscript. University of Wisconsin–Milwaukee.

Marquez, B. (1993). *LULAC: The evolution of a Mexican American political organization.* Austin: University of Texas Press.

Meier, K. J., & Stewart, Jr., J. (1991). *The politics of Hispanic education.* Albany: State University of New York Press.

Mladenka, K. R. (1989). Blacks and Hispanics in urban politics. *American Political Science Review,* 83, 165–192.

Moore, J., & Pachon, H. (1985). *Hispanics in the United States.* Englewood Cliffs, NJ: Prentice-Hall.

National Association of Latino Elected Officials. (1990). *National roster of Hispanic elected officials.* Washington, DC: NALEO.

National Association of Latino Elected Officials. (1996). *National roster of Hispanic elected officials.* Washington, DC: NALEO.

Oboler, S. (1995). *Ethnic labels, Latino lives: Identity and the politics of (re)presentation in the United States.* Minneapolis: University of Minnesota Press.

Orfield, M. (1997). *Metropolitics: A regional agenda for community and stability.* Washington, DC: Brookings Institution Press.

Padilla, F. (1985). *Latino ethnic consciousness.* Notre Dame, IN: University of Notre Dame Press.

Padilla, F. (1993). The quest for community: Puerto Ricans in Chicago. In J. Moore & R. Pinderhughes (eds.), *In the barrios: Latinos and the underclass debate,* (pp. 129–148). New York: Russell Sage Foundation.

Parra, R., Rios, V., & Gutierrez, A. (1976). Chicano organizations in the Midwest: Past, present, and possibilities. *Aztlan,* 7, 235–254.

Polinard, J.P., Wrinkle, R.D., Longoria, T., & Binder, N. (1994). *Electoral structure and urban policy: The impact on Mexican American communities.* Armonk, NY: M.E. Sharpe.

Rusk, D. (1993). *Cities without suburbs.* Washington, DC: Woodrow Wilson Center Press.

Salces, L.M., & Colby, P.W. (1988). Manana will be better: Spanish American politics in Chicago. In F.C. Garcia (ed.), *Latinos and the political system* (pp. 195–200). Notre Dame, IN: University of Notre Dame Press.

Saldana, D.H. (1995). Acculturative stress: Minority status and distress. In A.M. Padilla (ed.), *Hispanic psychology: Critical issues in theory and research* (pp. 43–56). Thousand Oaks, CA: Sage Publications.

Smith, S.R., & Lipsky, M. (1993). *Nonprofits for hire: The welfare state in the age of contracting.* Cambridge, MA: Harvard University Press.

Statistical record of Hispanic Americans. (1995). M.A. Reddy (ed.) New York: Gale Research Inc.

St. John, C., & Miller, S.M.B. (1995). The exposure of black and Hispanic children to urban ghettos: Evidence from Chicago and the Southwest. *Social Science Quarterly,* 76, 562–576.

Tedin, K.L., & Murray, R. (1994). Support for bi-racial political coalitions among blacks and Hispanics. *Social Science Quarterly,* 75, 772–789.

Urban Affairs Institute. (1974). *National roster of Spanish surnamed elected officials.* Los Angeles: Aztlan Publications.

U.S. Bureau of the Census. (1992, February). *1990 Census of Population and Housing.* Summary Tape File 1c, United States Summary.

Valdes, D. (1991). *Al norte: Agricultural workers in the great lakes region, 1917–1970.* Austin, TX: University of Texas Press.

Welch, S., & Sigelman, L. (1993). The politics of Hispanic Americans: Insights from national surveys, 1980–1988. *Social Science Quarterly,* 74, 76–94.

CHAPTER 9

Asian Pacific Americans and the Pan-Ethnic Question

JAMES S. LAI

INTRODUCTION

Discussion of Asian Pacific Americans in state and local politics has traditionally centered around their aggregate population numbers, and thus their political potential as a "swing vote" (Nakanishi, 1991; Ong & Nakanishi, 1996; Nakanishi, 1998). Despite this potential, Asian Pacific Americans have been hampered by comparatively low voter registration and turnout rates during the nineties (Field Institute Poll, 1994; Asian Pacific American Legal Center of Southern California, 1996). Ironically the factors that have inhibited Asian Pacific Americans from higher voter participation rates stem from the very root of their potential—the growing population and demographic diversity among Asian and Pacific Islanders. California is on the nation's cutting edge for these recent changes. According to U.S. census figures, during the period from 1960 to 1980, the California Asian Pacific American population increased from less than one-third of a million to 2.8 million. By 1980, Asian Pacific Americans held a 10 percent share of California's population (Nakanishi, 1998). In 1990, 40 percent of the nation's Asian Pacific American population (almost ten million people) resided in California, and in turn, nearly 34 percent of the state's Asian Pacific Americans lived in Los Angeles County (Shinagawa, 1996).

Paralleling this overall growth, the Asian Pacific American community has also become more demographically diverse as a result of the 1965 amendments to the Immigration and Naturalization Act. According to the 1994 Current Population Survey, there are over thirty ethnic groups that fall within the category of Asian and Pacific Islanders. In Los Angeles County, nearly 80 percent of those Asian Pacific Americans ten years or older are foreign born (Ong & Azores, 1991). One of the characteristics of this ethnically diverse and foreign-born population is their low voter turnout rates.[1] Asian Pacific Americans have the lowest voter registration of all racial groups, with a registration rate of 39 percent, constituting only 4 percent of California's voters, compared to a 65 percent registration rate for whites (non-Hispanics), 58 percent for African Americans, and 42 percent for Hispanics (Ong, Espiritu & Azores, 1991). Ethnic diversity and low voter registration rates complicate any discussion of an Asian Pacific American "swing vote."

Whether Asian and Pacific Islanders can coalesce into a unified political bloc is an important question that will be explored in this chapter.[2] Indeed, in this chapter I argue that the extent of Asian Pacific American political influence in the next millennium will be determined, in part, by their ability to unite their diverse interests in pan-ethnic coalitions. Pan-ethnicity is a social concept that entails a collective vision bridging diverse identities and interests. I explore the potential for a pan–Asian Pacific American coalition in electoral politics by examining two case studies: the 1991 California 46th Assembly District special primary election; and the 1993 Los Angeles mayoral election. These case studies were selected because at least one major Asian American candidate ran in both instances, and because a large and diverse Asian Pacific American constituency was present in both election districts. I contend that the creation of pan-ethnic coalitions depends on the efforts of those who view elections as opportunities for bridge building rather than "go it alone" roads. In Los Angeles, the important players are community-based organizations; individuals who are perceived as "leaders"; the ethnic media; and candidates who strategically seek cross-ethnic support. I examine general patterns of campaign contributions made to the Asian Pacific American candidates to determine whether pan-ethnic coalitions were generated in either of the two cases.[3] The data suggest that a pan-ethnic coalition was not created in the 1991 46th Assembly District special primary election; monetary support for candidates was ethnic-group specific. On the other hand, pan-ethnic support for Michael Woo was evident among his Asian American contributors in the 1993 Los Angeles mayoral election.

PAN-ETHNICITY AND ITS ORIGINS

The term pan-ethnicity dates from the late 1960s, and was originally used in the context of social movements led by second and third generation Chinese American and Japanese American college students. It connotes the ability of diverse ethnic groups to view their interests and identities as a collective racial group (Espiritu, 1992; Wei, 1993; Espiritu & Ong, 1994). For Asian Pacific Americans, this concept has been operationalized by sociopsychological factors such as perceived discrimination due to race; knowledge of their leaders; support for race-based policy issues (e.g., affirmative action and the Redress Movement for Japanese Americans); and intermarriage (Lien, 1997). The underlying goal of those who embrace pan-ethnicity is to unify diverse groups based on their common racial categorization rather than their ethnic heritage.

Scholars have argued that the pan-ethnic movement among Asian Pacific Americans symbolizes the movement away from an ethnic-based paradigm to a racial formation paradigm, in which the latter represented a means to make policy demands on the racial state (Omi & Winant, 1986). The main purpose of this strategy is simple: there is power in numbers. A collective group identity could transform (under certain circumstances) the separate elements of the Asian Pacific American community into a more cohesive unit which, in turn, could increase their effectiveness in influencing policy outcomes or political elections.

Early political studies on immigrant racial and ethnic groups argued that race and ethnicity became less important factors over time as the groups became more assimilated (Dahl, 1961; Wolfinger, 1965; Verba & Nie, 1972). Race and ethnicity in today's political environment, however, has taken on a heightened salience. Bruce Cain, for example, has observed a trend in California politics for ethnic groups to "go it alone" (Cain, 1991). This is particularly the case among recent immigrant Asian ethnic groups (post-1965) who do not necessarily identify with issues that marked the political struggles of more established Asian American groups during the sixties.

Factors that diminish the potential for a pan-Asian identity among recent Asian immigrants include differences in socioeconomic background such as education and income, generation issues, and homeland politics (Espiritu, 1992; Wei, 1993; Espiritu & Ong, 1994; Lien, 1997). For example, many Vietnamese who came to the United States during the seventies, entered as refugees (those who flee from homeland persecution under life or death circumstances), whereas Koreans who arrived in subsequent decades did so as immigrants under non–life threatening circumstances. Both groups have had different political experiences in their respective homelands and in the United States, therefore they do not share identical perspectives. As a result, cross-ethnic unity in the electoral arena can by no means be taken for granted; pan–Asian Pacific American coalitions do not automatically materialize. They are a constructed phenomenon shaped by the efforts of the following strategic-minded players: community-based organizations; individuals seen as leaders in the Asian Pacific American community; the ethnic press; and candidates running for office. The next section explores how they prevented the development of a pan-ethnic coalition in the 1991 46th Assembly District special primary election.

THE 1991 CALIFORNIA 46TH ASSEMBLY DISTRICT SPECIAL PRIMARY ELECTION: PAN-ETHNIC POLITICAL COALITION FAILURE

The 1991 46th Assembly District primary election was a "special" election held to fill the mid-term retirement of the incumbent, Mike Roos. The 46th Assembly District was solidly Democratic; approximately 64 percent of its voters were registered Democrats and 22 percent of its voters were registered Republicans (*California Journal,* 1990). At that time, the population was reported to be 40 percent Latino, 38 percent White, 16 percent Asian and Pacific Islander, and 5 percent African American (*Rafu Shimpo,* 1991). As a result of Roos' sudden retirement announcement, the Democratic characteristics of this assembly district, and the fact that it contained large portions of Koreatown and Filipino Town, three Asian Americans entered the race: T.S. Chung (Korean American), Keith Umemoto (Japanese American), and Joselyn Geaga Yap (Filipino American).[4] Both Chung and Yap were political novices. Chung was an attorney and Yap was a social worker. Umemoto was a consultant to the California Senate Committee on Budget and Fiscal Review. His father, Kaz Umemoto, once ran for the same Assembly District seat in 1977. Barbara Friedman was also one of the fifteen candidates who sought the Democratic nomination. Friedman had a prior history of public service: she served as Chief of Staff for Assemblyman Burt Margolin and Chief Deputy to Los Angeles City Controller Rick Tuttle.

The final result of the June 4th special election, as seen in Table 9.1, was that Barbara Friedman finished in first place. T.S. Chung, Joselyn Geaga Yap, and Keith Umemoto finished, respectively, in second, third, and fifth place.

Table 9.1. 1991 46th Assembly District Primary Election Results

Candidates	Barbara Friedman	T.S. Chung	Joselyn Geaga Yap	Keith Umemoto
Total Votes—At Polls	2,838	1,186	1,376	1,263
Total Votes—Absentee	589	1,087	604	428
Finish Total	3,427	2,273	1,980	1,691
Primary Finish	First	Second	Third	Fifth

Source: Los Angeles County Registrar Recorder's Office: Office of Campaign Reporting, California Long Form 490, Schedule A, 1991.

The Role of Asian Pacific American Leadership in Community-Based Organizations and the California Democratic Party

Community-based organizations can play a role in the construction of a pan-ethnic coalition. In the 1991 46th Assembly District primary, community-based organization leaders, who were worried about Asian voter support splintered between the three Asian candidates, tried to find one consensus candidate. The negotiation effort was led by Asian Pacific American leaders from various Northern and Southern California community-based organizations as well as the Asian Pacific American Caucus of the California Democratic Party. There were two meetings in Los Angeles on the issue, both initiated by leaders from these two groups. The first meeting took place over lunch with several community leaders present. According to Jai Lee Wong, a consultant for the Los Angeles County Human Relations Commission who was involved with planning the Southern California meetings:

> The first meeting was a closed meeting over lunch that did not involve any of the candidates. I called a meeting at Bill Tan's office to strategize how to get the three candidates together, to try to get a different reading on the candidates. (J. L. Wong, interview conducted October 24, 1993)

It was decided that a second, mediating meeting, with all three candidates present, should be held. The hope was that in-person pressure and persuasion from California's Asian Pacific American community elite would convince two candidates to withdraw from the race.

The second meeting occurred in the law office of Violet Rabaya (a prominent figure in the Asian Pacific American Caucus) and was attended by approximately fifteen leaders and professionals from various community-based organizations, along with the three candidates. The outcome was a disappointment to those who arranged the mediation session. None of the three candidates would concede, and all affirmed their desire to stay in the race.

Why did Asian Pacific American community leaders fail in their attempt to produce a consensus candidate, which would have facilitated a pan-ethnic electoral coalition? One reason is that post-1965 ethnic groups (e.g., Koreans, Filipinos, Vietnamese) resent the relative power and status held by more established ethnic groups (e.g., Chinese and Japanese). Consequently many of these recent immigrant groups may not view pan-ethnic coalitions as a viable means to pursue their political interests, particularly in winning a "voice of their own." As Joselyn Geaga Yap succinctly put it:

> As a function of having been here longer, the Japanese and Chinese communities are in more places of power and influence. So there is a degree of envy by Filipinos and the Koreans when they see that the mainstream views all of us as the same way: a monolithic, homogenous group. . . . Because of a lack of understanding among these coalitions, the fragmentation becomes almost inevitable. (J. G. Yap, interview conducted October 24, 1993)

Ethnic-Specific Media Coverage

The ethnic media did little to promote cross-ethnic support for the three Asian American candidates. Given the large Asian bilingual population in Los Angeles, the ethnic media has the potential to play an important role in educating their respective communities about the political necessity of cross-ethnic coalitions. However, in this election, the three major Los Angeles newspapers that serve the Korean American, Filipino American, and Japanese American communities focused on candidates believed to be of special interest to their readers. This was particularly the case for the Filipino American and Korean American newspapers.

The *Los Angeles Filipino Bulletin* gave exclusive coverage to Joselyn Geaga Yap's campaign. It even published an article authored by Yap, which gave her an opportunity to communicate "personally" to readers her qualifications as a potential officeholder. Yap also discussed the relationship of Filipino Americans' socioeconomic visibility to their political status:

The Filipino American community's lack of social and economic visibility has, in the past, translated to a lack of political presence and,
consequently, to a politically weakened community. As the largest
Asian American population group in the country and in California, we
are determined to establish a stronger political presence and take a
more active role in charting our political future. (*Los Angeles Filipino
Bulletin*, 1991, p. 1)

Moreover, the May 1991 edition of the *Los Angeles Filipino Bulletin* (a
monthly paper) contained three pro-Yap pieces. On the front page were
two items urging Filipino Americans to vote for Yap. One was a boxed
statement situated at the top right section of the front page that simply
stated: "Get the vote out for Joselyn Geaga Yap Assemblywoman 46th
District. Vote on June 4." The other front page item was a short editorial
piece entitled "Joselyn Yap's Candidacy Is a Victory for Us." The term
"us" was a clear reference to Filipino Americans as the editorial argued
that the community would greatly benefit from electing Yap to office.

The *Korea Times*'s coverage of the 46th Assembly District primary
was designed to mobilize Korean American support for T.S. Chung's
campaign. The newspaper simply ignored other candidates, including
Umemoto and Yap. One article prominently featured an interview with
T.S. Chung, who emphasized the political urgency for the Los Angeles
Korean American community:

Everyone in the Korean American community with whom I have spo-
ken feel we have to run in this election. When a vacancy opens in the
district with the largest number of Koreans living in, if we don't assert
our rights and build our candidates, we are never going to be treated as
a serious player. (*Korea Times*, 1991a, p. 1)

Rafu Shimpo's coverage of the 1991 46th Assembly District primary
election was more equitable. *Rafu Shimpo* ran three election-related articles covering all three Asian candidates. The difficulty in developing a
pan-ethnic coalition was suggested in the front-page headline of the May
22 edition: "46th District Tests Ethnic Loyalties: Three Candidates, Representing Different Asian Pacific Ethnic Groups, Test the Community's
Ethnic and Personal Alliances." This article analyzed the three Asian Pacific American candidates' campaigns and their political impact on voters. Unlike the *Korea Times* and the *Los Angeles Filipino Bulletin*, the
Rafu Shimpo article also mentioned non-Asian candidates such as Barbara Friedman (*Rafu Shimpo*, 1991).

Ethnic-Specific Monetary Campaign Contributions

Campaign contribution patterns indicate that a pan-ethnic coalition did not exist in the 1991 46th Assembly District primary election. To assess the extent to which campaign contributions were ethnic-specific, I analyzed data from Chung, Yap, and Umemoto's campaign disclosure forms for the filing period of January 1, 1991 to June 30, 1991. Official monetary contributions were coded into the following categories: race and ethnicity, amount per contribution, individual versus business, and geographic location. The category of race was divided into three subcategories: Asian, Non-Asian, and Unknown. The Asian subcategory was further divided into Asian ethnicities. A surname dictionary was used to identify ethnicity.[5] These data indicate that all three candidates received ethnic-specific contributions. However, Chung and Yap received a greater proportion of their money from co-ethnics than did Umemoto.

According to Table 9.2, T.S. Chung received a total of $237,807 from 626 contributors. Over three-quarters (76.7 percent) of these contributors were Korean American individuals or businesses. Their donations comprised 77 percent of the total contributions made to Chung. The second largest category of contributions (15 percent) was Unknown individuals and businesses, whose donations were 17.2 percent of the money received by Chung. Only 5.4 percent of Chung's contributors were non-Asian, and they provided 4 percent of his money.

Table 9.3 shows that Joselyn Geaga Yap received a total of $64,146 from 352 contributors. Almost 83 percent of these contributors were Filipino American individuals, businesses, and community-based organizations. Their donations were 88.1 percent of the total contributions made

Table 9.2. T.S. Chung Campaign Contributions

Ethnic Group	# of Contributors	% of Contributors	Total $	% of Total $
Total	626	100.0	237,809	100.0
Korean American	480	76.7	183,234	77.1
Non Asians	34	5.4	9,475	4.0
Unknown	94	15	40,900	17.2

Source: Los Angeles County Registrar Recorder's Office: Office of Campaign Reporting, California Long Form 490, Schedule A, 1991.

Table 9.3. Joselyn Geaga Yap Campaign Contributions

Ethnic Group	# of Contributors	% of Contributors	Total $	% of Total $
Total	352	100.0	64,146	100.0
Filipino American	290	82.4	54,491	88.1
Other Asians	16	4.5	1,175	1.8
Non Asians	46	13.1	6,480	10.1

Source: Los Angeles County Registrar Recorder's Office: Office of Campaign Reporting, California Long Form 490, Schedule A, 1991.

to Yap. Non-Asians constituted the second largest category of contributors (13.1 percent); they gave 10 percent of the money received by Yap. Other Asians were 4.5 percent of Yap's contributors and they provided just 1.8 percent of the money she received during the primary campaign cycle.

As Table 9.4 indicates, Keith Umemoto received a total of $137,983 from 324 contributors. Half of these contributors (50.3 percent) were non-Asian. They donated 72.1 percent of the money received by Umemoto. A plurality (42.3 percent) of Umemoto's contributors were Japanese American individuals, businesses, and community-based organizations, and they provided 25.5 percent of his campaign money. About 7 percent of Umemoto's contributors were Other Asians, and they provided just 2.4 percent of his war chest.

Table 9.4. Keith Umemoto Campaign Contributions

Ethnic Group	# of Contributors	% of Contributors	Total $	% of Total $
Total	325	100.0	137,983.98	100.0
Japanese American	137	42.3	35,190	25.5
Other Asians	24	7.4	3,350	2.4
Non Asians	163	50.3	99,443.98	72.1

Source: Los Angeles County Registrar Recorder's Office: Office of Campaign Reporting, California Long Form 490, Schedule A, 1991.

The geographic location of contributors further illuminates the pattern of ethnic-specific contributions. The contribution data were coded into six areas: within Los Angeles County, Southern California (outside of Los Angeles County), Northern California (within Sacramento County and vicinity), Northern California (Bay Area and vicinity), Outside of California (within the United States), and Not Available. Most of the campaign contributions given to all three Asian Pacific American candidates came from within Los Angeles County (the location of the 46th Assembly District). Eighty-two percent of Chung's contributors, 59.4 percent of Yap's contributors, and 58.6 percent of Umemoto's contributors were located in Los Angeles County. Northern California was the second largest source of contributions for both Umemoto and Yap. About 20 percent of Umemoto's contributions came from the greater Sacramento County area, while 24.4 percent of Yap's contributions lived in the Bay Area and vicinity. Five percent of Chung's contributions (his second largest geographic category) lived in Southern California, outside of Los Angeles County.

The ethnic composition of T.S. Chung and Joselyn Geaga Yap's contributors from their primary and secondary geographic sources was predominantly Korean and Filipino, respectively. In contrast, the ethnic composition of Keith Umemoto's secondary geographic source of contributors, Northern California (within Sacramento County and vicinity), was not primarily Japanese Americans but rather non-Asian individuals and professional/labor associations. These findings indicate differences in the three candidates' political connections. Umemoto tapped into his work-related contacts at the State Capitol, while Chung and Yap drew upon more local and ethnic-specific resources. Chung, for example, received contributions from international Korean corporations with Los Angeles headquarters.[6]

What might explain ethnic-specific campaign contributions during the 1991 46th Assembly District primary election? First, the political stakes were much greater for the Los Angeles Filipino American and Korean American communities than for the Japanese American community. The 46th Assembly District encompassed all or large portions of both Filipino Town and Koreatown, whereas Little Tokyo was situated in the neighboring 47th Assembly District. Filipino Americans and Korean Americans represented over 53 percent of the Asian and Pacific Islander population in over forty-eight census tracts situated in the 46th Assembly District (Lai, 1994). Therefore, a critical mass of both Filipino American and Korean American constituents existed in the 1991 46th Assembly

District that could be tapped for both monetary contributions and votes. Secondly, the district's political landscape thus led candidates to believe that their individual (and their group) interests would be best advanced by pursuing an ethnic-specific campaign strategy. Chung's campaign manager, Charles Kim, indicated their goal was to attract contributions and votes from the Korean American community, which was seen as favorably predisposed towards a Korean American candidate (C. Kim, interview conducted February 8, 1994).

Korean Americans and Filipino Americans were acutely interested in electing a candidate of their "own" to the State Assembly because Chinese Americans and Japanese Americans have historically dominated Asian electoral politics. In fact, one criticism leveled at pan-Asian organizations is that Chinese Americans and Japanese Americans have tended to dominate leadership positions (*Korea Times,* 1991b; Espiritu & Ong, 1994). There is some evidence, at least in Los Angeles, that post-1965 ethnic groups are aware they need to work together to increase their political clout—both within the Asian Pacific American community and in electoral politics in general. Shortly after the 1991 46th Assembly District primary, the *Korea Times* reported that Chung and Yap had said they would try not to run against each other in the future. Their discussion marked ". . . the first time that an Asian subgroup has been targeted by Koreans as an ally in pursuing political office" (*Korea Times,* 1991b).

The 1991 46th Assembly District primary election illustrates a situation where three Asian candidates rejected the well-coordinated request of community leaders for a consensus candidate, and instead pursued independent, ethnic-specific support. The ethnic press focused coverage on candidates of interest to their readers and largely eschewed the subject of cross-ethnic electoral collaboration. In contrast, Michael Woo's 1993 mayoral campaign provides us with an example of a broadly focused strategy that sought support from all Asian Pacific American groups. Woo's campaign also suggests that, under certain circumstances, symbolic leadership can be used as a way to bridge diverse ethnic interests.

THE 1993 LOS ANGELES MAYORAL ELECTION: TRANSCENDING ETHNIC DIFFERENCES THROUGH A PAN-ETHNIC CAMPAIGN STRATEGY AND THE SYMBOLIC LEADER

The 1993 Los Angeles mayoral election represented the end of the liberal, biracial coalition that had kept Mayor Tom Bradley in office for

Table 9.5. 1993 Los Angeles Mayoral General Election Exit Poll Results

Race (% of total voters)	Riordan (%)	Woo (%)
White liberals (22)	31	69
White moderates (31)	75	25
White conservatives (20)	92	8
African Americans (12)	14	86
Latinos (10)	43	57
Asian Americans (4)	31	69
Jews (19)	49	51

Source: *Los Angeles Times*, June 10, 1993, A25.

twenty years, and simultaneously marked the shift to a multiracial electoral paradigm (Sonenshein, 1993). This nonpartisan election pitted Michael Woo, the first Chinese American to be elected to the Los Angeles City Council in 1985, against the multimillionaire businessman Richard Riordan. Woo decided to participate in the city's public finance and matching funds program, while Riordan self-financed his campaign.

According to Table 9.5, the general election exit poll results indicated that Asian Americans supported Woo over Riordan, 69 percent and 31 percent, respectively. Riordan received 54 percent of the overall vote compared to 46 percent for Woo.

As the previous case study suggested, a candidate's campaign strategy can either facilitate or hinder the formation of a pan-ethnic coalition. In nonpartisan elections candidates have complete latitude to decide whether to follow a narrowly or broadly-focused campaign strategy. To counter Riordan's deep pockets, Woo pursued a broad-based campaign finance strategy and appealed to Asian Pacific American contributors both in Los Angeles County and nationwide. David Lang, Woo's campaign finance co-director, contends that there was a deliberate effort to solicit potential Asian Pacific American donors:

> We specifically targeted Asian Americans outside of California, particularly Chinese Americans. . . . Our strategy was based on cultivating and developing a relationship with Asian Americans, Chinese Americans in particular. (D. Lang, interview conducted November 7, 1995)

Clearly the strategy paid off. Woo's selective courting of Chinese Americans, and playing upon an ethnic connection, helps to explain why they gave the most money to his campaign. Woo's appeal was not limited to Chinese Americans, however.

In the eyes of many Asian Pacific Americans, Woo's mayoral candidacy represented a historic opportunity because Los Angeles is home to the mainland's largest Asian and Pacific Islander populations. The symbolic importance of electing an Asian Pacific American to Los Angeles's top office was widely understood. In fact, Asian Pacific Americans held fundraisers for Woo's Los Angeles mayoral campaign in cities as far away as New York City.

To determine whether there was substantive pan–Asian American support for Woo's candidacy, I analyzed campaign contributions he received in the following five months: September 1992, November 1992, January 1993, March 1993, and May 1993. Table 9.6 shows Woo's total contribution amount was $1,989,246. Non-Asians contributed the largest share of Woo's money (39.1 percent). Businesses followed in second place; they gave Woo almost 35 percent of his total contributions. Asians

Table 9.6. Woo Campaign Contributions

	Total Contributions ($)	**% of Total**
All Groups	1,989,246	100.0
Asians	494,731	24.8
Chinese	375,423	18.9
Japanese	44,875	2.3
Korean	43,075	2.2
Asian Indian	22,328	1.1
Vietnamese	7,600	0.4
Filipino	1,430	0.07
Non-Asians	778,294	39.1
Other	25,220	1.3
Businesses	691,001	34.7

Source: Los Angeles City Ethics Commission, California Long Form 490, Schedule A, 1993.

Table 9.7. Woo's Asian American Contributions by Geographic Source

Geographic Location	Total Number of Individual Contributions	% of Total Individual Contributions
All Areas	913	100
Within Los Angeles County	621	68
Outside Los Angeles County	113	12.4
Outside California	179	19.6

Source: Los Angeles City Ethics Commission, California Long Form 490, Schedule A, 1993.

constituted the third largest category of donors and provided Woo with 24.8 percent of his contributions. Within this category, Chinese Americans dominated by giving 19 percent to Woo, while the other Asian ethnic groups (combined) contributed 6 percent.

Table 9.7 indicates that over two-thirds of Woo's contributions came from within Los Angeles County. This geographic concentration can be explained in two ways. First, the Los Angeles mayoral race was a local election, so Woo focused his media advertisements and direct mailings on voters within the city. Second, a significant number of Asian American voters and contributors lived in Los Angeles. According to the 1990 census, the largest Asian Pacific American population of any mainland U.S. city was that of Los Angeles, where 9.8 percent of the population was Asian Pacific American (Ong & Azores, 1991).

Almost 20 percent of Woo's campaign contributions came from Asian Americans living outside California. Woo received 179 contributions (19.6 percent of his total Asian American contributions) from the following seventeen states: Illinois, Ohio, New York, Virginia, Texas, Maryland, Washington, Michigan, New Jersey, Arizona, Wisconsin, Missouri, Pennsylvania, Florida, Minnesota, Louisiana, and Arkansas. According to 1990 U.S. Census figures, none of these states contained an Asian and Pacific Islander population greater than 4 percent of the total population.

A Pan-Ethnic Pattern among Woo Contributors

Table 9.6 suggests a pattern of pan-ethnic support among Woo's Asian American contributors. To reiterate, Asian Americans provided about 25 percent of Woo's campaign contributions. Chinese Americans were the dominant source of this money. They gave Woo $375,423, which was nearly 76 percent of all Asian American contributions. However, other Asian American ethnic groups made substantial donations. In particular, Japanese Americans and Asian Indians contributed amounts proportionate to their share of Los Angeles' Asian American population. Japanese Americans provided 9.1 percent of the money contributed to Woo by Asian Americans ($44,874), and they represented 13.3 percent the city's Asian and Pacific Islander population. Asian Indians provided 4.5 percent of the money contributed to Woo by Asian Americans ($22,328), and they were approximately 5 percent of the Asian and Pacific Islander population (Ong & Azores, 1991).

The Asian American contributions to Woo's mayoral campaign may be viewed as significant in two ways. First, the findings illustrate the salience of campaign contributions among Asian Americans. According to the *Los Angeles Times* general and primary election exit polls, Asian Americans represented only 4 percent of the total voter turnout, the lowest of all racial groups (*Los Angeles Times,* 1993). At the same time, Asian Americans were almost one-quarter of Woo's campaign contributors. Secondly, the diversity of Woo's Asian American contributors is an encouraging indication that a pan–Asian American identity may have existed in the context of his campaign. Such diversity has been nonexistent in past local elections with an Asian American candidate. For example, in 1988, Judy Chu, a Chinese American, ran for Monterey Park (CA) City Council. Chu received $14,698 in campaign contributions. Most of this money (89 percent) was given by Chinese Americans and Japanese Americans. She did not receive contributions from members of other Asian American ethnic groups.

POLITICAL AGENTS AND PAN-ETHNIC COALITIONS: THEIR ROLE IN BUILDING FUTURE ALLIANCES

The 1991 46th Assembly District primary and the 1993 Los Angeles mayoral election indicate that certain factors—community-based organizations, the ethnic media, candidate strategy, and symbolic leadership—affect the development of pan-ethnic coalitions. In the 46th Assembly District primary election, community-based organizations and their leadership were unable to convince ambitious candidates that a unity campaign was the "best" course of action. While unsuccessful in this instance, leadership rooted in community-based organizations still has tremendous potential to mobilize Asian and Pacific Islander groups around various political issues.

Asian Pacific American community-based organizations represent one of the fastest growing areas in the Southern California public service sector. Asian Pacific American community-based organizations attempt to meet the needs of the diverse ethnic groups; their work ranges from job training and placement to immigrant and refugee assistance. In 1997, there were over 250 such pan-Asian organizations in Los Angeles and Orange counties (*Asian and Pacific Islander Community Directory for Los Angeles and Orange Counties,* 1997). Civil rights and electorally oriented pan-Asian organizations such as the Asian Pacific American Legal Center of Southern California, the Asian Pacific American Labor Alliance, and the Korean American Coalition play integral roles in the political education of Asian Pacific Americans through a broad range of political activities such as "get out the vote" drives, exit polling of Asian and Pacific Islanders, political education forums, and litigation. Thus these grassroots organizations may play a critical role in the forging of new cross-ethnic alliances.

The ethnic media could also play a vital role in nurturing pan-ethnic coalitions. It certainly did not encourage collaborative or mutually supportive relationships in the 1991 46th Assembly District primary election. The *Korea Times* and the *Los Angeles Filipino Bulletin* both emphasized the importance of getting "one of their own" elected into the State Assembly. In contrast, the *Rafu Shimpo*'s coverage of the 1991 46th Assembly District primary election stressed the importance of pan-ethnic coalition building. Los Angeles County has a network of more than 195 Asian and Pacific Islander media outlets that provide news and information to their respective bilingual populations (*Asian and Pacific Islander Community Directory for Los Angeles and Orange Counties,* 1997). With the cooperation of this extensive media network, community-based organizations could inform the larger Asian Pacific American community about pertinent issues and the benefits of pan-ethnic coalitions. Furthermore, community-based organizations and the ethnic media could work together to gather information on the needs and concerns of post-1965 ethnic groups in order to foster cohesiveness.

Another political agent that can either inhibit or facilitate the development and maintenance of inter-ethnic/racial coalitions is an effective leader or leadership (Stone, 1989; Browning, Marshall & Tabb, 1990; Sonenshein, 1993). The symbolic leader may promote a collective Asian American identity, as demonstrated by Michael Woo's 1993 Los Angeles mayoral campaign. For many Asian Pacific Americans, Woo's campaign represented a galvanizing political force, which allowed him to transcend ethnic divisions. The lack of a well known and trusted symbolic leader in the 1991 46th Assembly District primary election would partially explain the failure of a consensus candidate strategy. Stewart Kwoh, the executive director of the Asian Pacific American Legal Center of Southern California, supports this position and argues that:

> [A] candidate that is going to receive the backing of a cross-section of Asian Pacific Americans has to represent the aspirations and the hopes of those people. Much of the time that will mean that the person has to have some track record in the other Asian and Pacific Islander communities, fighting for certain interests, being visible in the community, having some sort of track record on issues or services, representing certain existing politicians, and providing certain constituent services. (S. Kwoh, interview conducted January 25, 1994)

The three Asian Pacific American candidates who ran in the 1991 46th Assembly District primary were political novices and did not have the experience, proven track record, or visibility that would be required for a unity campaign.

Asian Pacific American political leaders must possess crossover appeal to other groups besides Asian Pacific Americans (Brackman & Erie, 1995). Michael Woo was such a candidate as he received nearly 86 percent, 54 percent, and 43 percent of the African American, Latino, and white liberal votes, respectively (Sonenshein, 1993). Perhaps the future's most prominent political leaders will come from the large pool of Asian Pacific American political aides (Brackman & Erie, 1995). However, many of these aides often do not choose to run for office, and must be encouraged by the state parties and Asian Pacific American community leadership to do so. Another source of future political leadership is community-based organizations. As the number of Asian Pacific American electorally oriented community-based organizations increase, these groups will incubate Asian Pacific American political leaders with experience in coalition politics (Park, 1998).

Given California's weak political party system, a candidate's campaign strategy in mobilizing voters and contributors helps to determine whether or not a pan-ethnic coalition will develop. In the 1991 46th Assembly District primary election, candidates mobilized voters and contributors from their respective ethnic groups, and ignored the warning of

Democratic party and community leaders that to do so would split the Asian American vote. In contrast, Woo's campaign strategy during the 1993 Los Angeles mayoral election was to target a broad spectrum of Asian American ethnic contributors from Los Angeles County and outside of California. This, along with the symbolic nature of his candidacy, would explain why a pan-ethnic trend emerged from Woo's Asian American campaign contributors.

Other political factors with potential to impact the formation of future pan-ethnic coalitions include race-based policy issues such as hate crimes against Asian Pacific Americans, affirmative action, and anti-immigration policies. According to a 1996 national survey of Asian Pacific American voters, ethnic unity exists on race-based policies (*AsianWeek*, 1996). Pan-Asian coalitions have been successfully created around such issues. An example is the pan-Asian organization American Citizens for Justice that was formed in 1984 to monitor hate crimes against Asian Pacific Americans across the country. This organization consisted of liberal and conservative American-born and immigrant Chinese, Japanese, Filipinos, and Koreans (Zia, 1984). Since then, other pan-Asian organizations such as the National Asian Pacific American Legal Consortium in Washington DC, continue to monitor hate crimes. Race-based public policies may also provide a stimulus for Asian Pacific Americans to develop coalitions with other groups and to seek greater elected representation (Preston & Lai, 1998).

If pan-ethnic coalitions can be developed and maintained around key issues at the local and state levels, the political implications for Asian Pacific Americans are significant. For example, the development of a pan-Asian identity has been found to facilitate voter turnout. During the nineties, Southern California Asian Pacific American voters who personally experienced discrimination because of their race/ethnicity were more likely to vote than Asian Pacific Americans with higher education or socioeconomic attainment (Lien, 1997).

Efforts to build pan-ethnic coalitions may also be bolstered by increases in Asian Pacific American elected representation. There are more candidates of various Asian ethnicities running for office and winning federal, state, and local positions than ever before. During the June 1998 primary elections in California, a record twenty-four candidates ran for such positions, with fourteen winning nominations. There are currently over 2,000 Asian and Pacific Islander elected and appointed officials from over thirty-one states compared to less than 500 in 1978 (*National Asian Pacific American Political Almanac*, 1998–1999). As the numbers of elected Asian Pacific American candidates grow, the urgency of post-1965 Asian Pacific American groups to work only on behalf of "one of their own" will diminish. In turn, this should enhance the likelihood that ethnic groups would support each other's candidates at the ballot box.

The future of Asian Pacific American electoral politics—and gains in empowerment via pan-ethnic identity and collaboration—will most likely be shaped and influenced by community-based organizations, the ethnic media, symbolic leadership, and candidate campaign strategy. Scholars of Asian Pacific American politics argue that it is necessary to extend traditional approaches towards political behavior (e.g., voting) to include nontraditional actors and their influences on Asian Pacific American behavior and attitudes (Nakanishi, 1986; Lien, 1997; Nakanishi, 1998; Saito, 1998). Growth in the size and ethnic diversity of the Asian Pacific American population presents special challenges to scholars and activists alike. Building pan-Asian coalitions designed to increase Asian Pacific American political influence is a difficult task, but one with potentially high rewards. For that reason, it is well worth our attention in the next millennium.

REFERENCES

Alexander, H.E. (1991). *Reform and reality: The financing of state and local campaigns.* New York: Twentieth Century Fund Press.

Asian and Pacific Islander Community Directory for Los Angeles and Orange Counties, 7th ed. (1997). Los Angeles: UCLA Asian American Studies Center.

Asian Pacific American Legal Center of Southern California (1996). *1996 Southern California Asian Pacific American exit poll report: An analysis of APA voter behavior and opinions.*

Asian Week. Asian Americans on the issues: The Results of a national survey of Asian American voters. (1996, August 23), pp. 14–17.

Brackman, H., & Erie, S. P. (1995). Beyond 'Politics by Other Means': Empowerment strategies for Los Angeles' Asian Pacific Community. In M.P. Smith & J. R. Feagin (eds.), *The bubbling cauldron: Race, ethnicity, and the urban crisis* (pp. 282–303). Minneapolis: University of Minnesota Press.

Browning, R.P., Marshall, D.R., & Tabb, D.H. (1990). Minority mobilization in ten cities: Failures and successes. In R.P. Browning, D.R. Marshall, & D.H. Tabb (eds.), *Racial politics in American cities* (pp. 8–32). New York: Longman.

Cain, B.E. (1991). The contemporary context of ethnic and racial politics in California. In B.O. Jackson & M.B. Preston (eds.), *Racial and ethnic politics in California,* Vol. 1 (pp. 9–24). Berkeley, CA: Institute of Governmental Studies Press.

Cain, B.E., & MacDonald, K. (1998). Race and party politics in the 1996 U.S. presidential election. In M.B. Preston, B.E. Cain, & S. Bass (eds.), *Racial and ethnic politics in California,* Vol. 2 (pp. 199–232). Berkeley, CA: Institute of Governmental Studies Press.

California Journal. (1990). Legislative district maps of California supplement.

Dahl, R. (1961). *Who governs?* New Haven, CT: Yale University Press.

Erie, S.P., & Brackman, H. (1993). *Paths to political incorporation for Latinos and Asian Pacifics in California.* University of California: The California Policy Seminar.

Espiritu, Y.L. (1992). *Asian American panethnicity: Bridging institutions and identities.* Philadelphia: Temple University Press.

Espiritu, Y.L., & Ong, P.M. (1994). Class constraints on racial solidarity among Asian Americans. In P.M. Ong, E. Bonacich, & L. Cheng (eds.), *The new Asian immigration in Los Angeles and global restructuring* (pp. 395–322). Philadelphia: Temple University Press.

Field Institute Poll. (1994). In J.S. Lai (ed.), *1996 national Asian Pacific American political almanac,* 7th ed. (pp. 187–188). Los Angeles: UCLA Asian American Studies Center.

Horton, J. (1989). The politics of ethnic change: Grass-roots responses to economic and demographic restructuring in Monterey Park, California. *Urban Geography,* 10, 578–592.

Jennings, J. (1994). Changing urban policy paradigms: Impact of black and Latino coalitions. In J. Jennings (ed.), *Blacks, Latinos, and Asians in urban America* (pp. 3–16). Westport, CN: Praeger.

Korea Times, Coalition in the making: Koreans and Filipinos close ranks for future elections. (1991b, July 21), p. 1.

Korea Times, Son of Koreatown: T.S. Chung seeks seat in Sacramento. (1991a, March 20), p. 1

Lai, J.S. (1994). *At the threshold of the golden door—Ethnic politics and Pan-Asian Pacific American coalition building.* Unpublished master's thesis, University of California, Los Angeles, CA.

Los Angeles City Ethics Commission. (1993). Michael Woo for Los Angeles Mayor. California Long Form 490, Schedule A.

Los Angeles County Registrar Recorder's Office: Office of Campaign Reporting. (1991). Tong Soo Chung for 46th Assembly, California Long Form 490, Schedule A.

Los Angeles County Registrar Recorder's Office: Office of Campaign Reporting. (1991). Keith Umemoto for 46th Assembly, California Long Form 490, Schedule A.

Los Angeles County Registrar Recorder's Office: Office of Campaign Reporting. (1991). Joselyn Geag Yap for 46th Assembly, California Long Form 490, Schedule A.

Los Angeles Times. (1993, June 10). Exit poll, p. A25.

Lien, P. (1997). *The political participation of Asian Americans: Voting behavior in Southern California.* New York: Garland Publishing.

Los Angeles Times. 1993 Los Angeles mayoral election general and primary exit poll results. (1993, June 10), A25.

Nakanishi, D.T. (1986). Asian American politics: An agenda for research. *Amerasia Journal, 12,* 1–27.

Nakanishi, D.T. (1991). The next swing vote? Asian Pacific Americans and California politics. In B.O. Jackson & M.B. Preston (eds.), *Racial and ethnic politics in California,* Vol. 1 (pp. 25–54). Berkeley, CA: Institute of Governmental Studies Press.

Nakanishi, D.T. (1998). When numbers do not add up: Asian Pacific Americans and California politics. In M.B. Preston, B.E. Cain, & S. Bass (eds.), *Racial and ethnic politics in California,* Vol. 2 (pp. 3–43). Berkeley, CA: Institute of Governmental Studies Press.

National Asian Pacific American Political Almanac, 8th ed. (1998–1999). Los Angeles: UCLA Asian American Studies Center.

Omi, M., & Winant, H. (1986). *Racial formation in the United States: From the 1960s to the 1980s.* New York: Routledge.

Ong, P.M., & Azores, T. (1991). *Asian Pacific Americans in Los Angeles: A demographic profile.* Los Angeles: LEAP Public Policy Institute and UCLA Asian American Studies Center.

Ong, P. M., & Nakanishi, D. T. (1996). Becoming citizens, becoming voters: The naturalization and political participation of Asian Pacific immigrants. In B.O. Hing & R. Lee (eds.), *Reframing the immigration debate* (pp. 275–305). Los Angeles: LEAP Public Policy Institute and UCLA Asian American Studies Center.

Ong, P.M., Espiritu, Y.L., & Azores, T. (1991). *Redistricting and political empowerment of Asian Pacific Americans in Los Angeles: A position paper.* Los Angeles, CA: LEAP Public Policy Institute and UCLA Asian American Studies Center.

Park, E. (1998). Competing visions: Political formation of Korean Americans in Los Angeles, 1992–1997. *Amerasia Journal, 24:* 1, 41–58.

Preston, M.B., & Lai, J.S. (1998). The symbolic politics of affirmative action. In M.B. Preston, B.E. Cain, & S. Bass (eds.), *Racial and ethnic politics in Cal-*

ifornia, Vol. 2 (pp. 161–198). Berkeley, CA: Institute of Governmental Studies Press.

Rafu Shimpo, 46th district tests ethnic loyalties: Three candidates, representing different Asian Pacific ethnic groups, test the community's ethnic and personal alliances. (1991, May 22), p. 3.

Saito, L.T. (1998). Beyond numbers: Asian American and Latino politics in Los Angeles' San Gabriel Valley. In M.B. Preston, B.E. Cain, & S. Bass (eds.), *Racial and ethnic politics in California,* Vol. 2 (pp. 45–72). Berkeley, CA: Institute of Governmental Studies Press.

Shinagawa, L.H. (1996). The impact of immigration on the demography of Asian Pacific Americans. In B.O. Hing & R. Lee (eds.), *Reframing the immigration debate* (pp. 59–130). Los Angeles: LEAP Public Policy Institute and UCLA Asian American Studies Center.

Sonenshein, R.J. (1993). *Politics in black and white: Race and power in Los Angeles.* Princeton, NJ: Princeton University Press.

Stone, C.N. (1989). *Regime politics: Governing Atlanta,* 1946–1988. Lawrence, KS: University of Kansas Press.

Tachibana, J. (1986). California's Asians: Power from a growing population. *California Journal,* 17, 534–543.

Verba, S., & Nie, N. (1972). *Participation in America.* New York: Harper & Row.

Wei, W. (1993). *The Asian American movement.* Philadelphia: Temple University Press.

Wolfinger, R.E. (1965). The development and persistence of ethnic voting. *American Political Science Review,* 59, 898–908.

Yap, J.G. (1991, April). Lack of visability spells a weakened voice in politics. *Los Angeles Filipino Bulletin,* p. 1.

Zia, H. (1984). The new violence. *Bridge,* 9:2, 18–23.

NOTES

[1]Asian Pacific Americans, and other minorities, have usually been under-sampled in most statewide and local election exit polls (Lien, 1997; Cain & Mac-Donald, 1998). As a result, estimates of Asian Pacific American voter turnout have been subject to criticism by scholars of Asian Pacific American politics (Ong & Nakanishi, 1996).

[2]This is not to downplay the significance of the need for Asian Pacific Americans to coalesce with other racial groups in California and elsewhere. The ability of Asian Pacific Americans to develop and maintain advantageous coalitions with other racial and ethnic groups will be central to their future political incorporation (Erie & Brackman, 1993; Jennings, 1994).

[3]Asian Pacific Americans have a history of being large campaign contributors to federal, state, and local campaigns (Tachibana, 1986; Nakanishi, 1991; Lai, 1994; Lien, 1997). This is primarily because one does not have to be a citizen or a registered voter to give a campaign contribution. One only needs to be a legal permanent resident in the United States at the time the contribution was given (Alexander, 1991). Given their proclivity toward campaign contributions combined with the limitations of exit poll data (i.e., the absence of exit poll data at the voter level that operationalizes for Asian ethnicity; the undersampling of Asian and Pacific Islander respondents; and their low voter turnout rate), analyzing campaign contribution data allows one to address pan–Asian Pacific American coalitions more effectively.

[4]The author wishes to clarify the spellings of the ethnic enclaves and groups that will be discussed throughout this chapter. The spellings of "Koreatown" and "Filipino Town" are adopted from the respective ethnic communities. The term "Filipino American" will be used as opposed to "Pilipino American," as it is more commonly used.

[5]Several limitations are associated with the surname identification method. One limitation of surname identification was that some surnames could be either Asian or non-Asian (e.g., Lee). These contributions were placed in the Unknown category. Another limitation in surname identification involved interracial marriage, whereby surnames of contributors could have been changed.

[6]Official campaign contribution reports for T.S. Chung indicate he received monetary contributions from the following international Korean corporations with headquarters in the United States: Hyundai Corporation USA (5/20/91); Sangyong International, Inc. (5/20/91); and Dongkuk International, Inc. (5/20/91).

CHAPTER 10

Gay and Lesbian Incorporation into Four Urban Regimes in Upstate New York

DONALD B. ROSENTHAL

There has been a considerable increase in the visibility of lesbians and gay men in American politics and society in the past twenty years. Beyond visibility, the record of social and political incorporation is mixed. Nonetheless, there continue to be sufficient victories and near-victories to sustain commitment to a gay and lesbian identity movement. Many of those victories have taken place in local political arenas, where lesbian and gay voters are increasingly courted by officeholders and candidates for office and where a small but increasing number of lesbians and gay men have been elected to municipal office. There is also a mounting body of local ordinances designed to provide civil rights protections. According to one recent study, at least 100 cities and 25 counties currently have such ordinances (Button, Rienzo & Wald, 1997). In those and other places, lesbians and gay men increasingly have become "players" in local politics and government.

While the incorporation experiences of gays and lesbians parallel those of other groups that have sought individual and collective opportunities through participation in municipal politics, ethnic and racial groups have received the bulk of attention in the incorporation literature. Furthermore, such groups have been seen through the lens of what Bullard and Feagin (1991, p. 59) characterize as "assimilation-progress models." Whether reflected in the early work of Dahl (1961) on ethnic group assimilation in New Haven or, more recently, in the research of Browning, Marshall, and Tabb (1984) on racial group incorporation in ten Northern California cities, the underlying appeal of the incorporation model is its concordance with democratic ideals.

Yet, in practice, as Bullard and Feagin argue, and as a number of the contributors to the recent collection edited by Browning, Marshall, and Tabb (1997) illustrate, the incorporation efforts of important groups like African Americans and Latinos/as in most cities have yielded limited benefits for group members. What substantive benefits have been distributed—most commonly, political appointments and public service jobs in local government—have gone mainly to a small middle-class. At best, most members of the group have received only those psychological benefits that flow from symbolic recognition of their communities.

That is not to suggest that symbolic benefits may not contribute to the long-term economic and social advancement of a group. Insofar as symbolic recognition initiates a process by which the larger population reconstructs its evaluations of a minority group, it may constitute an important first step toward substantive incorporation. Yet, that leaves open what benefits social and political incorporation actually provide to members of a marginalized group. Furthermore, the process of incorporation may be a much more tortuous and fragile one than Browning, Marshall, and Tabb have recognized. It may be marked by frustrations and blockages even where governing coalitions and local governments are nominally sympathetic.

For the purpose of understanding some of the problems of gay and lesbian political incorporation, I report here the results of more than seventy-five interviews conducted with leading local activists and political observers, and draw on published and unpublished materials collected over the past eight years. These materials focus on lesbian and gay social and political mobilization and political participation in four medium-sized metropolitan areas in upstate New York: Albany, Buffalo, Rochester, and Syracuse. After briefly introducing readers to some general themes bearing on the development of the gay and lesbian movement and patterns of political incorporation of gays and lesbians into local governing coalitions, I will review how regimes in the four central cities proceeded from repression in the 1960s to varying degrees of incorporation by the 1990s.

THE GAY AND LESBIAN MOVEMENT

Like ethnic and racial groups that have placed claims on local governments before them, gay and lesbian progress in urban political arenas needs to be understood not only in terms of the obstacles overcome and the victories won, but also in relation to the special problems involved in constructing and mobilizing the political community for which political activists claim to speak and in shaping the demands put forward by those leaders.

One of the special challenges to the lesbian and gay population is defining the boundaries of the group. Given the silences, ambiguities, and repressions associated historically with homosexuality in American society, it is impossible to estimate the size of the gay and lesbian (as well as bisexual and transgendered) population in the United States as a whole or in any particular locality. (In that connection, see, Bailey, 1999; D'Emilio, 1996.) Furthermore, there are important class and racial differences among lesbians and gay men. Most local political organizing tends to be dominated by middle-class white men and women. Undoubtedly, the advances made by those who claimed to speak politically or socially for the larger collectivity may have made it easier for some people to think of themselves as gay, lesbian, or bisexual in the past thirty years, but visibility continues to represent a personal challenge to those who struggle with their own identities even in otherwise supportive environments. To the leadership of this ambiguously delimited and internally fragmented population, the situation presents an enormous problem both in terms of community building and the formulation of political demands.

Compared to many other movements for political change (Darnovksy, Epstein & Flacks, 1995; Morris & Mueller, 1992; Tarrow, 1994), material considerations have been only marginally implicated in the gay and lesbian movement. That is not to deny the claim that many lesbians and some gay men (particularly those of color or from working-class backgrounds) have been discriminated against in terms of economic opportunities. However, a shared sense of economic deprivation has not been as central to the mobilization efforts of the movement nor to the goals the movement's spokespeople have laid out as have issues of social and political equality. As a result, while nondiscrimination in employment has found a place among the demands of the movement (along with nondiscrimination in housing and public accommodations), what the gay and lesbian movement has promoted is equal opportunity rather than any measure of affirmative action for lesbians and gay men in the workforce—a classically moderate and middle-class ideological position in American politics.

A second generation of demands—those having to do with the recognition of domestic partnerships for purposes such as paid leave for family-related emergencies and health insurance coverage—has entered a somewhat more complex realm of discourse. Obtaining such recognition has entailed political bargaining for equality of treatment in regard to material benefits that are otherwise accorded only to legally sanctioned marriages.

While a small proportion of movement intellectuals and national political leaders seek to reach out to potential coalition partners on what remains of the political left or to those who represent minorities or the poor (Cohen, 1997; Vaid, 1995), most political activists—both nationally and locally—have come to focus increasingly on an assimilationist agenda that calls for equality of treatment in governmental and nongovernmental arenas. (For the assimilationist position, see Bawer, 1993; Kirk & Madsen, 1989; and Sullivan, 1995.)

Although gay and lesbian policy demands are sometimes treated by opponents as the expression of a well-articulated national gay and lesbian movement, in reality that movement is both fluid and decentralized. These characteristics are not peculiar to the gay and lesbian movement but have been observed in other social movements in the United States, notably the women's movement (Costain, 1992) and the African American civil rights movement of the 1950s and 1960s (McAdam, 1982).

Contributing to the decentralized and fluid character of the gay and lesbian movement and the way its demands are presented and promoted is a history of weak national organizations that have never developed effective structures for reaching down to localities to mobilize broad support. Unlike the civil rights movement, which was able to draw on local black churches for significant resources, the lesbian and gay movement has achieved a measure of political expression in hundreds of localities without the development of well-articulated relationships between national organizations and local activists. What national organizations have helped to do is frame issues for the movement which are then pursued or ignored by local political activists as they see fit. At the same time, however, the behaviors of local activists have been shaped in significant measure by their own political values and the character of the political environments within which they have chosen to work.

LOCAL REGIMES AND INCORPORATION PROCESSES

In order to assess the extent and character of local lesbian and gay political incorporation, it is necessary to understand not only how members of that population have been mobilized, but the nature of the established institutional arrangements they have attempted to enter and influence. In that regard, we will follow the practice of Browning, Marshall, and Tabb

(1984) and many of the contributors to their more recent edited volume (1997) of focusing on local electoral politics and the governing coalitions that operate municipal governments. I would argue that the behaviors of local governments reflect long-established value patterns that operate in local communities. In this usage, I follow David Easton's (1965, p. 193) formulation of "regime," which emphasizes the "values" and "norms" that circumscribe the behaviors of a political system.[1] As Easton wrote,

> . . . [V]alues serve as broad limits with regard to what can be taken for granted in the guidance of day-to-day policy without violating deep feelings of important segments of the community. The norms specify the kinds of procedures that are expected and acceptable in the processing and implementation of demands.

For present purposes, it is important to view incorporation as involving the overcoming of established social and cultural barriers associated with the operations of local regimes. This extends to influencing changes in the behaviors of important culture-shaping institutions like local media and religious bodies as well as removing more specific institutional barriers to influence in political and governing coalitions. In that connection, we will postulate four phases in the incorporation process, in general, and then examine the relations that have developed between gays and lesbians and local regimes in the four cities we examined. The four phases are: 1) *repression;* 2) *exclusion;* 3) *symbolic recognition;* and 4) *substantive incorporation.*

Under *regime repression,* the subject population is not only excluded from participation in politics and government, but it experiences severe deprivations and institutionalized use of force, including imprisonment and harassment by the instruments of the regime, particularly the police. This is done in the name of societal control of behaviors unacceptable to the dominant political culture. Such experiences are familiar to students of African American history. On a lesser scale, the history of lesbians and gay men in many communities is similar. Thus, the police were regularly employed in the past (and still are in some places) to invade gay spaces—bars, bathhouses, and cruising areas—and to arrest people on a variety of charges (Chauncey, 1994; D'Emilio, 1983; Duberman, 1993; Kennedy & Davis, 1993).

In this repressive atmosphere, it was relatively easy to lose one's job or one's home without political or legal recourse. While these disabilities were generally treated as outside the purview of government, the fact that recourse was not available to local regimes reflected the pervasiveness of anti-gay values. Under the circumstances, the principal route for survival for some gays and lesbians was to burrow even further underground. Others chose to stay aloof from the social networks that existed within the underground, especially during periods of high repression.

There is considerable speculation about the causes that led to the creation of a gay and lesbian movement in the United States (Adam, 1987; Cruickshank, 1992; D'Emilio, 1983). Nonetheless, in cities across the country in the 1950s and 1960s, but particularly in New York (Duberman, 1993) and San Francisco (Shilts, 1982), repression began to be regularly challenged by an emerging gay and lesbian community. Where these challenges were successful, regimes adopted a posture of *exclusion* as a first line of response. Regulation by the police was no longer as commonplace (though police might continue to maintain surveillance near gay bars or cruising areas). More broadly, exclusion meant official regime indifference to the presence of lesbians and gay men so long as members of that population remained "discreet" in their behaviors. Contemporaneously, however, leaders of nongovernmental institutions like the media and many of the religious organizations that helped shape local culture asserted traditional values by expressing strong antipathy toward members of the group.

It was during this period of exclusion—beginning in some larger cities in the 1970s—that greater freedom for community building occurred. As a result, gays and lesbians created a multitude of affinity groups (e.g., sports clubs; choruses; religious groups; addiction and psychological support groups; hobby clubs; drag performance organizations) and strengthened existing friendship networks. These came to play an important role in defining social opportunities for lesbians and gay men. Among these organizations, only a tiny proportion were explicitly concerned with partisan politics or with "political issues" more broadly understood, but they all had at their core the promotion of collective identities and they came to make up the building blocks of local lesbian and gay communities.

Depending on the effectiveness of local political mobilization, some gay and lesbian activists began to feel sufficiently empowered to make limited claims on the political system. In the four cities studied, most of these initiatives involved reactions to particular events—a police raid on a gay bath house; the murder of a gay man for which the attacker was convicted only of burglary; homophobic comments by public officials.

Such instances resemble forms of *demand-protest* described by Browning, Marshall, and Tabb for some of their Northern California cities during the 1960s and 1970s.[2]

While lesbians and gay men began to be recognized as legitimate participants in local politics in some places before the 1980s, local political mobilization and incorporation processes were complicated by AIDS and the rise of AIDS activism in the early 1980s. We cannot begin to address that connection here (see Rosenthal, 1996b), but one aspect of AIDS activism was that it provided a vehicle for intense mobilization by gay men and lesbians in all four of the communities studied here and fostered occasional episodes of demand-protest in its own right. While it was feared at the outset of the epidemic that AIDS would set the gay and lesbian movement back, the serious public policy concerns of the community in regard to the epidemic actually appear to have tapped into a vein of governmental and public support (at least in New York State) that enhanced gay and lesbian visibility and political self-confidence. In a way that still remains to be analyzed in detail, the epidemic may have contributed to mobilizing gay men and lesbians' political concerns on issues distinct from AIDS.

Even before AIDS activism became commonplace, connections began to be made between some local politicians and public officials and leaders of the gay and lesbian community. This rapprochement depended both on the level and character of lesbian and gay political mobilization in each locality and the incentives members of existing local electoral coalitions (both incumbent and oppositional) or governing coalitions had to gaining political support from the group. Much like the experience of coalition building described by Browning, Marshall, and Tabb, lesbians and gay men gradually came to be seen as useful resources in putting together liberal electoral and governing coalitions.

The initial steps toward incorporation took the form of *symbolic recognition.* In exchange for electoral support (including financial contributions and campaign work), those associated with the political regime or those engaged in contesting against incumbent regimes reached out through symbolic gestures. Supportive appearances at community events (e.g., community picnics or forums; Gay Pride events) or official proclamations recognizing Gay Pride celebrations contributed to establishing bonds between members of the lesbian and gay population and local political leaders. With time, these bonds were extended to include invitations to participate more directly in the political process. Given the importance of partisanship in framing politics in New York

State, lesbian and gay participation in electoral politics (as campaign workers, party committee members, and, ultimately, as candidates for office and participants in party decision making) has been an important route to incorporation into governing coalitions.

At a point that may be rather subtle in some places, taking lesbians and gay men "into account" as legitimate participants in the distribution of symbolic recognition crosses the line into *substantive incorporation.* There are various forms such incorporation may take, including: 1) *individual material benefits* such as appointments to government offices, including various municipal boards and commissions; 2) *collective material benefits* that provide the group with organizational resources that can be used to advance various aspects of the social mobilization and service activities of the community; and 3) *collective policy benefits* that advance the communal concerns of lesbians and gay men in relation to the larger population. (For the derivation of these distinctions, see Clark & Wilson, 1961; and Wilson 1960, 1973.) Such efforts might also encourage better formal and informal administrative relations with local government agencies such as the police department, the schools, or other agencies with important roles in providing social or cultural services.

INCORPORATION INTO THE FOUR REGIMES

In three of the four localities examined here (Albany, Buffalo, and Rochester), significant regime changes have taken place since the 1970s that have allowed for the political incorporation of gays and lesbians into local politics and government. In the fourth city, Syracuse, a measure of symbolic accommodation has taken place, but the regime has not moved toward incorporation to the same extent.

Before addressing the character of regime accommodations, it is useful to highlight a few features of local politics and government that the four regimes share in common and a few ways they differ. Party government is strong in New York State and in its larger municipal jurisdictions. Over the past twenty years, the Democratic party has been the predominant political force in the four cities, but factionalism within that party and the ambitions of local party politicians have created opportunities for party dissidents to win occasional elections.

Albany, until recently, has operated under a machine-dominated regime. In the other cities, the Democratic party has operated as an umbrella under which a variety of patronage-oriented and reformist forces have jostled along with ethnic and racial groups to gain a measure of political advantage. Reflecting differences in local political traditions and cultures, Rochester's Democratic party has assumed a more open "good government" tone, whereas Buffalo's Democratic party has reflected more emphasis on conflicts among racial and ethnic groups. (Nonetheless, the Rochester Democratic party has had to accommodate a growing African American population which has challenged the middle-class "good government" traditions of the city.) Syracuse's Democratic party falls somewhere between the two, but also reflects the generally conservative values of a predominantly white working-class population for whom voting Republican is an increasingly acceptable political behavior. Except for Syracuse, however, the other cities remain overwhelmingly Democratic.

Demography and electoral behaviors are filtered through governmental structures that are generally nonreformist in character. Except for Rochester, which tried a city-manager system from the 1960s until 1985, all of the cities currently have strong-mayor systems. At the same time, all of them have accepted a measure of reformist ideas about legislative representation promoted earlier in the century. Thus, their municipal councils are relatively small (nine to fifteen members) and include some at-large representation, though each council has a majority of members elected from districts.

Rochester: Pluralist Politics and Reformist Government

Among the four cities, Rochester's regime has been historically the most *pluralistic* culturally and *reformist* politically (Rosenthal, 1999). Not only government but the business sector has been open to diversity for the last decade, as industries like Eastman Kodak and Xerox—companies with long-established ties to the area—have led the way (not only locally but nationally) in adopting gay-friendly employment policies.

While these behavior patterns reflect middle-class traditions once found locally in both the Democratic and Republican parties, Rochester's politics also has had to take into account the city's economic decline and the changing composition of the city population. Thus, as Tables 10.1 and 10.2 indicate, not only did the city experience a substantial decline in population between 1970 and 1990, but by 1990 it had the second highest percentage of individuals (23.5 percent) living below the poverty line among the four cities (only slightly ahead of Buffalo's 25.6 percent). Indeed, despite its past reputation as a center of white-collar employment, by 1990 it was third among the four cities in terms of the percentage of population holding BAs or higher degrees (19 percent). The city also had the highest percentage of minorities by 1990 among the four cities.

Table 10.1. City Populations 1970 and 1990 (Totals and by Race)

Location	Total 1970	Total 1990	White 1970	White 1990	African American 1970	African American 1990	Other 1970	Other 1990
Albany	115,781	101,082	100,851	76,323	14,132	20,869	798	3,890
			(87%)*	(75%)	(12%)	(20%)	(1%)	(5%)
Buffalo	462,768	328,123	364,367	212,449	94,329	100,579	4,072	15,095
			(79%)	(65%)	(20%)	(30%)	(1%)	(5%)
Rochester	296,233	231,636	244,118	141,503	49,647	73,024	2,468	17,109
			(82%)	(61%)	(17%)	(32%)	(1%)	(7%)
Syracuse	197,208	163,860	173,611	122,867	21,383	33,320	2,214	17,109
			(88%)	(75%)	(11%)	(20%)	(1%)	(5%)

Source: U.S. Census 1970 and 1990.
*percentage of total

**Table 10.2. Economic and Educational Characteristics for
City Populations 1970 and 1990**

Location	Per Capita Income 1990	Persons below Poverty Line 1970	Persons below Poverty Line 1990	BA or Higher 1970	BA or Higher 1990
Albany	13,742	14.2%	18.3%	12.4%	29.5%
Buffalo	10,445	15.2%	25.6%	6.7%	16.0%
Rochester	11,704	12.4%	23.5%	7.8%	19.0%
Syracuse	11,351	14.1%	22.7%	13.1%	22.0%

Source: U.S. Census 1970 and 1990.

Perhaps as much because of its political culture and traditions of liberalism as its contemporary demographics, Rochester was viewed as gay friendly from early in the history of the national gay and lesbian movement. That movement took root with relatively little opposition from the time in October 1970 that the first meeting was held on the campus of the University of Rochester that led ultimately to the creation of the Gay Alliance of the Genesee Valley (GAGV) in 1973. GAGV continues to serve as an interorganizational network drawing together a number of affinity groups. Shortly after its creation, lesbians and gay men affiliated with GAGV created what later became the city's Lesbian and Gay Political Caucus.

After a period where Democratic and Republican majorities had alternated in controlling Rochester's city council and in selecting Rochester's city manager, Democratic candidates for municipal office won a firm governing majority in 1973 and turned Rochester into a one-party Democratic city. This was done by accommodating African Americans, women, and gay men and lesbians into the party structure and then into city government. From the beginning, Democratic candidates for office sought campaign support from the lesbian and gay community. In symbolic exchange, they attended leading community events, and appeared at election meetings sponsored by gay groups or held in gay and lesbian–operated locations. In this environment, lesbians and gay men found it easy to win seats on Democratic party committees and become a recognized part of the party structure.

This situation provided opportunities for lesbians and gay men to gain both symbolic and substantive benefits. Proclamations recognizing gay events were easily achieved by the late 1970s. Equally important, a formal liaison with the Rochester Police Department was established—one that has remained in place. About the same time, the community received its first (and, thus far, only) direct public benefit from the city government in the form of a two-year grant under the federal Comprehensive Employment and Training Act which was used by GAGV to hire staff and strengthen the administrative operations of the organization.

It was an exclusionary act of the local Chamber of Commerce that mobilized lesbians and gay men to seek formal legislative recognition from the municipal government. In 1982, the Chamber refused to rent space to GAGV to hold an awards dinner. While the city council did not act against the chamber, members of the council felt they had to display some measure of support for the gay and lesbian community. That support took the form of passing an ordinance protecting the rights of municipal employees against discrimination. Until 1994, that was the only legislative measure passed by the Rochester City Council aimed directly at protecting gays and lesbians.[3]

In 1985, one of the leaders of the Lesbian and Gay Political Caucus, Tim Mains, ran for the city council. Although he did not receive the endorsement of the party organization in the Democratic primary, he was able to mobilize sufficient backing to win a narrow victory for an at-large seat. He then went on to win easily in the general election, thereby becoming the first openly gay elected official in New York State. (Mains was elected to his fourth term in 1997.)

Political incorporation in Rochester does not mean that the lesbian and gay community always gets what it wants or that what it gets comes without a struggle. Thus, GAGV battled for three years with the city administration to gain a property tax exemption (as a not-for-profit organization) for the community center it opened in 1990. The mayor, who had a mixed record of policy leadership generally and a lukewarm attitude toward the lesbian and gay community during his two terms, supported the city assessor on this issue. The latter strongly opposed the tax exemption (as he did for claims by most organizations seeking them). As a result, the matter was referred to the state courts where an appellate court ruled in favor of GAGV in February 1994. By the time of that ruling, the new mayor, William Johnson, had gone on record in support of the exemption.

Johnson, an African American, had emerged out of a crowded field of Democrats in 1993 that included other African Americans, several whites, and one Latina. Gay and lesbian activists divided among several of the contestants, but Johnson was not among their leading choices. Nonetheless, he succeeded in winning narrowly in the primary and then easily in the general election.

Johnson could have remained silent in 1994 when Council member Mains introduced legislation to extend health benefits to the domestic partners of city employees and to establish a register of domestic partners for all city residents.[4] Instead, the mayor went on record that he would sign both measures if they were passed by the council. The first passed by a vote of 7 to 2, the second by 6 to 3. Indeed, by 1997, Mayor Johnson was so popular both among the general public and in the lesbian and gay community that he was re-elected without opposition.

On the whole, Rochester gays and lesbians have been slow to seek either significant individual or collective material advantages from their participation in the local governing coalition (unless one counts domestic partnership benefits for government workers among significant movement victories). No senior administrative appointments have flowed to leaders of the community under the Johnson administration nor have material benefits gone directly to GAGV. On the one hand, it could be argued, that because neither Mayor Johnson nor his predecessor owed political debts to the gay and lesbian community, there was no reason to expect such actions to be taken. On the other hand, the predominantly middle-class gay and lesbian activists who might have staked claims to such rewards shared "good government" values with the regime in which the price of participation and support for the regime was not measured in terms of individual or collective material benefits.

Albany: Machine Politics Old and New

For much of this century, Albany was governed by one of the most famous political machines in American history (Erie, 1988; Robinson, 1977; Swanstrom & Ward, 1987). That machine drew its major support from conservative working-class and, later, middle-class Irish Catholics. However, it began to lose some of its support in the early 1970s as older voters left the city or died. While the machine did cultivate votes in the African American population, the rewards to that community were minor. In addition, few women held elected or appointed offices under the machine.

A more cosmopolitan subculture began to emerge in the 1960s as middle-class migrants to Albany were lured by the rapid growth in state government employment under Governor Nelson Rockefeller. It was during the Rockefeller years that major construction projects got underway in the city and nearby suburbs, including a new campus of the state university. As a result of these new investments and employment opportunities, the city's per capita income by 1990 was the highest of the four cities and it had the highest percentage of persons with BAs. (See Table 2.) It also tied with Syracuse for the lowest percentage of nonwhites (25 percent).

Finding themselves unwelcome politically in a city where the machine was firmly in control of local government, some of the newcomers came together in the mid-1970s at the neighborhood level to form block clubs in two of the city's gentrifying neighborhoods. Later, this self-styled "progressive" coalition was joined in uneasy alliance by a few African American politicians who resented the marginalization of their community by the machine. Politically active gays and lesbians were welcomed into these efforts to create an oppositional electoral coalition.

The attitudes of the local regime were mainly ones of exclusion toward lesbians and gay men. There were occasional episodes of repression like a raid conducted by the police department that shut the city's only gay bathhouse in the late 1970s, but such episodes were relatively isolated. They also did not so much generate demand-protest by gays and lesbians as they did efforts to form a political organization independent of the machine. That organization emerged as the Eleanor Roosevelt Democratic Club (ERDC) in 1983.

The death in office in the same year of long-time mayor, Erastus Corning, set off a prolonged period of jockeying for leadership within the machine. For nearly a decade, this infighting went on even as the machine continued to control the mayor's office and the city council. Thus, in their first electoral effort in 1985, the progressive coalition managed to elect only two members to the fifteen-member city council: one, a neighborhood activist; the second, an African American from a poor ward of the city. As a further indicator of the weakness of that coalition, they were able to get only two votes for a gay rights amendment to a pending civil rights ordinance in 1988 which would have provided protections against discrimination in employment, housing, and public accommodations. The machine majority cast twelve votes against the measure; one member abstained.

In the municipal elections of 1989, the ERDC and their coalition partners endorsed four candidates who supported gay and lesbian rights. Three went on to win, among them Keith St. John, who became the first gay African American elected to municipal office in the United States. The progressive caucus in the city council again brought the gay rights amendment to a vote in January 1991 and was again defeated, this time by a vote of 10 to 5.

Despite that setback, the mayor, who was a contestant for Democratic party leadership, chose to reach out to the lesbian and gay community in his January 1992 "State of the City" address when he expressed his support for a slightly revised gay rights ordinance. Negotiations ensued in which St. John took a leading role on behalf of the gay and lesbian community.[5] Although the proposal attracted heated opposition from religious conservatives, the ordinance passed in December 1992 by a vote of 8 to 6.

The mayor's actions proved to be irrelevant to the party's decision about its endorsement in 1993. He was denied renomination. The primary contest for mayor that followed pitted two long-time Democrats against each other. Running against the endorsed candidate of the machine was Gerald Jennings, who had served in the past on the council as a party-backed candidate. Jennings had been denied endorsement in 1989 but had run as an independent Democrat. During that campaign, he received strong ERDC support, despite a mixed record on gay rights. (As a machine-supported member of the council in 1988, Jennings had voted against the ordinance; in 1991 he shifted his vote when he sat on the council as an independent Democrat elected with ERDC backing.) By 1993, both mayoral candidates sought gay and lesbian support, but Jennings won that endorsement and was elected easily, along with nine other candidates endorsed by ERDC. In the only seat where a candidate endorsed by ERDC lost, all three candidates had indicated their commitment to gay rights.

By the municipal elections of 1997, some of the leaders of the ERDC had become part of the electoral coalition associated with Mayor Jennings and served as advisors and leading political organizers for the mayor. However, they did not press for individual or material benefits. The only new piece of legislation they promoted was a measure that passed in the spring of 1996 (by a vote of 12 to 3) that established a domestic partnership register for city residents much like the one passed earlier in Rochester. This legislation did little more than confirm the electoral influence that lesbians and gay activists were perceived to have in the city of Albany.

Indeed, by 1997, ERDC had so identified itself with the governing coalition led by Mayor Jennings that it had begun to lose some of its standing with its former progressive allies, including some lesbian and gay activists who viewed ERDC as being too close to what they perceived as the mayor's efforts to revitalize the machine. While Mayor Jennings rewarded ERDC leaders with symbolic appointments to city boards (one to the commission charged with reviewing complaints against the Albany Police Department; another on a city charter revision commission), few discernible benefits flowed to the community from its support of the mayor.

Nonetheless, ERDC (and much of the gay and lesbian community) backed Jennings for re-election in 1997. He won easily. Along with him, a leader of ERDC, who received some support from the Jennings electoral coalition, was elected to the city council. In the same electoral cycle, however, Keith St. John was defeated in the primary by another African American candidate. His defeat came about despite the support of the predominantly white progressive coalition and at least the nominal support of ERDC.[6] (Few of the members of these electoral organizations resided in his district.)

Buffalo: Intergroup Politics and Limited Government

For the last twenty years, city politics in Buffalo has been marked by conflicts among three fragments within the Democratic party: (1) a group of (predominantly white) centrist-to-liberal politicians who identified with the liberal wing of the national party and the organization led in New York State by Governor Mario Cuomo (who served in that office from 1983 to 1995); (2) neighborhood-based working-class politicians rooted in ethnic communities (Irish, Italian, Polish) and loosely tied together by a shared conservative outlook on social issues; and (3) a group of African American politicians led by State Assemblyman Arthur Eve, who found it impossible to work with the second group and difficult to cooperate on a sustained basis with the first. For most of the period, however, the first group controlled the machinery of the Democratic party in Buffalo.

While the first group usually held a majority in the Buffalo City Council (particularly when a coalition could be formed with the Eve faction), from 1977 to 1993, the mayor of Buffalo was Jimmy Griffin, whose base lay in the second group. His appeal was that of the pugnacious social conservative fighting the party organization on behalf of the "little" (white) man. Much of his political energy was focused on maintaining a low-tax, low-expenditure approach to government services. At the same time, he saw no contradiction in turning to the county, state, and national governments in order to gain external resources to sustain the minimal services the city was prepared to provide. At the same time, Griffin's racism was barely disguised and his homophobia clearly stated.

Griffin took office shortly before the city entered a period of radical economic decline. Reflective of that situation, by 1990 it had the lowest per capita income of the four cities examined here ($10,445 to Albany's $13,742). Its future prospects were also grim. Only 16 percent of its population over twenty-five years of age held BAs in 1990 compared to nearly 30 percent in Albany. As one might expect, it also had the greatest number of persons living below the poverty line (25.6 percent).

The concerns of lesbians and gay men did not figure much in local political calculations for most of the Griffin years. Indeed, the Democratic party organization throughout much of the 1980s (partly out of fear of a Griffin-inspired backlash) assumed a "public face" of indifference to issues affecting gays and lesbians. Nonetheless, a few party and government officials had reasonably friendly personal relationships with lesbian and gay activists and drew on their support to run campaigns. However, they stopped short of visible association.

The lesbian and gay community was mobilized only episodically to engage in demand-protest activities during the Griffin years. For the most part, these protests were responses to the mayor's verbal attacks on the community or to the behaviors of his police department which launched regular crackdowns on gay men in public areas. Indeed, legal suits from Buffalo led to striking down, first, the state's sodomy law, and, later, its vaguely worded loitering law, both of which were used to arrest gay men (Rosenthal, 1996a).

Despite this repressive climate, in 1983, the president of the city council, George Arthur, shepherded a resolution through the council to provide antidiscrimination protections for gay and lesbian city employees. This was done by Arthur, an African American affiliated with the Democratic party, on his own without consulting the party leadership (Arthur, 1997). Nor did it involve mobilization by the gay and lesbian community. Rather, it grew out of personal conversations with a few gay friends. Working quietly on his own, Arthur succeeded in gaining passage of the ordinance. It was promptly vetoed by Mayor Griffin. The ordinance was then re-passed over the mayor's veto by a vote of 9 to 2 (with two abstentions). Despite its symbolic value, it proved ineffective because Mayor Griffin refused to implement its provisions.

It is unclear how much the ordinance was designed to mobilize lesbian and gay support for Arthur's candidacy for mayor in the election of 1985. In reality, the strength of the gay and lesbian vote in the city was very difficult to estimate and it did not appear to count for much in the elections of that year. For, while Arthur defeated Griffin in the Democratic primary, he went on to lose to him in the general election where Griffin ran as the endorsed candidate of the Republican party and the small (but influential) state Conservative party. Griffin also benefited from the defection of the Eve forces which pointedly encouraged abstention from the mayoral vote by the African American community.

It was not until 1993 that a scandal in city government forced Mayor Griffin to decide that it was time to retire. This opened the way for Anthony Masiello, a state senator whose district included a substantial African American population, to emerge as the party choice. Masiello and a new party chair were able to reconcile differences with the Eve group, which helped Masiello easily win both the Democratic primary and the general election.

During the campaign, Masiello went out of his way to court gay and lesbian support, though he could have easily won without it. Yet, he had been a supporter of gay rights while in the state legislature and was now engaged with the party chair in constructing an electoral coalition that would include not only African Americans but the small Latino/a population as well as lesbians and gay men. Once in office, however, Masiello was unprepared to undertake policy initiatives that reflected the concerns of gay men and lesbians. Even at the symbolic level, he refused to designate a mayoral liaison to the gay and lesbian community at the same that he was establishing such liaisons to the African American and Latino/a communities.

Gays and lesbians were so delighted by the change of tone at city hall, however, that they were willing to accept even minor symbolic gestures as major achievements. Gay Pride events were now acknowledged at city hall and, indeed, for the first time, Pride events were held on the steps of that building, though it was not until his (successful) re-election campaign in 1997 that Masiello addressed a Pride rally.

In contrast to Albany and Rochester, where years of political mobilization within the lesbian and gay community preceded entry into local electoral coalitions, the community's political mobilization in Buffalo was constrained during the Griffin years. The arrival of Mayor Masiello on the scene and the encouragement that lesbians and gay men received to participate in the state elections of 1994 began to change matters. For, in the course of his twelve years in office, Governor Cuomo had grown increasingly close to the lesbian and gay community. In his 1994 re-election campaign, Cuomo actively solicited their involvement, including establishing campaign liaisons to the community. Furthermore, in the Democratic primary for state attorney general, the victor in a three-way race was an unendorsed candidate, Karen Burstein, a New York City–based lesbian. While both Cuomo and Burstein went down to defeat, lesbians and gay men were visibly involved in both campaigns. In recognition of their role in Erie County, the Democratic party chair appointed the first openly gay person to the party's executive committee in early 1995.

After the 1994 election, an intraparty conflict surfaced between the incumbent Democratic county executive of Erie County Dennis Gorski, who sought party endorsement for re-election in 1995, and the party chair. The latter was doubtful of Gorski's chances for re-election and prevailed on the party to deny the endorsement to Gorski. That set off a major battle not only at the county executive level but for nominations for other county and city offices (including the Buffalo City Council) as both factions reached out for allies. Among those who took advantage of these conflicts were a number of newcomers to politics, including younger African Americans associated with a newly created political group that was beginning to challenge Assemblyman Eve's leadership and the city's first Latino candidate for municipal office.

Most important for our purposes, however, an openly identified lesbian, Barbara Kavanaugh, decided to run for one of the three at-large seats up for election to the city council. Kavanaugh had established a reputation as an attorney working on behalf of poor people, particularly on housing issues, and she had connections to neighborhood organizations in the city. She was not particularly prominent in the gay and lesbian community nor in party circles. Nonetheless, she mobilized support from a variety of segments of the city, including gays and lesbians, and created a strong campaign organization that overcame the fact that she did not receive the official party endorsement. She succeeded in forging informal relationships with some of the minority candidates running for ward seats and received the support of politicians associated with both sides of the intraparty conflict. Indeed, as the campaign proceeded, Kavanaugh gained the quiet support of some of Gorski's political workers. In the primary, Kavanaugh coasted to a strong second-place finish in a multicandidate race. She won easily in the general election.

Within a short time, Kavanaugh established herself as a highly visible personality in local politics and an articulate leader on housing and education policy. However, she took few legislative initiatives directed specifically at benefiting gay men and lesbians. On the other hand, the gay and lesbian community did not pressure her or the regime to move beyond symbolic public gestures. At the same time, lesbians and gay men quietly added to their numbers on party committees and became a much more visible presence in local politics and government than they have ever been before.[7]

Syracuse: Mixed Signals from a Conservative Regime

Gays and lesbians in Syracuse currently confront a conservative regime in which Republicans hold influence in the governing coalition and Democratic politicians treat identification with lesbians and gay men with considerable caution. While acts of repression are rare, lesbians and gay men are still largely excluded from participation in the local regime, though certain anomalies (discussed later) illustrate a regime uncertainly poised between exclusion and recognition.

Like Buffalo, Syracuse has been hurt badly by the economic changes that took place in upstate New York in the 1970s. Its industrial base was substantially eroded, though not to the same extent as Buffalo's. As Table 2 illustrates, the per capita income in Syracuse in 1990 fell between those of Rochester and Buffalo. The percentage of its population living below the poverty line was 22.7 percent, which actually put it second to Albany's low of 18.3 percent. In terms of racial composition, Syracuse was similar to Albany in having a predominantly white population (see Table 1).

Until the mid-1980s, the gay and lesbian community was largely excluded from the political process in Syracuse. A 1985 controversy that arose when activists attempted to use a downtown square to hold a small Gay Pride rally illustrates that exclusionary behavior. Municipal authorities, who had allowed rallies to occur in the square in the past without charge, insisted that the sponsoring organization pay $1,000 toward an insurance premium to cover the use of the space for one hour. The committee sued and won based on evidence that the requirement had been applied selectively and constituted an infringement of free speech.

Aside from this episode, the political energies of the gay and lesbian community were largely focused on AIDS activism during the 1980s. Indeed, the emerging political voice of the community was briefly organized under the banner of a local chapter of the AIDS activist group, ACT UP. Thus, ACT UP was responsible for organizing Gay Pride events in June 1989. In that connection, they approached the Democratic mayor of Syracuse, Thomas Young, about issuing a proclamation in recognition of the occasion. Young, who had been studiously silent on gay and lesbian issues, refused to do so. In response, ACT UP organized an "action" in which they piled cardboard boxes around city hall to symbolize the "wall of silence" that the mayor had maintained both on AIDS and on other gay and lesbian concerns. They also supported one of their members in the Democratic primary for mayor held later that year. While this candidacy was only symbolic, it made the local Democratic party sufficiently nervous to lead them to challenge the candidate's nomination petitions and to get him declared off the primary ballot. However, he ran in the general election on a third-party ticket where he received about 3.3 percent of the vote—not enough to defeat Young but enough to cause concern among Democratic party leaders.

Demand-protest was not put to rest. Instead, the events of 1989 inspired activists in 1990 to seek symbolic endorsement of Gay Pride from members of the city council rather than the mayor. A proposed proclamation was brought to the council in June by its most gay-friendly member, the only African American member of that body. Both Republicans and Democrats (on a body controlled by the Democrats) found fault with the proposed document and deleted portions. Representatives of the gay and lesbian community refused to accept the watered-down terms of the proclamation. Ultimately, the council killed the resolution.

Angered at this treatment, gays and lesbians created a Fair Practices Committee that initiated a campaign to mobilize the support of an array of religious, legal, and professional groups behind an ordinance to prohibit discrimination in employment, housing, and public accommodations in the city. That ordinance was introduced in August 1990. The Cuomo administration used the opportunity to associate itself with these efforts (coming as they did just before the state elections) by dispatching state officials—including Cuomo's official liasion to the gay and lesbian community and a senior government official with many years of service to the lesbian and gay community—to Syracuse to speak and lobby on behalf of the proposed ordinance.

To the surprise of many observers, the council passed the ordinance 5 to 4 on October 1. While one Democrat refused to vote for it, one of the four Republicans on the council supported the measure. Passage was made easier by the "cover" provided by the endorsements of numerous "establishment" groups and by limited media coverage of the process. Only at a public hearing held by the mayor prior to deciding whether to sign the measure did representatives of conservative groups make strong public presentations. Nonetheless, Mayor Young signed the ordinance, declaring that his decision rested on respect for individual freedom.[8] Whatever the symbolic gains, the ordinance has had relatively little direct effect on the operations of politics and government in Syracuse. For one thing, the law's enforcement mechanism depends entirely on suits filed by individual complainants; thus far, no such suits have been litigated.

In 1993, voters elected a 5 to 4 Republican majority to the council and, for the first time in twenty-four years, a Republican mayor. The new mayor, Roy Bernardi, was a conservative minor officeholder who did not mention gay and lesbian issues during the campaign. Neither he nor the council were prepared to rescind the ordinance after the election, however, even though two members of the new council majority had been openly hostile in some of their public comments at the time of passage of the ordinance. Within a year, the council majority again shifted as one Republican crossed the aisle to join the Democrats.

There has been little effort by the Democratic party in Syracuse to recruit lesbians and gay men. At the same time, after Democrats regained control of the city council, they passed Gay Pride resolutions in 1995 and 1996 with little controversy. In the spring of 1997, community activists pressed further, however, when they sought a proclamation that explicitly extended coverage to bisexuals and transgendered persons. The council majority had difficulty accepting these additions and the proclamation was eventually withdrawn, but the nature of the controversy illustrates that gay and lesbian politics has moved to a slightly different plane. Second, even as members of the council were dividing over this proclamation, Mayor Bernardi acceded to a request from a few gay individuals that the Gay Pride Parade route for 1997 be marked by a lavender line painted down the center of the street by the city's Department of Public Works. This practice was repeated in 1998 after Mayor Bernardi's easy re-election.

THE ENDS OF LOCAL INCORPORATION

So, what have lesbian and gay political activists in the four cities accomplished through their investment of time, energy, and money in city politics over the last twenty years?

From one perspective, the tangible results of their efforts appear to be rather limited: one gay man or lesbian has held a seat on the multi-member city councils of Albany, Buffalo, and Rochester (although in the Albany case two *different* persons from different wards have held a seat over the last three terms); Albany and Syracuse have passed broad ordinances protecting lesbians and gay men against discrimination in employment, housing, and public accommodations, while Buffalo and Rochester have passed ordinances protecting city workers against employment discrimination. More recently, Rochester has extended domestic partnership benefits to its employees, and both Rochester and Albany have established domestic partnership registers.

Furthermore, even as lesbians and gay men have come to be an accepted part of the electoral coalitions supporting candidates for various local offices, their participation has yielded few substantive benefits to members of the group, though a few staff appointments have been given to particular activists. None of the cities have senior lesbian or gay administrators; none have extended governmental resources to services for gay men and lesbians; none have engaged in systematically changing the operations of their municipal bureaucracies, although some agencies—notably the police departments in Albany, Buffalo, and Rochester—have made tentative efforts to be more sensitive to the needs of gays and lesbians (Rosenthal, 1996c, 1997).

From a slightly different perspective, the efforts of lesbian and gay activists have been rewarded with a clear shift in the climate of opinion in the four cities. Even in Syracuse, the level of hostility appears to be increasingly moderated. Gays and lesbians are also more visible in the local media and in the political fabric of that city as well as in the three other cities.

Lesbian and gay activism has achieved a significant measure of symbolic recognition, most markedly in Albany and Rochester, less in

Buffalo, and least in Syracuse. The achievements of these local movements are much less complete with respect to substantive incorporation. While part of the explanation for this reflects the resistance of other elements in existing governing coalitions and the persistence of bureaucratic traditions within government agencies, a large part of it also reflects uncertainty among lesbians and gay political activists and their constituents about what they really want out of political participation. For many lesbian and gay citizens, as well as for political activists, symbolic recognition is sufficient. Thus, passage of the 1994 domestic partnership ordinance and creation of registers in Rochester and Albany seemed to be less a response to grassroots demands for policy change than a vehicle for re-energizing local movements that were flagging because their support base had largely lost interest in political mobilization.

Similarly, the establishment of a political beachhead for lesbians and gay men in Buffalo, first in electoral politics and then in city government, has been independent of any concrete policy demands. Indeed, no one (including the lesbian member of the city council) has put forward a demand for ordinances of the character passed in any of the three other cities. Nor has the 1983 ordinance protecting city employees against discrimination been deemed worthy of more vigorous enforcement.

What is most striking about the current state of lesbian and gay movements in the four cities is that they are led by ideological centrists for whom working "within the system" is either an opportunity for career advancement or an avocation. In none of the cities does there appear to be a contingent of programmatic activists who challenge this leadership. The closest there is to an internal opposition within the movement in any city is a group of activists in Albany who more closely identify with the "progressive" wing of the Democratic party than they do with the current leadership and direction of ERDC. These dissidents complain about the degree to which ERDC has become part of what they see as a reconstituted political machine led by Mayor Jennings. However, they do not represent a significant departure from the ERDC on policy matters. Rather, they have worked for candidates more closely associated with the progressive wing of the party, while ERDC, on occasion, has been more willing to work for candidates with poor records on gay and lesbian issues because they are favored by the Jennings organization.[9]

Indeed, the conflict between the two groups in Albany illustrates an emerging challenge for local lesbian and gay movements that echoes the experiences of other movements that have achieved some of the insignia of political incorporation. For, the opening of greater political opportunities to lesbians and gay men, at least in Albany, Buffalo, and Rochester, has encouraged the political involvement of lesbians and gay men with different personal goals than some of those who helped to mobilize lesbian and gay communities originally in pursuit of community building (Rosenthal, 1997).

Among the new generation of activists are those whom we would characterize as *careerists* and *avocationalists*.[10] Careerists include individuals who pursue paid opportunities in politics or government as a major part of their professional lives; avocationalists treat political involvement as a form of volunteerism done more for the personal excitement and sociability involved than for any notion of personal gain or collective benefits for their community. In both cases, engaging in electoral and governing coalitions tends to enforce caution with respect to advancing lesbian and gay concerns. The result is that both types of political activists appear to be increasingly engaged in activities that have the effect of de-mobilizing lesbian and gay activism or mobilizing it in a very constrained fashion.

For political careerists, being gay or lesbian is not a major barrier to personal advancement in politics or government. Indeed, identification with the lesbian and gay community may be a political resource to be used to mobilize voters and campaign workers, and to solicit financial support, in much the same way that being of Irish, Italian, Polish, or African extraction was once (and in some places still is) an electoral asset to be exploited in staking a claim to government patronage. For such individuals, getting ahead in politics may carry little policy baggage. Thus, for the people who have been appointed to staff positions in government (including mayoral, councilmanic, and state legislative staffs), being openly lesbian or gay may be career-enhancing. (At the same time, such appointments confirm the outreach activities of the gay or straight politicians who make them.)

A similar phenomenon appears to be occurring among political avocationalists. These include lesbians or gay men who gain personal satisfaction from participating in the mechanics of electoral politics or by playing some advisory role to party or government officials. As one such activist in Albany, who was a leader of ERDC and an advisor to the mayor, commented, "I don't see myself as a representative of a movement. I see myself as a leader in the community" (Getto, 1996).

Whether political careerist or avocationalist, when pressed, none of these political leaders had anything approaching a coherent "agenda" that might serve as a platform for pursuing either specific or general policy benefits for the lesbian and gay community. Furthermore, in none of the cities does there presently appear to be a mobilized community pressing at their heels to achieve certain goals through the machinery of government. Nonetheless, lesbians and gay men continue to participate not only in local electoral politics but in state politics, including in the increasingly routinized work of lobbying the New York State legislature (unsuccessfully, thus far) for antidiscrimination laws.[11]

And so, does local political incorporation end more with a whimper than a bang? It is entirely possible that lesbian and gay activists, having made their peace with local regimes, will simply settle for being "good soldiers" in the trenches of urban politics and policy. Although they may still make occasional efforts to bring about small adjustments in regime practices, most issues of collective importance to gays and lesbians will be left to the courts or to the actions of other levels of government. At the same time, many lesbians and gay men have come to feel that their lives have been made a little better because they have visible spokespeople, political leaders whose names regularly appear in the newspapers and are favorably treated by the local media, and that policies are adopted on occasion by local governments that express positions favorable to the lesbian and gay population, even if the benefits they provide are limited.

No doubt, lesbians and gay men now have "a seat at the table" in Albany, Buffalo, and Rochester—albeit a smaller one in Buffalo than in the other two cities. However, maintenance of even that degree of incorporation is dependent on their association with sympathetic Democratic party officials. There is no assurance that they are so critical to the maintenance of electoral or governing coalitions in those cities, however, that lesbian and gay influence might not be substantially reduced with a shift in local electoral or governing coalitions much as has happened to African Americans in major cities like Chicago, Los Angeles, and New York (Browning, Marshall & Tabb, 1997). Even where gay and lesbian fortunes have reached a plateau, however, it is hard to see a full-scale return to the repressive or exclusionary practices of the past in the cities examined here.

NOTES

*I would like to thank Diane Costlow-Oyler for her assistance in preparing this chapter.

[1]Easton's formulation differs significantly from the one advanced by Clarence Stone (1989, p. 6), who uses the term "regime" to highlight "the informal

arrangements by which public bodies and private interests function together in order to be able to make and carry out governing decisions." Rather than emphasizing private sector economic forces and their role in constituting a local regime, we focus here on the ways that different local political cultures and practices—including different value systems—encourage or discourage the incorporation of different groups, including lesbians and gay men.

[2]Neither in their original study nor in their more recent work do Browning, Marshall, and Tabb (1984; 1997) examine the repressive or exclusionary practices of the 1960s and 1970s in the cities they studied. It might be hypothesized, for example, that the character of demand-protests reflected the nature and intensity of regime behaviors toward minorities during that period. Pinderhughes (1997, p. 129) implies as much in her comments about the way the demand-protest activities of young black men both in Oakland and Chicago were met with "violence and political repression by public officials" during the 1960s. For another perspective on the clearly exclusionary (if not repressive) nature of the Oakland regime during that period, see Pressman, 1975.

[3]Some Rochester informants argue that the regime has been so supportive generally of lesbians and gay men that they have not felt it necessary to mobilize to try to pass a general antidiscrimination ordinance. Indeed, there is some uncertainty about the legal authority of municipal governments in New York State to pass such ordinances. Nonetheless, a number of municipalities (including Albany, Ithaca, New York City, and Syracuse) have passed broad-based ordinances while others have not done so even when lesbians and gay men have achieved a measure of political influence. Thus far, the constitutionality of such ordinances has not been tested in the courts of New York State.

[4]Partnership registries of the kind created in Rochester (and in Albany) provide an opportunity for both same-sex and opposite-sex couples to affirm their relationships publicly. They provide no additional benefits to the couples involved, but they constitute a movement response to the attacks that have been made on the concept of gay and lesbian marriage.

[5]In the midst of these negotiations, the machine issued a symbolically important invitation to ERDC to take part for the first time in the annual Albany County Democratic party picnic. ERDC participation has been a routine matter ever since.

[6]St. John lost the Democratic primary to a candidate with stronger ties in the African American community and a better electoral organization within the ward. Informants from both the ERDC and the progressive coalition conceded even before the primary that St. John lacked the political skills to fend off this challenge.

[7]Kavanaugh resigned from her council seat early in 1999 to accept a position as Assistant Attorney General for the Buffalo region after a Democrat was

elected State Attorney General in 1998. The seat was left open pending the municipal elections of 1999, but no gay or lesbian appeared to be in line to claim a seat on the council for a member of that community.

[8]More cynical informants suggest his turnaround may have resulted from passage of a referendum in the 1989 mayoral election that limited Syracuse mayors to two terms. That meant that Young was a lame duck at the time he signed the ordinance.

[9]Reflective of the differences of approach of the two groups was a disagreement that arose over the best strategy to employ in passing the city ordinance in 1996. Because it knew it had the votes, ERDC favored the (ultimately successful) approach of avoiding a public hearing and relying on its influence with city council members. Other activists favored using public hearings as a way of mobilizing community support and strengthening the community's public reputation for influence.

[10]I have avoided application of the term "amateur" employed by Wilson (1962) to the latter type given Wilson's somewhat derogatory use of that term and also in recognition of the considerable political skills some of these activists possess.

[11]The New York State Assembly (controlled by Democrats) now regularly passes antidiscrimination laws and does so by increasingly larger margins that reflect the growing support of moderate Republicans from the New York City metropolitan area. The New York State Senate, which is controlled by Republicans, has consistently refused to consider gay rights legislation.

REFERENCES

Adam, B.D. (1987). *The rise of a gay and lesbian movement.* Boston: Twayne.

Arthur, G. (1997, November 6). Interview.

Bailey, R.W. (1999). *Gay politics, urban politics.* New York: Columbia University Press.

Bawer, B. (1993). *A place at the table.* New York: Poseidon.

Browning, R.P., D.R. Marshall, & D.H. Tabb. (1984). *Protest is not enough.* Berkeley: University of California Press.

———. (eds.). (1997). *Racial politics in American cities.* 2nd ed. New York: Longman.

Bullard, R.D., & J.R. Feagin (1991). Racism and the city. In M. Gottdiener & C. Pickvance (eds.), *Urban life in transition* (pp. 55–76). Thousand Oaks, CA: Sage.

Button, J.W., B.A. Rienzo, & K.D. Wald. (1997). *Private lives, public conflicts.* Washington, DC: CQ Press.

Chauncey, G. (1994). *Gay New York.* New York: Basic Books.

Clark, P.B., & J.Q. Wilson. (1961). Incentive systems: A theory of organizations. *Administrative Science Quarterly.* 6 (2), 219–266.

Cohen, C. (1997). Straight gay politics: The limits of an ethnic model of inclusion. In I. Shapiro & W. Klymicka (eds.). *Ethnicity and group rights* (pp. 572–616). New York: New York University Press.

Costain, A. (1992). *Inviting women's rebellion.* Baltimore: Johns Hopkins University Press.

Cruickshank, M. (1992). *The gay and lesbian liberation movement.* New York: Routledge.

Dahl, R.A. (1961). *Who governs?* New Haven: Yale University Press.

Darnovsky, M., B. Epstein, & R. Flacks, (eds.) (1995). *Cultural politics and social movements.* Philadelphia: Temple University Press.

D'Emilio, J. (1983). *Sexual politics, sexual communities.* Chicago: University of Chicago Press.

———. (1996). *Power at the polls.* Washington, DC: National Gay and Lesbian Task Force.

Duberman, M. (1993). *Stonewall.* New York: Plume.

Easton, D. (1965). *A systems analysis of political life.* New York: Wiley.

Erie, S. (1988). *Rainbow's end.* Berkeley: University of California Press.

Getto, D. (1996, July 30). Interview.

Kennedy, E., & M. Davis. (1993). *Boots of leather, slippers of gold.* New York: Routledge.

Kirk, M., & H. Madsen. (1989). *After the ball.* New York: Doubleday.

McAdam, D. (1982). *Political process and the development of black insurgency.* Chicago: University of Chicago Press.

Morris, A.D., & C.M. Mueller, (eds.). (1992). *Frontiers in social movement theory.* New Haven: Yale University Press.

Pinderhughes, D. (1997). An examination of Chicago politics for evidence of political incorporation and representation. In R.P. Browning, D.R. Marshall, & David H. Tabb (eds.), *Racial politics in American cities* (pp. 117–135). 2nd. ed. New York: Longman.

Pressman, J.L. (1975). *Federal programs and city politics.* Berkeley: University of California Press.

Robinson, F. (1977). *Machine politics: A study of Albany's O'Connells.* New Brunswick, NJ: Transaction Books.

Rosenthal, D.B. (1996a) Gay and lesbian political mobilization and regime responsiveness in four New York cities. *Urban affairs review.* 32 (1), 35–70.

———. (1996b). Who 'owns' AIDS service organizations? *Polity.* 29 (1), 97–118.

———. (1996c). The ends of gay and lesbian politics: Issues in the articulation of movement goals with local politics. Paper presented at the 28th Annual

Meeting of the Northeastern Political Science Association, Boston, MA, Nov. 14–16.

———. (1997). Community building, bridge building and political opportunities for lesbians and gay men in four New York cities. Paper presented at the 1997 Annual Meeting of the American Political Science Association, Washington, DC, August 28–31.

———. (1999). Regime change and gay and lesbian politics in four New York cities. In E.B. Sharp (ed.), *Culture wars and local politics* (pp. 63–80). Lawrence: University Press of Kansas.

Shilts, R. (1982). *The mayor of Castro street.* New York: St. Martin's Press.

Stone, C. (1989). *Regime politics.* Lawrence: University Press of Kansas.

Sullivan, A. (1995). *Virtually normal.* New York: Knopf.

Swanstrom, T., & S. Ward. (1987). Albany's O'Connell organization. Paper Presented at the annual meeting of the American Political Science Association, Chicago, September 1–4.

Tarrow, S. (1994). *Power in movement.* Cambridge: Cambridge University Press.

U.S. Bureau of the Census. (1971). *1970 Census of population, Volume 1: Characteristics of the population, part 34: New York,* Tables 16, 33, 83, and 90. Washington DC: U.S Government Printing Office.

U.S. Bureau of the Census. (1992). *1990 General population characteristics: Summary population and housing characteristics: New York,* Table 3, Washington DC: U.S. Government Printing Office

———. (1992) *Social and economic characteristics of New York,* Tables 171, 177, 178. Washington DC: U.S. Government Printing Office.

Vaid, U. (1995). *Virtual equality.* New York: Anchor Books.

Wilson, J.Q. (1960). *Negro politics.* New York: The Free Press.

———. (1962). *The amateur democrat.* Chicago: University of Chicago Press.

———. (1973). *Political organizations.* New York: Basic Books.

CHAPTER 11

A Long and Uncertain Path
Looking Ahead to the Twenty-first Century

KATHERINE UNDERWOOD

This volume's essays address different facets of a seemingly straightforward question: "Why does political equality remain a challenge to be conquered?" Those seeking clear-cut answers may be disappointed because incorporation is a complex phenomenon that defies easy characterizations and pat answers. Nevertheless, three general observations illuminate the conceptual terrain covered by the preceding chapters.

First, struggles for equality have revolved around two goals: Equal treatment under law, and public policies that reflect the interests of previously excluded groups. An ongoing dialectic in U.S. politics has been between minority groups seeking equality and the majority power holders—at all levels of government—who have not readily shared the fruits of democracy. Public debate has typically centered on questions such as "How much will it cost (the majority) in terms of power and status?" "How much will it cost in terms of scarce public resources?" "How far should the government go to ensure equal opportunities for all citizens?" These have been always been controversial issues, generally evoking passionate responses, and all too often, violence against the groups seeking inclusion and equality.

Second, while there have been important common aims, specific incorporative goals depend on the context. Group-level factors, geographic location, and time periods affect what is sought by minorities. Specific group agendas are partly shaped by issue salience and partly by the values of group leadership. Browning, Marshall, and Tabb (Chapter 6) and Longoria (Chapter 8) suggest that economic considerations, such as affirmative action in public sector employment, minority contracting programs, and minority economic development, have been priorities for African Americans and Latinos. In contrast, Rosenthal argues that leaders of the gay and lesbian movement have generally promoted "equal opportunity rather than any measure of affirmative action . . . in the workforce . . . " (Chapter 10, p. 229). And Lai's research indicates that different Asian Pacific American ethnic groups residing within a single-member district may disagree over *which* group should be descriptively represented in a legislative body (Chapter 9).

A federal system in which states have granted cities home rule combined with considerable variation in local electoral rules, political institutions, and informal practices means that we should *expect* group goals to vary among cities. Longoria (Chapter 8) observes that the study of Latino politics has focused on the Southwest where the Latino struggle for equality has been shaped by particular historical, social, and political factors not operative elsewhere (such as the Midwest). The implication, then, is that the salient issues for Latinos living in suburban Illinois are not the same for those living in small Texas cities. Even within a given state, differences in local institutional and cultural practices determine the range of a group's strategic targets and the degree to which resistance to change might be expected, as indicated by Rosenthal's investigation of gay and lesbian politics in Albany, Buffalo, Syracuse, and Rochester.

Another relevant contextual issue is the period of time under study. Minority and majority group expectations of incorporative outcomes can be viewed as a continuing dialogue. Over time minority group collective action and evolving social norms have gradually altered the majority's conception of what is "realistic." Thus today's starting points for policy debate and proposals are different than those at the midpoint of this century.

Prior to the passage of the Voting Rights Act and the Civil Rights Act of 1964, states had the leeway to do as they saw fit with respect to the civil and political rights of communities of color. There were virtually no civil rights guarantees in *any* state. For example, after World War II, fair employment practices (FEP) legislation was a major goal for coalitions of African American civic organizations and churches, and white liberals who worked to secure its passage at the city and state level. Progressives in Los Angeles failed in three attempts to have the city council establish a municipal FEP commission. The *Los Angeles Times* and conservative interest groups opposed a local FEP law because social relations were "a process that can't be accelerated by law" (*Los Angeles Times,* 1949). White conservatives in southern California saw nondiscrimination in employment as "unrealistic" and even dangerous. In the same vein,

Southern Democrats viewed equal voting rights for African Americans as anathema.

Transforming the status quo required considerable, sustained collective action directed at racist and discriminatory practices (Morris, 1984). At each step of the way conservatives and some moderates challenged the civil rights movement's legitimacy and their goals. Martin Luther King's eloquently passionate "Letter from a Birmingham Jail" was a pointed response to white clergy who counseled him to wait. In their eyes, the Southern Christian Leadership Conference's campaign was ill-advised and poorly timed, socially subversive, and not at all pragmatic. King said:

> Frankly, I have yet to engage in a direct action campaign that was "well-timed" in the view of those who have not suffered unduly from the disease of segregation. For years now I have heard the word "Wait!" It rings in the ear of every Negro with piercing regularity. This "Wait" has almost always meant "Never." (King, 1963, p. 768)

The Birmingham campaign continued and the Southern Christian Leadership Conference was able to secure concessions from the local white power structure (Morris, 1984).

Subsequent events in the South, many of them tragic, prodded a reluctant President Kennedy into endorsing civil rights legislation that provided uniform treatment under law. Yet Congress passed it only after Kennedy's assassination and in response to President Johnson's persuasive leadership. Less than a year later, after the bloody Selma to Montgomery march, President Johnson quickly sent Congress powerful voting rights legislation; it was enacted within five months. The Voting Rights Act of 1965 has been seen as the capstone of the "second Reconstruction" (Davidson, 1992; Kousser, 1992; Davidson & Grofman, 1994a) because "it secured for black Americans what the Fourteenth and Fifteenth Amendments passed during the first Reconstruction, had not— the right to vote, the very bedrock of democracy" (Davidson, 1992, p. 7). While this discussion has centered primarily on the African American civil rights movement, ethnic minorities, women, and gays and lesbians have fought similar battles for social and political equality and faced similar sets of questions—"Are these changes really necessary?" "Is this realistic?" "Shouldn't you wait?"—from policymakers at all levels.

Mid to late twentieth-century activism—and national legislation that prevents states from discriminating on the basis of race and ethnicity—

profoundly changed the status quo. Issues such as discrimination against individuals in voting, *de jure* segregation, and openly racist employment practices belong to the past. Symbolic of this sea change are prominent public figures who were vehement segregationists and supporters of the South's ancien regime, but who have since recanted and embraced civil rights, for example, Strom Thurmond, George Wallace, and Joe Smitherman (former mayor of Selma). Therefore, today's activists work from a different foundation, but with an eye to protecting, consolidating, and institutionalizing often fragile victories. Securing legislation and court decisions favorable to minorities is one thing, but their thorough implementation is yet another. To summarize, the aggregate picture of minority political power in the United States is much improved when compared to points in the not-so-distant past, but a closer look at individual cities and/or particular policy areas gives us a different perspective.

Thus, a third general observation is that minority groups have experienced mixed success in their pursuit of incorporation. On the positive side, liberal, biracial coalitions have replaced conservative governing city council majorities, and facilitated the election of African American and Latino mayors (Browning et al., 1984, 1990, 1997). Changes in local electoral rules have facilitated further increases in minority representation in city halls large and small. New players in the policy process have worked to change bureaucratic practices and tried to secure a more progressive delivery of municipal services. There are also more grassroots players in the local politics, and therefore more mechanisms that low-income groups and communities of color may use to articulate their concerns and pressure government (Howard, Lipsky & Marshall, 1994). Moreover, as Engstrom (Chapter 2) and Fleischmann (Chapter 5) point out, we have not reached a dead end in terms of thinking creatively about how to overcome the problems of minority political invisibility and social immobility.

Yet each step taken toward a more egalitarian political society can be countered with pessimism. Minority representatives on city councils may not be included in governing coalitions, and mayors remain more concerned with improving their city's tax base and pursuing growth than substantively addressing increases in concentrated poverty. Altering bureaucratic practices and institutional norms requires mayors and councils to work collaboratively towards common and clearly delineated ends, and requires resolute and long-term "political will." Without this direction, municipal agencies have considerable room to maneuver in their daily operations. Community-based organizations, which have the potential to be many things—empowerment vehicles for immigrants and new citizens, government watchdogs and whistle blowers, policy incubators—frequently suffer from lack of resources and may work at cross-purposes with one another. Finally, the only time elected officials are inclined to experiment with policy innovations is during crisis. Incrementalism remains the norm for the U.S. policymaking process. The hard reality is that the institutional deck is stacked against rapid, substantive change; it arrives in bits and pieces and only in response to concerted electoral and interest group pressure.

Our contributing authors have suggested the process of securing greater voice in and responsiveness from the political system has not followed a predictable path. Some changes are institutionalized, while others are more controversial and face resistance, and, in some cases, rollback. We encourage readers to view the mixed bag of results discussed herein as the most recent iteration of a decades-long and continuing struggle. In the remainder of this chapter, I sketch four thematic explanations for why incorporation has been such a long and uncertain path, suggest factors that will shape urban minority politics early in the next millennium, and identify areas that should receive scholarly attention.

ELECTORAL RULES AND INSTITUTIONAL ARRANGEMENTS SHAPE MINORITY OPPORTUNITIES FOR REPRESENTATION

Gerber, Morton, and Rietz (1998) affirm the position held by a number of scholars (Browning et al., 1984, 1990, 1997; Welch & Bledsoe, 1988; Heilig & Mundt, 1984; Bridges,1997; Polinard et al., 1994) that descriptive and substantive representation are connected. They argue that ". . . if features of the political system prevent one demographic group from achieving descriptive representation, then it may be highly unlikely that the group will be able to achieve substantive representation of its interests" (Gerber et al., 1998, p. 127). Progressive-era reformers and nineteenth-century Southern Democrats were quite conscious of this linkage among institutional design, politics, and policy. Morgan Kousser and Amy Bridges have meticulously described how state legislatures in the South (Kousser, 1974, 1992) and Southwest (Bridges, 1997) enacted franchise restrictions that deliberately winnowed African Americans, Latinos, and poor whites from the electorate.

Subsequently, homogenous electorates supported state and local segregation laws (Kousser, 1974) and, in the Southwest, voted for local charter reform designed to promote "good government" (Bridges, 1997). At-large (multimember districts) elections for city council were a central component of such reform. In racially polarized settings they were, not coincidentally, a significant barrier to communities of color seeking elected representation.

Including those who had been excluded from politics has required another round of rule changes (Bridges, 1997; Heilig and Mundt, 1984). Minority groups seeking electoral power and elected representation have been able to use the Voting Rights Act to their advantage.[1] While the legislation was originally focused on removing barriers to individual voting, minority vote dilution has been the centerpiece of its protections since the 1970s (Davidson 1992; Davidson & Grofman, 1994). Single-member majority-minority districts, as Engstrom points out (Chapter 2), have been the predominant remedy for vote dilution.

Political science research shows that single-member districts have a positive impact on the election of African Americans and, to a somewhat lesser extent, on the election of Latinos to office (Welch & Bledsoe, 1988). Yet Bridges and Underwood (Chapter 3) suggest that the question of how structural change (the move from at-large to district elections) might affect municipal policymaking remains incompletely answered. One underexplored issue is the dynamic of mayoral interaction with minority council representatives. What are the ways in which executives might build and nurture support for their programs? What are the quid pro quos at their disposal? In what ways might these negotiated, elite agreements benefit (or hurt) communities of color?

Browning et al.'s research has focused less on racially discriminatory structural arrangement and more on what happens when minorities are part of liberal council majorities or are elected as mayors (1984, 1990, 1997). In Chapter 6 they argue that *who* controls the formal apparatus of government affects the distribution of public resources. When black mayors or biracial coalitions are defeated in elections, there are "real losses" to African American interests such as cutbacks in funding to programs and community organizations, fewer appointments to boards and commissions, and a reduced share of city employment (Chapter 6, p. 147). Yet Browning, Marshall, and Tabb explicitly recognize that "the contemporary nature and context of political incorporation are more complex than the simple model of a biracial coalition with an African American mayor that emerged from the 1960s and 1970s" (Chapter 6, p. 134).

Keiser (Chapter 7) examined the issue of mayoral control in New York and Philadelphia and found that the elections of Rudoph Giuliani and Ed Rendell, which are considered cases of conservative rollback by journalist Jim Sleeper, were actually a continuation of previous electoral patterns. In New York, David Dinkins was unable to institutionalize his fragile base of support; Giuliani was elected by the same sturdy coalition of groups that kept Ed Koch in power. Ed Rendell's election represented a continuation of the liberal, biracial coalition that supported Wilson Goode. Keiser's research on New York and Philadelphia also provides support for Browning, Marshall, and Tabb's contention that "in some cities, city councils are powerful, and representation there can be employed to mobilize significant policy and spending initiatives or to ward off policy rollbacks attempted by unsympathetic mayors" (Chapter 6, p. 144). This line of research should be extended to other major (and smaller) cities where African American and Latino mayors have been replaced by (conservative) whites: Are the electoral bases of white replacement mayors similar to or different than the defeated (minority)? Does conflict between white replacement mayors and city councils with minority representatives take a generalizable form? What are its variations?

PARTIES AND COMMUNITY-BASED ORGANIZATIONS SHAPE MINORITY POLITICAL OPPORTUNITIES

Parties, nonpartisan slating groups, interest groups, and community-based organizations operate "informally" within the space created by electoral rules and political institutions. The interaction between players and formal structure often creates a web of barriers to groups seeking additional voice and policy influence. Steven Erie's research (1988) on political machines indicates that party organizations in the nineteenth and early twentieth centuries did not seek out ever-increasing sources of new voters. Parties strategically added to their base: their most aggressive naturalization, registration, and mobilization drives occurred when organizations had not yet consolidated power. Once a reliable winning majority was constructed, machines conserved their scarce resources by curtailing voter efforts. In other words, strong party organizations did not automatically embrace newly arrived ethnic groups, nor did they empower them as full political partners in the governing process.

More recent studies corroborate Erie's debunking of the myth that political parties are equal opportunity vote seekers. Keiser's investigation of African American political incorporation in Atlanta, Chicago, Gary, and Philadelphia found that the greatest gains were made in electorally competitive situations. When neither major party organization held a monopolistic advantage, African Americans provided critical swing votes, and were rewarded substantively with nominations to office and policy benefits (Keiser, 1997).

Rosenthal's four-city study of gay and lesbian attempts to win political power in New York State yields similar findings. His research shows that factionalism within the Democratic party along with local candidate ambitions have created opportunities for electoral victories. Rosenthal also suggests that local political culture has affected regime change. Rochester's pluralistic political culture, for example, produced candidates who actively sought support from gay men and lesbians (and African Americans) during the early 1970's when the parties alternated control of local government. In exchange for electoral support, Democrats attended community events and election meetings sponsored by gay groups. Moreover, "In this environment, lesbians and gay men found it easy to win seats on Democratic party committees and become a recognized part of the party structure" (Chapter 10, p. 237). In Albany, Buffalo, and Syracuse, where the Democratic party was both more conservative and less vulnerable to electoral competition, gay men and lesbians have had to more forcefully pressure the party organization and candidates for symbolic recognition and policy benefits.

Most large cities in the United States, however, hold nonpartisan rather than partisan elections (see Chapter 3, Table 1), which means that political parties do not play a role in municipal politics. In the nonpartisan cities of the Southwest, Anglo community leaders failed to mount efforts to bring new voters into the electorate (Bridges, 1997). Where informal nonpartisan slating groups operated, demobilized minority voters found it nearly impossible to exert influence over the nomination process (Bridges, 1997; Fraga, 1988). The mobilization of minority voters in nonpartisan cities has generally been undertaken by ethnic community-based organizations, such as the Community Service Organization in post–World War II Los Angeles, and the more recent Communities Organized for Political Service in San Antonio (Underwood 1997; Sekul, 1975). Community-based voter registration and mobilization efforts may also enhance the competition in partisan elections. For example, the election of Harold Washington to the mayor's office in 1983 resulted from grassroots activity that ignited the interest of new voters in the electoral process (Grimshaw, 1992; Rivlin, 1992).[2] Within this volume, DeSipio (Chapter 4), Lai (Chapter 9), and Rosenthal (Chapter 10) indicate that community-based organizations continue to play important roles in mobilizing new voters both in partisan and nonpartisan contexts.

Because political parties do not energetically expand their bases unless forced by electoral necessity, it should not be surprising that neither major organization has rushed to embrace the nation's immigrant communities. Republicans have, at best, a mixed record. In the early 1980s, the Reagan administration was supportive of Cuban-led naturalization drives in Miami (Portes & Stepick, 1993) but did not actively reach out to low-income Latinos in California and Texas. More recently, presidential candidate Robert Dole aired TV and radio ads opposing undocumented immigration during the final weeks of his 1996 campaign in California. Republicans in states with large immigrant populations have adopted exclusionary stances, such as California's Governor Pete Wilson who was allied with pro–Proposition 187 forces (DeSipio & de la Garza, 1998; Pachon, 1998).[3]

The Democrats' record on supporting naturalization efforts is somewhat better. The Clinton administration launched "Citizenship USA" in 1995, which was a $77 million program to eliminate a huge backlog of legal residents who had applied for citizenship (Mogelonsky, 1997). Unfortunately, a small percentage of those naturalized in the expedited process were ineligible for citizenship, and several hundred of these individuals had criminal records (Mogelonsky, 1997; Pachon, 1998). In 1996, congressional Republicans hammered the Immigration and Naturalization Service (INS) by delaying funding and requiring the agency to revamp their background check procedures. Since then a combination of an INS slowdown, changes in federal law that eliminated public benefits to (legal) noncitizens, and anti-immigrant rhetoric have created a record-breaking backlog of applicants waiting for naturalization (Ojito,1998).

Community-based organizations, immigrant rights groups, and public educational institutions—not political parties—have taken the lead in educating post-1965 immigrants on the importance of naturalization and tried to lower the costs of applying for citizenship in various ways. Latinos in southern California may access a network of organizations and institutions such as the National Association of Latino Elected Officials (NALEO) and Los Angeles city schools and community colleges that encourage and help "Latino immigrants to become new Americans" (Pachon, 1998, p. 419). It should also be noted that southern California Latino elected officials (*not* party organizations per se) have "hosted naturalization workshops" (Pachon, 1998, p. 419). Community-based leadership that promotes naturalization and subsequent voter education and registration efforts is a critical part of the political socialization process.

DeSipio (1996) has argued that the *context* in which immigrants become citizens is important because naturalization alone does not produce politically active citizens. Because political parties mount voter registration only episodically (immediately before elections), community organizations can perform ongoing educative functions and generate a sense of political efficacy among the newly naturalized. Latino and Asian Pacific American elites have recognized the power of grassroots action in boosting participation levels among newly arrived ethnic groups, and scholars should expect community-based citizenship campaigns to continue well into the future (particularly if anti-immigrant rhetoric remains strident). Therefore, social scientists should focus their attention on the funding and strategy of community-based immigrant outreach—in what ways does it vary between cities? How might variation be explained? How are nonpolitical actors (media, the church, labor unions) involved? Nor should we ignore the strategy of state and local party organizations in states with large immigrant populations: What conditions facilitate inclusionary efforts? What conditions facilitate exclusionary stances? How might political parties interact with grassroots organizations to expand voter bases in election and nonelection years?

While record numbers of immigrants are applying for and receiving citizenship, DeSipio points out that "High rates of noncitizenship in many immigrant communities preclude regular influence by these groups on electoral politics" (Chapter 4, p. 95). For this reason, community-based organization will continue to be the primary avenue through which immigrant needs are communicated to government officials. These organizations have an ability, both individually and collectively, to assess immigrant needs, articulate issue positions, publicly voice concerns, and offer ideas designed to solve policy and service problems (Lai, Chapter 9; DeSipio, Chapter 4).

Given that public discourse has become highly polarized and that today's voters tend to make decisions based on issues, minority groups must successfully oppose arguments for policies that penalize immigrants, people of color, and gays and lesbians. Therefore, we should anticipate that community-based ethnic and gay and lesbian organizations and group-specific media will assume higher, more outspoken profiles, and will more aggressively try to influence the broader opinion climate and the rhetoric of policy debates. Doing so will require minority groups to coalesce around shared issue positions, and here again community-based organizations could be fundamental components of cross-ethnic, umbrella coalitions.

A research agenda in this area should include comprehensive attitudinal surveys of all minority communities (both immigrant and citizen). We need to have more information about the policy preferences of new immigrants and whether they are substantially the same or different than those of white and minority citizens. We should also be investigating cross-ethnic political collaborations on issues of common concern, and the circumstances that facilitate their successes or failures. Particular attention might be paid to how group-specific media and mainstream media frame policy debates, minority group issue stands, and mobilization efforts.

NATIONAL AND STATE-LEVEL DECISIONS SHAPE MINORITY POLITICAL OPPORTUNITIES

Up to this point, my discussion has centered on formal political structures and informal groups (parties and community organizations) at the municipal level Yet national-level partisan trends, and legislative and judicial decisions profoundly impact grassroots minority political opportunities.[4] The U.S. Supreme Court has the ability to strike down laws passed by Congress. It also has the power to interpret legislation in narrow or expansive fashion. The courts—as an appointed, anti-majoritarian institution—are theoretically insulated from political winds, but ideology is one factor taken into account in the nomination process. Currently, seven of the nine Supreme Court justices were appointed by Republican presidents.

It is generally accepted that the Supreme Court's "center of gravity has shifted to the right in recent years" (Greenhouse, 1997). This does not bode well for minority groups seeking legal redress for discrimination such as vote dilution. In Chapter 2, Engstrom shows how "the" Supreme Court has placed new constraints on the creation of majority-minority districts, and also made it more difficult for minorities to force local governments to change from at-large to SMD arrangements" (Chapter 2, p. 22). He argues that in the near future increases in minority electoral power and officeholding may rest on the implementation of the "alternative" electoral arrangements, specifically, limited, cumulative, and preference voting (Chapter 2, pp. 30–31).[6]

Whether these "modified multiseat election systems" are enthusiastically adopted by minority groups and local governments will depend on how they are politically "marketed." Advocates might want to emulate progressive reformers who worked tirelessly to restructure local governments across the Southwest (Bridges, 1997). Scholars could mine a rich vein by examining the campaigns in support and opposition in cities where such changes have been implemented and where they are being proposed. What are the interest group coalitions and the type of arguments advanced by each side? How might supporters convince voters of the superiority of new electoral rules? Where have alternative electoral systems been defeated—and why? Finally, what are the long run electoral and policy consequences of alternative electoral arrangements?

Just as high court decisions limiting the use of single-member districts as a remedy for minority vote dilution will affect local institutional landscapes, national immigration laws will continue to reshape urban demography. In Chapter 6, Browning, Marshall, and Tabb point out the future of urban politics is multiracial, not biracial. This diversity has been largely driven by the Immigration and Nationality Act of 1965, which eliminated national origin quotas and established a family reunification policy (DeSipio & de la Garza, 1998, p. 42). Important for our purposes is that immigrant residential patterns are heavily concentrated in just a few states and, within these states, cities are the receiving ground for the vast majority of the nation's new residents (DeSipio, Chapter 4, pp. 80–81).

Therefore, a relative handful of cities and counties have found themselves responsible for providing basic services (emergency health care, education, transportation, police and fire protection) to growing low-income and non-English-speaking populations. Obtaining sufficient funding from other levels of government is problematic for three reasons. First, as Keiser argues in Chapter 1, national Democrats are no longer reliable allies for urban constituents. Second, state governments have tried to recover the costs of service provision to undocumented immigrants by filing suit against the federal government, but these attempts have been denied by federal courts (DeSipio & de la Garza, 1998). Third, unless local elected officials find a compelling appeal, Republican controlled state governments are not likely to provide social assistance to urban, Democratic constituencies.[7]

The bottom line is that national-level decisions have helped to generate a zero-sum game at the local level in which racial and ethnic groups compete for, and clash over, increasingly slender pieces of the public-sector pie and private space. This is a problem from our perspective because conflicts within and among ethnic groups both complicate and slow the incorporation process. Intergroup conflict—between different ethnic and racial groups and between minorities and whites—has emerged over jobs, neighborhood space, and the distribution of public resources and officeholding (McClain & Stewart, 1995, p. 129).

Moreover, DeSipio (Chapter 4) and Lai (Chapter 9) observe that increased diversity *within* ethnic groups means that intragroup distrust and conflict is not uncommon. Ethnic group fragmentation retards the development of coherent issue agendas and, as Lai's research indicates, can forestall the construction of voting blocks with the potential to influence electoral outcomes. In the Midwest, according to Longoria, Latino diversity might impair electoral efficacy "when national origin remains a crucial voting cue and Latino candidates divide Latino votes and advantage white candidates"(Chapter 8, p. 182).

State-level policy decisions that negatively impact minority communities may be a spur to local collective action and ethnic-group unity. This has been the case in California, where statewide ballot initiatives Propositions 187 (in 1994) and 209 (in 1996) had unanticipated political consequences. As noted above, the network of Latino grassroots organizations engaged in naturalization efforts have been expanded and strengthened (Pachon, 1998). Moreover, the 12 percent Latino voter turnout in the state's 1998 primary was a record high (Del Olmo, 1998). The long-term effects of lawmaking by ballot box on the political behavior of ethnic groups has yet to be determined, and should be measured via longitudinal studies. In election years where there is not a commonly perceived threat to minority communities, solidarity and high levels of participation may be difficult to sustain.

As noted above, a priority for researchers should be surveys of immigrant communities to determine areas of potential intra- and intergroup collaboration. DeSipio reports that "the absence of survey data on the policy needs of immigrant populations other than Latinos makes it impossible to say whether issue-based coalitions can form to create an urban immigrant political agenda" (Chapter 4, p. 94). Issues of common concern may be a starting point for the resolution of group conflict, but such resolution also requires the time and energy of enlightened and patient leadership. The dialogues and negotiated understandings that take place between ethnic community elites, and between elites and policymakers need to be communicated to the grassroots. Therefore, another set of questions that deserves careful investigation and cross-city comparison are: Who facilitates intragroup and intergroup dialogues and coalition building? Under what conditions? Are they ad hoc, issue based, or ongoing and institutionalized collaborations? How might we measure their successes?

SUBURBANIZATION AND GLOBALIZATION CONTINUE TO RESTRUCTURE SOCIAL AND POLITICAL RELATIONSHIPS

Not only has minority incorporation been shaped by decisions made by national political institutions, but it has also been affected by metropolitan land-use patterns. The post–World War II acceleration of suburbanization will continue as the nation's dominant developmental paradigm. In Chapter 1, Keiser documents the move of the nation's population to the suburbs and the corresponding increase in suburban political power. This process has affected the strategic calculus of the national Republican *and* Democratic parties. Keiser argues that in recent presidential elections Democrats have stopped tailoring policy stances to the preferences of urban (minority) voters, and have begun to court suburban independents and Republican leaners (Chapter 1, p. 11).

Moreover, suburbanization has increased disparities between the life chances of urban, minority residents and those of suburban residents. In Chapter 5, Fleischmann reviews the leading scholarly assessment of problems associated with suburbanization: Fragmented metropolitan areas (central cities surrounded by autonomous, incorporated suburbs) have higher levels of racial and economic segregation, and a very limited ability to grow and increase their tax bases. Moreover, Fleischmann notes, the drawing of governmental boundaries is not a neutral process: "In fact, they often are drawn for motives related to race, class, and political power" (Chapter 5, p. 111). How should this problem be resolved to provide a more level economic playing field for minority groups? Fleischmann reports that David Rusk (the most prominent voice in the debate over the costs of suburbanization) recommends regional policy solutions, which require cooperation and collaboration between cities and their suburbs (Chapter 5, p. 109). Yet the history of suburban antipathy to the city's fate leaves us pessimistic about the prospects for such collaboration.

Minority empowerment in this context is a good news/bad news situation. The good news, according to Fleischmann, is that data shows approximately the same rates of minority officeholding in elastic and inelastic cities. The bad news is that:

> Having Latinos and blacks elected to local offices does not guarantee that the interests of their respective groups will be addressed . . . . There is no guarantee that minority representation will be more effective in either type of city. In elastic Columbus, poverty has continued to

grow in the central city as black and white middle-class residents move to newer neighborhoods. (Chapter 5, p. 118)

The conundrum, in a nutshell, is that the problems of central city minority-elected officials and their constituents are not salient to suburban-area residents—who literally exist in a different world. Suburban residents enjoy new infrastructure, good schools, low crime rates, and relative social homogeneity (and, therefore, lower levels of ethnic group conflict). If regionwide collective action and interjurisdictional efforts are required to promote substantive economic development in central cities and to minimize chronic jobs–housing mismatches, then urban elected officials face an enormous task. How do they effectively appeal to the self-interest of suburban and state policymakers? Fleischmann says that "in inelastic areas, experience thus suggests that regionalism may spread piecemeal. . . ." (Chapter 5, p. 122)

Questions that should be addressed by those who study regionalism are: Who takes the lead on crafting these institutions and processes? What do they look like? What issues are most frequently common grounds for interjurisdictional efforts? When do state elected officials get involved? What are notable successes and failures, and what lessons do they provide?

Longoria (Chapter 8) contends that the suburban and regional context is relevant in a second way: It may shape the attitudes and issue stances of ethnic groups (specifically Latinos), and also structure availability of political resources. This is pertinent, Longoria says, because the number of minority groups living in the suburbs has grown since the 1980s. Suburbs are not all the same, however. Longoria says, "While Latinos are better off in absolute terms in some suburbs, this is not true in less affluent inner-ring suburbs" (Chapter 8, p. 196). Differences in socioeconomic standing suggests that some suburban Latinos occupy a more privileged position than others, and this may have an impact on the construction of group identities and issue agendas. A hypothetical example: Affluent Latinos living in Oak Brook, Illinois, might not view at-large election structures as an obstacle to increased political influence, while working-class Latinos in Cicero, Illinois, might see district representation as a political imperative.

Researchers would be well-advised to survey policy attitudes of minority residents of inner- and outer-ring suburbs, and to compare them with minority central city residents. How might attitudinal similarities or differences affect cross-ethnic, cross-class coalitional opportunities? What forms do group-specific and cross-ethnic mobilization efforts take in the suburbs? What difference might regional context make? How does the intersection of race and class play out in suburban empowerment campaigns?

Finally, the new global economy has exacerbated domestic income inequalities, which makes the intertwined problems of class and race increasingly intractable. Ameliorating economic disparities borne primarily by ethnic and racial minorities is perhaps the biggest social challenge facing the nation. A number of scholars have documented the local impacts of an internationalized and service-based economy (Sassen, 1991, 1998; D. Wilson, 1997; Goldsmith & Blakely, 1992).[7] A bifurcated income distribution has produced a shrinking middle class. Simultaneously occurring de-industrialization and re-industrialization have created, on the one hand, high-poverty neighborhoods where most residents are unemployed (W. J. Wilson, 1997; Soja, 1996), and on the other hand, a new class of working poor (Ong & Blumberg, 1996; Goldsmith & Blakely, 1992). Because education and income are the greatest predictors of political participation, we appear to be well on our way to two separate political societies—each with divergent needs, and unequal levels of participation and access to elected officials and policymakers. Research should continue to investigate how local policymakers and citizens, individually and collectively, attempt to mitigate the most devastating aspects of these enormous structural changes.

To summarize, powerholders have always asked minority groups why their demands for equality require change. Throughout the history of this nation, demands for minority equality have been generally contested on the grounds they are not sufficiently "realistic." There are broad common denominators in what has been sought by minorities, but group-specific factors, geographic location, and the historical time period help determine specific aims. While the overall status quo for minority groups at the end of this century is considerably different than at its beginning, outcomes have been mixed and it is not clear whether future generations of equality seekers will travel an easier road than their predecessors.

What, then, might we expect in the early decades of the next century? It is realistic to anticipate continued efforts to increase numbers of minority elected representatives and an escalation of conflict over electoral arrangements. Political parties will play a minimal role in mobilizing central city communities of color, while community-based organizations will assume a more prominent role in mobilization, issue articulation, and cross-racial, cross-ethnic coalition building. Given the rightward ideological shift among voters, national institutions will continue to make decisions that render local minority inclusion more problematic (although we will not revert to the dire conditions following the first Reconstruction). Suburbanization (and the new global economy) will still generate disparities between central cities and their suburbs in the area of income, education, and racial–ethnic composition; this will also have an impact on who participates in the political process. Both Democrats and Republicans will woo suburban rather than urban voters, and thus the federal and state governments will not play "knight in shining armor" to the central cities.

The sobering reality is that scholars and activists alike have much work to do in the next millennium. But in the words of Martin Luther King, Jr., "Human progress never rolls in on the wheels of inevitability . . ." (King, 1963, p. 770). We think a substantively inclusive political system and a socially tolerant society remain worthy goals, and challenge our readers to advance this cause actively.

NOTES

[1] For case studies on how African Americans in southern states and Latinos (in Texas) have used the Voting Rights Act to change discriminatory electoral systems, see C. Davidson and B. Grofman (eds.), *Quiet Revolution in the South* (1994), "Part One: View from the States."

[2] Chicago holds nonpartisan elections for its council. Through 1995, Chicago's citywide offices were partisan; beginning in 1999 these offices will also be filled in nonpartisan elections.

[3] Proposition 187 was a 1994 statewide ballot initiative designed to curtail undocumented immigration into California by denying immigrants and their children access to public services (education, health care, and income assistance).

[4] For a discussion of how national partisan dynamics affected political opportunities for southern Republicans in the post–Reconstruction era, see Richard Valelly, "National Parties and Racial Disfranchisement" (1995).

[5] Gerber et al. (1998) designed a theoretical model that considers the voting equilibria in three-candidate elections in double-member districts under straight voting and cumulative voting. Their experimental evidence shows minority candidates win significantly more seats in cumulative than straight voting elections.

[6] As of summer 1999, Republicans held gubernatorial control in thirty-one states and legislative control in seventeen states. Democrats controlled twenty-one state legislatures. Partisan legislative control was split in eleven states (Nebraska's legislature is nonpartisan).

[7]For overviews of the new global economy's multidimensional urban consequences, see P.K. Kresl & G. Gappert (eds.), *North American Cities and the Global Economy* (1995), and D. Wilson (ed.), *Globalization and the Changing U.S. City* (1997).

REFERENCES

Bridges, A. (1997). *Morning glories: municipal reform in the southwest.* Princeton, NJ: Princeton University Press.

Browning, R.P., Marshall, D.R., & Tabb, D.H. (eds.). (1997). *Racial politics in American cities* (2nd ed.). White Plains, NY: Longman.

Browning, R.P., Marshall, D.R., & Tabb, D.H. (eds.). (1990). *Racial politics in American cities.* White Plains, NY: Longman.

Browning, R.P., Marshall, R.P., & Tabb, D.H. (1984). *Protest is not enough: The struggle of blacks and hispanics for equality in urban politics.* Berkeley: University of California Press.

Davidson, C. (1992). The voting rights act: a brief history. In B. Grofman & C. Davidson (eds.), *Controversies in minority voting: The voting rights act in perspective* (pp. 7–51). Washington, DC: Brookings Institution.

Davidson, C., & Grofman, B. (1994a). The voting rights act and the second reconstruction. In C. Davidson & B. Grofman (eds.), *Quiet revolution in the South* (pp. 378–387). Princeton, NJ: Princeton University Press.

Davidson, C., & Grofman, B. (eds.). (1994b). *Quiet revolution in the South.* Princeton, NJ: Princeton University Press.

Del Olmo, F. (1998, June 7). "Giant" is awake and is a force. *Los Angeles Times,* p. M5.

DeSipio, L., & de la Garza, R.O. (1998). *Making Americans, remaking America: Immigration and immigrant policy.* Boulder, CO: Westview.

DeSipio, L. (1996). Making citizens or good citizens?: Naturalization as a predictor of organizational and electoral behavior among Latino immigrants. *Hispanic Journal of Behavioral Sciences,* 18 (2), 194–213.

Erie, S.P. (1988). *Rainbow's end: Irish-americans and the dilemmas of urban machine politics, 1840–1985.* Berkeley: University of California Press.

Fraga, L.R. (1988). Domination through democratic means. *Urban Affairs Quarterly,* 23 (4), 528–555.

Gerber, E., Morton, R.B., & Reitz, T. A. (1998). Minority representation in multimember districts. *American Political Science Review,* 92 (1), 127–144.

Goldsmith, W.W., & Blakely, E.J. (1992). *Separate societies: Poverty and inequality in U.S. cities.* Philadelphia: Temple University Press.

Greenhouse, L. (1997, July 1). Benchmarks of justice. *New York Times,* p. A1.

Grimshaw, W.J. (1992). *Bitter fruit: Black politics and the Chicago machine, 1931–1991.* Chicago: University of Chicago Press.

Heilig, P., & Mundt, R.J. (1984). *Your voice at city hall: The politics, procedures, and policies of district representation.* Albany: State University of New York Press.

Howard, C., Lipsky, M., & Marshall, D.R. (1994). Citizen participation in urban politics: Rise and routinization. In G.E. Peterson (ed.), *Big city politics, governance, and fiscal constraints* (pp. 153–199). Washington DC: The Urban Institute Press.

Keiser, R.A. (1997). *Subordination or empowerment?: African American leadership and the struggle for urban power.* New York: Oxford University Press.

King, M. L., Jr. (1963). Letter from a Birmingham jail. *The Christian Century,* LXXX (24), 767–773.

Kousser, J.M. (1992). The voting rights act and the two reconstructions. In B. Grofman and C. Davidson (eds.), *Controversies in minority voting: The voting rights act in perspective* (pp. 135–176). Washington DC: The Brookings Institution.

Kousser, J.M. (1974). *The shaping of southern politics. Suffrage restriction and the establishment of the one-party South, 1880–1910.* New Haven: Yale University Press.

Kresl, P.K, & Gappert, G. (eds.). 1995. *North American cities and the global economy: Challenges and opportunities* (Urban Affairs Annual Review, vol. 44). Thousand Oaks, CA: Sage.

Los Angeles Times. (1949, September 23). Part II, p. 4.

McClain, P.D., & Stewart, J., Jr. (1995). *"Can we all get along?": Racial and ethnic minorities in American politics.* Boulder, CO: Westview.

Mogelonsky, M. (1997, March). Natural(ized) Americans. *American Demographics,* pp. 45–49.

Morris, A.D. (1984). *The origins of the civil rights movement: Black communities organizing for change.* New York: Free Press.

Ojito, M. (1998, April 20). A record backlog to get citizenship stymies 2 million. *New York Times,* p. A1.

Ong, P., & Blumberg, E. (1996). Income and racial inequality in Los Angeles. In A.J. Scott & E.J. Soja (eds.), *The city: Los Angeles and urban theory at the end of the twentieth century* (pp. 311–335). Berkeley: University of California Press.

Pachon, H.P. (1998). Latino politics in the golden state: Ready for the 21st century? In M. B. Preston, B.E. Cain, & S. Bass (eds.), *Racial and ethnic politics in California,* vol. 2 (pp. 411–438). Berkeley: Institute of Governmental Studies Press.

Polinard, J.L., Wrinkle, R.D., Longoria, T., & Binder, N.E. (1994). *Electoral structure and urban policy: The impact on Mexican American communities.* Armonk, NY: M.E. Sharpe.

Portes, A., & Stepick, A. (1993). *City on the edge: The transformation of Miami.* Berkeley: University of California Press.

Rivlin, G. (1992). *Fire on the prairie: Chicago's Harold Washington and the politics of race.* New York: Henry Holt.

Sassen, S. (1998). *Globalization and its discontents.* New York: New Press.

Sassen, S. (1991). *The global city: New York, London, Toyko.* Princeton, NJ: Princeton University Press.

Sekul, J. (1975). Communities organized for public service: Citizen power and public policy in San Antonio. In D.R. Johnson, J.A. Booth, & R.J. Harris (eds.), *The politics of San Antonio: community, progress, and power* (pp. 175–190). Lincoln: University of Nebraska Press.

Soja, E.W. (1996). Los Angeles, 1962–1992: From crisis-generated restructuring to restructuring-generated crisis. In A.J. Scott & E.J. Soja (eds.), *The city: Los Angeles and urban theory at the end of the twentieth century* (pp. 426–462). Berkeley: University of California Press.

Underwood, K. (1997). Pioneering minority representation: Edward Roybal and the Los Angeles City Council, 1949–1962. *Pacific Historical Review,* LXVI (7), 399–425.

Valelly, R.M. (1995). National parties and racial disfranchisement. In Paul Peterson (ed.), *Classifying by race* (pp. 188–216). Princeton, NJ: Princeton University Press.

Welch, S., & Bledsoe, T. (1988). *Urban reform and its consequences: A study in representation.* Chicago: The University of Chicago Press.

Wilson, D. (ed.) (1997, May). *Globalization and the changing U.S.. city* (The Annals of the American Academy of Political and Social Science, vol. 551). Thousand Oaks, CA: Sage.

Wilson, W.J. (1997). *When work disappears: The world of the new urban poor.* New York: Vintage Books.

Author Biographies

Amy Bridges is Professor of Political Science at the University of California, San Diego. A scholar of urban political history, Bridges is the author of *A City in the Republic: Antebellum New York and the origins of Machine Politics* (Cornell, 1986), and *Morning Glories: Municipal Reform in the Southwest* (Princeton, 1997).

Rufus P. Browning is Professor of Political Science and Director of the Public Research Institute at San Francisco State University. He has written on racial politics and other topics. His current work is on tolerance.

Louis DeSipio is an Assistant Professor in the Department of Political Science at the University of Illinois at Urbana-Champaign. He is the author of *Counting on the Latino Vote: Latinos as a New Electorate* (University Press of Virginia, 1996) and the co-author with Rodolfo O. de la Garza of *Making Americans/Remaking America: Immigration and Immigrant Policy* (Westview Press, 1998). He is also the author and editor of a five-volume series on Latino political values, attitudes, and behaviors published by Westview Press. The next volume in this series, *Awash in the Mainstream: Latino Politics in the 1996 Elections* (Rodolfo O. de la Garza and Louis DeSipio, eds.), will be published in 1999 by Westview Press. His research focus on the process of political incorporation of new and formerly excluded populations into U.S. politics.

Richard L. Engstrom is Research Professor of Political Science at the University of New Orleans. He has written extensively on the impact of election systems on minority voters. His articles on this topic, a number of which have been cited by the U.S. Supreme Court, have appeared in the *American Political Science Review, Journal of Politics, Social Science Quarterly, Electoral Studies,* and other journals. He is a former Chairperson of the Representation and Electoral Systems section of the American Political Science Association.

Arnold Fleischmann is Associate Professor of Political Science at the University of Georgia. His research has focused on the politics of urban development, including land use, annexation, and local economic development policies. He is currently collaborating on two book projects: one on economic development efforts by American cities, and a second comparing policies affecting gays and lesbians in Britain and the United States.

Richard A. Keiser is Associate Professor of Political Science at Carleton College. His published research has focused on African American political power in Philadelphia and Chicago. He is the author of *Subordination or Empowerment? African American Leadership and the Struggle for Urban Political Power* (Oxford University Press, 1997).

James S. Lai is currently a doctoral candidate in political science at the University of Southern California. He has researched and written on state and local Asian American politics, public policy, and multiracial coalitions. He is the editor of the 1998–1999 *National Asian Pacific American Political Almanac,* co-directed with Dr. Don T. Nakanishi and published by the Asian American Studies Center at the University of California, Los Angeles. His most recent work is the chapter "The Symbolic Politics of Affirmative Action," co-authored with Dr. Michael B. Preston, in *Racial and Ethnic Politics in California,* edited by Michael B. Preston, Bruce E. Cain, and Sandra Bass (1998). He has taught several courses at the University of California, Los Angeles, in the areas of urban politics and race relations. His dissertation will be a comparative study of Asian Pacific American political behavior in Los Angeles and San Francisco.

Thomas Longoria, Jr., is an Assistant Professor of Political Science at the University of Texas—El Paso. He has published articles in journals such as the *Urban Affairs Review,* the *Social Science Quarterly,* and the *Latino Studies Journal* and is co-author of *Electoral Structure and Urban Policy: The Impact on Mexican American Communities.* His recent work includes production of a documentary film on Latinos in the Midwest entitled "After the Immigrant: Now We're Hispanic?" funded by the Wisconsin Humanities Council.

Dale Rogers Marshall is President and Professor of Political Science at Wheaton College in Massachusetts. Previously she was academic dean at Wellesley College and before that was professor of political science and associated dean of the College of Letters and Sciences at the University of California at Davis. She has published widely in urban politics and has been active in the Western Political Science Association and the American Political Science Association.

Donald B. Rosenthal is a Professor of Political Science at the State University of New York at Buffalo. He is the author of several books and numerous articles dealing with American urban politics and intergovernmental relations. His recent research has included work on gay and lesbian politics and AIDS politics in the four cities discussed here. He is also presently engaged in editing a collection of research essays on AIDS politics and policy.

David Tabb, Professor of Political Science at San Francisco State University, has written or co-authored over twenty articles and three books on the politics of race and political incorporation. His current research involves assessing the variation in political capacity of local governments to deliver federal programs to disadvantaged minorities.

Katherine Underwood is an Assistant Professor of Political Science at the University of Wisconsin, Oshkosh. Her work, which has been published in *Urban Affairs Review* and the *Pacific Historical Review,* focuses on the intersection of race and ethnicity and political institutions. She is currently completing a book on the election of Latinos to the Los Angeles and Chicago city councils.

Index